REENTRY TODAY:
Programs, Problems, and Solutions

THE RESOURCE CENTER
ETR Associates
4 Carbonero Way
Scotts Valley, CA 95066
1-800-860-2684

American Correctional Association
Alexandria, Virginia

Mission of the American Correctional Association

The American Correctional Association provides a professional organization for all individuals and groups, both public and private, that share a common goal of improving the justice system.

American Correctional Association Staff

Gwendolyn C. Chunn, President
James A. Gondles, Jr., CAE, Executive Director
Gabriella M. Klatt, Director, Communications and Publications
Harry Wilhelm, Marketing Manager
Alice Heiserman, Manager of Publications and Research
Michael Kelly, Associate Editor
Dana M. McCoy, Graphics and Production Manager
Darlene Jones Powell, Graphics and Production Associate
Cover Illustration and Design by Joseph J. Fuller, II

Copyright 2006 by the American Correctional Association. All rights reserved. The reproduction, distribution, or inclusion in other publications of materials in this book is prohibited without prior written permission from the American Correctional Association. No part of this book may be reproduced by any electronic means including information storage and retrieval systems without permission in writing from the publisher.

Printed in the United States of America by United Graphics Incorporated, Mattoon, Illinois.

ISBN 1-56991-240-8

For information on publications and videos available from ACA, contact our worldwide web home page at: http://www.aca.org

This publication may be ordered from:
American Correctional Association
Customer Service
P.O. Box 201
Annapolis Junction, MD 20701
1-800-222-5646

Library of Congress Cataloging in Publication Data

Reentry today : programs, problems, and solutions
       p. cm.
   Includes bibliographical references.
   ISBN 1-56991-240-8
1. Ex-convicts. 2. Criminals-Rehabilitation 3. Community-based corrections. I. American Correctional Association.
HV9275.R44 2006

364.8-dc22   2006040659

TABLE OF CONTENTS

Foreword by James A. Gondles, Jr., CAE 5

Introduction by Terry Marshall 7

1. ACA Public Correctional Policy on Reentry of Offenders 9

2. Reentry is Public Safety
Gwendolyn C. Chunn 11

3. The Reentry Policy Council Reports 13

4. Confronting Recidivism: Inmate Reentry and The Second Chance Act
Reginald A. Wilkinson, Ed.D. and Edward Rhine, Ph.D. 17

5. Presidential Support Is a Start but Still Not Enough
Joey R. Weedon 23

6. Hard Time: Ex-Offenders Returning Home after Prison
Joan Petersilia, Ph.D. 25

7. Reentry/Reintergration Survey, 2004 35

8. Reentry Survey, 2005 53

9. Inmate Reentry: What Works and What to Do About It
Richard P. Seiter, Ph.D. 77

10. Informing Policy and Practice: Prisoner Reentry Research at the Urban Institute
Elizabeth C. McBride, Christy Visher, Ph.D., and Nancy G. La Vigne 91

**11. Developing Successful Reentry Programs:
Lessons Learned from the "What Works" Research**
Christopher T. Lowenkamp, Ph.D. and Edward Latessa, Ph.D. 99

12. Evidence-Based Practices in Reentry: Challenges and Opportunities
Arthur J. Lurigio, Ph.D. 107

**13. Making Inmate Reentry Safe and Successful:
Using the Report of the Reentry Policy Council**
Katherine Brown 113

**14. An Initial Comparison of Graduates and Terminated
Clients in America's Largest Reentry Court**
Jeffrey B. Spelman, Ph.D. 119

15. Assessing for Success in Offender Reentry
Kathleen A. Gnall and Gary Zajac, Ph.D. 125

16. Engaging Communities: An Essential Ingredient to Offender Reentry
Reginald A. Wilkinson, Ed.D. 133

**17. Citizens' Circles: Community Reentry: Does Working in
Prison Result in Greater Employment and Less Recidivism Upon Release?**
Edward Rhine, Ph.D., John R. Matthews, II, Lee A. Sampson, and Rev. Hugh Daley 139

18. Adding the Crime Victims to the Reentry Equation
Peter A. Michaud 145

**19. Correctional Industries Preparing Inmates for Reentry:
Recidivism and Post-Release Employment**
Cindy J. Smith, Ph.D, Jennifer Bechtel, M.S., Angie Patrick, M.S 151

20. Releasing Inmates with Mental Illness and Co-Occurring Disorders into the Community
Lance Couturier, Ph.D., Frederick Maue, Ph.D., and Catherine McVey, M.A. 159

21. Iowa Implements Mental Health Reentry Program
Larry Brimeryer 167

22. "Step Down" Programs: The Missing Link in Successful Inmate Reentry
Ralph Fretz, Ph.D. 173

23. New Study Proves Jails Are an Important Component of the Reentry Equation
Vanessa St. Gerard 183

24. Jail Inmates Bake Their Way to Successful Reentry
Susan Clayton, M.S. 187

25. Pennsylvania's Approach to Reentry
Jeffrey A. Beard, M.A. and Kathleen Gnall, MSW 193

26. NIC Provides Practitioners Skills to Help Offenders with Reentry
Shelly Morelock and Melissa Houston 201

27. Reentry Statistics Now Available on the Bureau of Justice Statistics' Web Site
Leon T. Geter 209

28. Reentry Resources, *National Criminal Justice Reference Service* 213

FOREWORD

James A. Gondles, Jr., CAE
Executive Director
American Correctional Association

Offender reentry has become a hot topic in the various sectors of the criminal justice field. When you know the majority of offenders will return to the community, how do you best prepare them to be successful and ultimately reduce recidivism? This reader gathers together some of the best thinking on this topic from a variety of viewpoints and disciplines. We hope it will be useful for practitioners, community leaders, researchers and students who wish to get involved in crafting successful reentry strategies and programs.

As history has taught us, no one program works for everyone. Each component must be structured to best meet the needs of the offender. This collection of articles and research offers descriptions of several programs and overall advice on what works.

ACA is committed to examining the issues and challenges surrounding reentry. We have dedicated issues of our magazine, *Corrections Today*, and journal, *Corrections Compendium*, to the topic. Last year, ACA published the book *Managing a Job Retention Program for Ex-Offenders: A Step-by-Step Guide* by Dr. Tony Ryan. This resource examined employment as a part of reentry and showed the link between what is taught in prison and what must be done after release.

Successful offender reentry is a goal shared by many. Only through education and partnership will this goal be met. I invite you to log onto ACA's Web site www.aca.org for more information about the American Correctional Association and the many resources we have for those working in corrections.

INTRODUCTION

Terry Marshall,
President
International Community
Corrections Association
Washington, DC

Many words have been used to describe the offender dispersion from American institutions--reintegration, resettlement, or reentry are a few of them. The words may vary but the intent is the same. They all reflect a "process" by which persons move from a setting of incarceration to one of discharge or community supervision.

Reentry will occur some 650,000 times this year. It is a process that occurs whether on a mandatory sentence, maximum sentence, or discretionary hearing. In other words, the process of reentry is not a result of any political stance. Offender issues of reentry and the numbers generated who are in need of the process are political and cultural in origin but what can and must be done can be defined in practical, pragmatic terms.

On its own, the number 650,000 can appear to be quite daunting, but we also must keep in mind that under current practices, most of those individuals will end up in a handful of zip codes in a given state. The good news is that this should provide policymakers an opportunity to grasp the situation, concentrate resources, and mobilize a response. The bad news, of course, is that this results in a return that currently presents one more challenge to communities already overwhelmed by need.

In the following compilation, you may find it useful to view reentry as operating between two traditional "entities." On one hand, we have institutions that often have to struggle to maintain safe, humane, and effective levels of incapacitation. To truly become an effective reentry partner, those institutions would have to assess needs, motivate offenders, and engage in the promotion of program fidelity to successful models often developed elsewhere—not an easy task but a necessary one.

Some of the most basic needs that would have to be met would include:

- Providing education skills that concentrate on basic literacy and computation

- Training offenders in job skills that reflect the needs of the present job market

- Having certified staff treat primary drug and alcohol issues

- Offering mental health stabilization, and

- Evaluating individuals medically for chronic conditions

Perhaps, most important of all would be an understanding that the elements essential for effective release planning begin on the day of admission.

The second entity is a vast array of resources that we cobble together under the term "community services." Some are formal such as probation/parole supervision and contracted programs and services. Others are informal such as family, employers, drug and alcohol support programs, mental health support systems, community health services, faith-oriented groups, neighborhood councils, and so forth. First and foremost, we must deal with the issues of food, clothing, and shelter before the person arrives in the community. Then, the process of reentry at a minimum must match the continuation of the gains already begun in the institution with the development and support of ongoing services in the community.

The next few years will be interesting as we will see different jurisdictions take various approaches to reentry. Some will see a model of institutions "reaching out" to community-based services. Others will see community- based services "reaching in" to institutions. Still others may see the evolution of process-oriented "brokers" that ensure continuity of care between institution and community-service entities.

Most returning offenders come back to challenged communities so any reentry model should have at its base the goal of strengthening that community. Persons in recovery, persons with stabilized mental health conditions, persons with an improved educational level, and persons with real job skills can bring assets not deficits back to our struggling neighborhoods.

The following readings will help you better understand the general issues of reentry, outline some program responses, and provide a few evaluations of programs to date. They are authored by a distinguished group of policymakers, researchers, and program operators.

ACA's Public Correctional Policy on Reentry of Offenders

Introduction:

Reentry programs are in the best interest of society because they help prepare offenders for community life, help reduce future criminal behavior, remove the barriers that make it difficult for offenders to reenter their communities and develop necessary community support.

Policy Statement:

The American Correctional Association fully supports reentry programs and encourages the elimination of any local, state, and federal laws and policies that place barriers on the offender's successful reentry. Therefore, public and private agencies at the federal, state, and local levels should:

A. Advocate for the review of existing laws and regulations that inhibit the successful reentry of offenders

B. Initiate transitional planning, consistent with the individual needs of the offender, during intake to the facility

C. Provide an expedited process to obtain appropriate legal identification prior to or upon release

D. Assist the offender in accessing appropriate housing upon release

E. Provide sufficient staff to supervise offenders released to the community

F. Develop community partnerships and support networks for providing a seamless and timely connection between pre- and post-release programs and services

G. Provide information and assistance to address health care needs, such as obtaining Medicaid, medical and substance abuse treatment, and other health and psychological services, to offenders in the community upon release. Provide a sufficient supply of prescription medication upon release

H. Provide information and assistance to offenders to gain employment upon release, such as pre-employment readiness training, job identification and retention skills training, and job placement services

I. Provide prerelease counseling to help reunite offenders with their families and communities

---

This Public Correctional Policy was ratified by the American Correctional Association Delegate Assembly at the Congress of Correction in Philadelphia, August 15, 2001.

Reentry is Public Safety

Gwendolyn C. Chunn
ACA President

First printed in *On the Line,* a publication of the American Correctional Association, November 2004

This year, as in other recent years, America's prisons will release more than 600,000 inmates back into the communities from which they came. These men and women are not being released early; they have served their time and paid their debt to society. Now, they will rejoin the nation's communities. Society must act to put the services in place that will allow these people to successfully rejoin their communities, while ensuring that those communities remain safe.

According to the U.S. Department of Justice, two out of three released inmates will be rearrested for new offenses within three years. Society as a whole must act to reduce this unacceptably high recidivism rate. Those released from the nation's prison systems often lack access to programs that provide assistance locating employment, and help finding a place to live, a relationship with a law-abiding mentor, and mental health and substance abuse treatment. By ensuring access to these types of programs, crime can be reduced and communities will be made safer.

In addition to reducing crime, even modest reductions in recidivism provide significant savings to taxpayers. Nationally, the cost of keeping people in state prisons (a number that continues to grow, in part because of such high recidivism) is more than $30 billion a year. Local government, community groups, and churches have vital roles to play in creating networks to help offenders leaving prison meet their varying needs during the critical transition period. With proper preparations and continuity of care, society can strengthen public safety and reduce the burden on taxpayers.

President Bush recognized the importance of improving services to those leaving the nation's correctional facilities. During the 2005 State of the Union address, he called for action "to expand job training and placement services, to provide transitional housing and to help newly released prisoners get mentoring, including from faith-based groups." The president concluded his appeal for action by saying, "America is the land of second chance, and when the gates of prison open, the path ahead should lead to a better life."

In September 2005, the Department of Justice convened the nation's first national conference on offender reentry. Entitled "Coming Together, Strengthening Partnerships and Planning for the Future," the conference featured discussions among public and private organizations, community groups, and others who work with newly released adult and juvenile offenders on issues impacting reentry, including employment services, housing, education, substance abuse and health care. Then, Attorney General John Ashcroft delivered the keynote address at the conference. This leadership from the president and the attorney general demonstrates a much-needed commitment to confront the challenge of reducing recidivism.

Congress also has a critical role to play on this issue. In 2005, a bipartisan group of members of Congress introduced The Second Chance Act (H.R. 4676) to provide grants to states and local governments for transitional services for reintegration into the community and for support to community-based organizations for mentoring programs and other transitional services. The legislation will also ask both federal and state governments to study barriers to offender reentry and report the findings back to Congress so further steps can be taken to remove undue restrictions on those released from U.S. correctional facilities.

The Second Chance Act (see next page for more information) is a good beginning towards improving public safety by better addressing the reentry of so many people back into society. It will save local, state, and federal governments needed money, and it will help hundreds of thousands of inmates and their families rebuild their lives as they reenter society. Advocates for the legislation, including ACA, hope to see this measure enacted in 2006.

In the meantime, consider the following question: In this time of public safety crises and budget shortfalls, can the nation afford to continue to ignore a simple and cost-effective solution to the nation's crime problem? I do not think so.

Gwendolyn C. Chunn is president of the American Correctional Association.

The Reentry Policy Council Reports

Originally printed in *On the Line*, a publication of the American Correctional Association, November 2004

The Reentry Policy Council Reports

Following a spurt of recent Congressional activity on the Second Chance Act (H.R. 1704/S. 1934), including the bill's introduction in the Senate and a hearing before the Subcommittee on Crime, Terrorism, and Homeland Security in the House, Congressional leaders have indicated that further action on the bill will be delayed until the legislature reconvenes in 2006. The bill enjoys broad bipartisan support from members of Congress in both chambers. Senate contacts indicate a possible hearing on the legislation in early 2006. Despite the delay, key Congressional leaders expect the bill to pass during the 109th Congressional session, which ends December 2006

The Second Chance Act is a bipartisan bill designed to combat recidivism by improving the coordination among federal and state agencies regarding offender reentry. The bill increases the support to states and community organizations to address the growing population of ex-offenders returning to communities. The main areas of focus within the bill are jobs, housing, substance abuse/mental heath treatment and strengthening families.

The bill was introduced in the U.S. House of Representatives on June 23, 2004, by Reps. Rob Portman (R-Ohio), Danny Davis (D-Ill.), Mark Souder (R-Ind.), and Stephanie Tubbs Jones (D-Ohio). The legislation has been introduced in both chambers of Congress. The House Judiciary Committee, and the Subcommittee on Crime, Terrorism and Homeland Security held a hearing on the issue of federal inmate reentry on October 6, 2004.

What is the total cost of the bill? The total authorized amount of the programs created is $112 million over a two-year period. The breakdown is as follows:

- $40 million per year for the Reauthorized Reentry Demonstration Program

- $15 million per year for community-based mentoring

- $1 million per year for state grants for research

How do these grants work? Do states apply? To what agency? There are two grant programs in this bill. First, the bill reauthorizes and expands the existing Reentry Demonstration Program. States and local governments can apply for funds through the Department of Justice. The authorized funding level for the demonstration program is $40 million per year.

Second, the bill provides a small grant program titled Mentoring Adult Prisoners to be administered by the Department of Labor. The authorized funding level for the mentoring program is $15 million per year.

Are faith-based groups eligible for funding? Only states and local governments are eligible for funding under the demonstration program. Community-based organizations or nonprofit organizations can apply for mentoring funds through the Department of Labor. In addition, faith-based, nonprofit organizations, such as Catholic Charities, have been providing reentry and mentoring services for years and have had significant successes.

What is the actual number of inmates released from prisons? In 2002, there were 632,183 inmates released from state and federal prisons.

Why is substance abuse treatment an important concern in dealing with reentry? A remarkably high portion of the state prison population—a little more than 80 percent—report a history of drug and/or alcohol use (this is also true of 70 percent of federal inmates). This same population, 70 percent to 85 percent of state inmates, report that they need treatment.

Is there any connection between recidivism and substance abuse? According to the Department of Justice, 52 percent of state inmates and 34 percent of federal inmates reported being under the influence of drugs and/or alcohol when they committed the offense that led to their arrest and incarceration. About 80 percent of inmates have a problem with illegal drugs or alcohol abuse.

How will this reentry initiative save taxpayer dollars? State prison operating expenditures totaled $28.4 billion in fiscal year 2001, or a nationwide average annual operating cost of $22,650 per inmate. [$23,397 in 2004 according to the 2005 *Directory of Adult and Juvenile Correctional Departments, Institutions, Agencies, and Probation and Parole Authorities* published by the American Correctional Association] And there is tremendous variation among the states. Some states spend on average as much as $44,379 (Maine) per inmate annually. The bottom line is that by reducing recidivism among this population, communities will be kept safer and state and federal costs for arrest, prosecution, and incarceration will be reduced.

How does the bill provide jobs? It authorizes the Department of Labor to educate employers about existing programs for former inmates such as the work opportunity tax incentive. The bill also provides grants to states and local units of government that may be used to facilitate collaboration among corrections and community corrections, technical schools, community colleges, and the workforce development employment services.

What does this bill do regarding housing? The bill provides grants to states and local units of government that may be used to provide post-release housing and transitional housing, including group homes for recovering substance abusers.

What does this bill do regarding substance abuse treatment? The Second Chance bill provides grants to states and local units of government that may be used to provide mental health services, substance abuse treatment and aftercare, and treatment for contagious diseases to offenders in custody and after reentry into the community.

Is there anything in the bill that deals with millions disenfranchised from voting? No. As for other barriers that exist, this bill establishes an interagency task force that will report to Congress on these barriers for this population. Congress needs the right information before it moves forward on any of these measures.

Confronting Recidivism:
Inmate Reentry and the Second Chance Act

Reginald A. Wilkinson. Ed.D. and Edward Rhine, Ph.D.

This chapter is an edited version of written testimony presented to the U.S. House of Representatives, Committee on Government Reform, Oversight Hearing, by Reginald A. Wilkinson on February 2, 2005 and was printed in *Corrections Today*, a publication of the American Correctional Association, August 2005.

There is a growing national movement in corrections embracing offender reentry. Remarkably, in a relatively short span of time, an impressive array of efforts have been launched at all levels of government and by public policy institutes and community organizations to build more effective and innovative responses to the myriad challenges presented by reentry. These efforts clearly demonstrate that reentry is not a fad; it is here to stay.

Since the late 1990s, the Urban Institute in Washington, D.C., has hosted a series of reentry roundtables to assess the state of knowledge and to publish specialized reports on this topic. Leaders in the field, academicians, policymakers, and many others have gathered periodically to debate and share what is known about the challenges and issues that must be addressed to ensure successful reentry transitions for offenders.[1]

The National Institute of Corrections has launched the significant *Transition from Prison to Community* project to offer technical assistance and support to a select number of states relative to transforming their systems governing reentry.

In 2001, the U.S. Department of Justice and a broad consortium of federal agencies forged a unique, path-breaking partnership by providing a total of $100 million in grant funding spread across all fifty states to address reentry planning and programming for serious, violent felony offenders. Known as the *Serious and Violent Offender Reentry Initiative*, its continuing importance to the field has been reinforced by additional funding for a comprehensive, multiyear, multisite evaluation of selected states' systems of reentry (see www.svori-evaluation.org).

President Bush, in his 2004 State of the Union address, urged Congress to allocate substantial funding over four years to support the reentry transition of offenders. His recitation that "America is the land of second chance" will resonate with corrections professionals for years to come.

In mid-September 2004, Cleveland was the site of the first National Conference on Offender Reentry sponsored by the U.S. Department of Justice and the other federal agencies involved in the Serious and Violent Offender Reentry Initiative. More than 1,400 attendees participated in the conference.

The Re-Entry Policy Council recently released the *Report of the Re-Entry Policy Council: Charting the Safe and Successful Return of Prisoners to the Community*, a landmark report that offers a comprehensive set of bipartisan, consensus-based recommendations for policymakers and practitioners interested in improving the likelihood that adults released from prison or jail will avoid crime and become productive and healthy members of both their families and communities. The Council of State Governments partnered with ten other national organizations to compile this report, which comprises hundreds of recommendations and research findings related to employment, public safety, housing, health, families, faith-based initiatives, and victims. These recommendations are consistent with the provisions proposed in landmark legislation known as the Second Chance Act.

Confronting Recidivism

The Second Chance Act: Community Safety Through Recidivism Prevention recognizes the many complex issues affecting individuals released from prison or jail that must be addressed to ensure that they are not rearrested after their return to the community. The legislation, which encourages state and local governments to craft solutions that span agencies and engage community-based partners, was introduced in the House of Representatives by Reps. Rob Portman, R-Ohio, Danny Davis, D-Illinois, Howard Coble, R-North Carolina, Stephanie Tubbs Jones, D-Ohio, Steve Chabot, R-Ohio, Chris Cannon, R-Utah, and Katherine Harris, R-Florida.

This bill, if adopted, will exert a substantial impact on reducing offender recidivism, save precious taxpayer dollars, provide tools to address substance abuse, mental health, and other problems that beset offenders who are confined behind prison walls, and serve to strengthen families and communities across the country. The comprehensive nature of this proposed legislation encourages states, through demonstration grants and other means, to design a seamless system of reentry transitioning for offenders characterized by support and accountability.

The bill speaks to sound public policy and effective correctional practice. It views reentry from a holistic framework, targets strengthening families and seeks to improve communities' quality of life. Most important, it also focuses on reducing barriers that confront offenders as they seek to return home following a period of confinement.

Offender Recidivism and Public Safety

It is notable that upwards of 700,000 offenders will be released annually from state and federal prisons to communities and neighborhoods across the country. What this means is that over the course of the next decade, nearly 7 million formerly incarcerated individuals will return home from confinement. The Second Chance Act recognizes that the reentry strategies, initiatives, and programs adopted by those in the field matter a great deal to the future well being of communities, victims, and offenders.

It is an unfortunate reality that a majority of offenders released from confinement are likely to re-offend. According to Joan Petersilia, a well-known California criminologist, the problem of offender recidivism remains quite serious. As she notes in her book *When Prisoners Come Home: Parole and Prisoner Reentry*: "From the available evidence ... persons being released from prison today are doing less well than their counterparts released a decade ago in successfully reintegrating into their communities. More of them are being rearrested; these arrests are occurring more quickly; and as a group, ex-convicts are accounting for a growing share of all serious crimes experienced in the United States." High rates of recidivism mean pronounced levels of victimization.

Viewing Reentry Holistically

It is critical to recognize that correctional systems cannot go it alone. To do so promises to repeat the failures of the past and guarantees continued high rates of offender recidivism. The Second Chance Act clearly acknowledges the importance of taking a holistic approach when dealing with offenders returning home. In Ohio, Washington, and in many other states, innovative initiatives are under way that emphasize building a continuum of services, programming, support, and offender accountability that extends from the time of sentencing well beyond release from prison to any period of supervision that may follow.[2] The Second Chance Act emphasizes that these strategies and initiatives must be developed in collaboration and partnership with community groups, faith-based organizations, service providers, citizens, victims and formerly incarcerated individuals. Their ownership and support at the local level are vital to achieving successful pathways for offender reentry.

In July 2002, the Ohio Department of Rehabilitation and Correction published a comprehensive report called *The Ohio Plan for Productive Offender Reentry and Recidivism Reduction*. The Ohio Plan views reentry as a philosophy, not a program. Consistent with this framework, the process of planning for reentry begins immediately at a reception center, not a few weeks, or even a few months, before release from incarceration. Reentry planning draws on a variety of risk and needs assessment tools for prioritizing programming and service delivery as offenders move through the system. The Second Chance Act recognizes the importance of such assessments in reducing the likelihood of offender recidivism through its provision for demonstration grants to state and local governments to adopt such tools.

Ensuring that offenders receive appropriate programming both during confinement and while they are under supervision in the community is an important component of the reentry transition. National statistics indicate that a significant percentage of offenders who enter state and federal prisons have previous histories of substance abuse and/or mental health problems. These offenders require effective intervention and service delivery in a manner that must be sustained both during and after incarceration. There is a provision in the bill offering funding supportive of such programming to assist states in addressing these offenders' unique needs.

Strengthening Families

One of the more significant costs associated with imprisonment is its impact on the families and children left behind. As research shows, a growing number of prison inmates are parents. During the past decade, the total number of parents in prison has increased sharply from an estimated 452,500 in state and federal facilities in 1991 to 721,500 in 1997—an increase of 60 percent. These inmates are parents to more than 1.5 million children. This figure represents a growth of more than one-half million children in the past decade, according to *But They All Come Back: Facing the Challenges of Prisoner Reentry* by Jeremy Travis.

One of the more sobering trends too often overlooked in correctional management discussions is the impact incarceration and reentry have on families, fathers, mothers, children, siblings, and others who are connected to a family network. The Second Chance Act recognizes the importance of engaging families in reentry by providing funding options to states and local jurisdictions to expand family-based treatment centers offering comprehensive treatment services for the family as a unit. Family case management that starts inside and continues following an offender's release serves to reinforce successful reentry transitions.

Improving Communities' Quality of Life

The Second Chance Act addresses the vital role that community and faith-based organizations can play in ensuring that returning offenders are productive and remain crime free. Communities and local citizens bring expertise, knowledge of resources, and often a willingness to assist offenders in navigating reentry in a positive manner. As the legislation recognizes, mentoring represents a particularly important component in this process. Mentors, whether through faith-based or other community organizations, offer guidance, direction, and often a compassionate commitment to work with ex-offenders as they reacquire the skills and competencies they need to make it once they are released.

The Department of Rehabilitation and Correction under the Ohio Plan on Reentry has created a "reentry mentor" as part of the volunteers program. The goal is to afford community and faith-based organizations the opportunity to work with offenders starting inside and carrying that relationship outside to the community. This is an area of corrections that will be greatly enhanced given the bill's authorization to provide grants to those community organizations and groups that provide transitional services and mentoring programs as offenders exit the prison system.

Collateral Sanctions and Barriers to Reentry

Offenders released from prison experience a range of barriers affecting their prospects for a successful return home. Since 1980, numerous laws have been passed restricting the kinds of jobs for which ex-inmates can be hired, easing the requirements for their parental rights to be terminated, restricting their access to public welfare and housing subsidies, and limiting their right to vote. Though the rationale for these changes may have been well intentioned, their impact has been cumulative and deleterious to offender reentry.

Jeremy Travis, president of John Jay College of Criminal Justice, labels these "invisible punishments" by which he means the extension of formal criminal sanctions through the diminution of the rights and responsibilities of citizenship and legal residency in the United States. Often referred to as collateral sanctions, they represent laws, regulations, and administrative rules that often operate largely out of public view. They may carry serious, adverse, and unfair consequences for the individuals who are affected.[3]

It is notable that one of the provisions in The Second Chance Act seeks to identify and address those federal barriers, or collateral sanctions, that may undermine offenders' efforts at reentry through the formation of a federal task force. The task force is required one year after the enactment of this bill to submit a report to Congress assessing the effects of such barriers on offenders and their children and families.

The Future of Reentry

There is good reason to be optimistic about the future of reentry. The scale and scope of the national focus on reentry is unique to the extent that it encompasses a holistic perspective. The commitment to reentry in the field of corrections remains strong and is growing. Several states, including Michigan and Ohio, have formed the equivalent of interagency reentry steering committees to guide their work.

Most recently, a unique organization was formed called the International Association of Reentry (IAR). Its mission is to foster victim and community safety through correctional reform and prison population management, cost containment, professional development and the successful reintegration of offenders. This association will serve as a catalyst, spurring active collaboration among correctional practitioners, allied justice professionals, the victim community, formerly incarcerated individuals, higher education, public policymakers, interfaith and family advocates, and community members.

The International Association of Reentry is committed to identifying, developing, and disseminating evidence-based "best practices" and those policies, programs, and protocols relevant to reentry. It recently hosted an Inaugural Summit in Columbus, Ohio. IAR will provide energetic advocacy and education targeting the many areas encompassed by reentry, including the issuing of action-oriented reports, position papers, and policy briefs. For now, the reach of the association is within North America. Eventually, IAR expects a worldwide membership.

There is a pressing need for information to be shared and disseminated regarding where reentry best practices may be found. It is equally vital to ensure that there are sufficient resources and mechanisms in place to provide staff training on what these best practices are and how they may be implemented. The Second Chance Act includes a provision calling for a national adult and juvenile offender reentry resource center. The existence of such a center will provide a clearinghouse and national database whereby all levels of government, local jurisdictions, communities, and stakeholders who have an interest may go to learn more about what works and what is effective relative to offender reentry. They also may solicit technical assistance and training to adopt evidence-based practices germane to reentry.

The Second Chance Act provides a very sensible balance that recognizes that reentry is about public safety as well as returning offenders home as tax-paying and productive citizens. In thinking about the past, and the promising changes already under way, embracing reentry represents the only viable option for corrections. Reentry, however, must be done correctly. That means drawing on reentry best practices, seeking active collaboration and sustainable community and faith-based partners, engaging families across the full spectrum of reentry, and reducing those barriers that undermine offenders' successful transitions from prison to home.

ENDNOTES

[1] Travis, J. 2005. *But They All Come Back: Facing The Challenges of Prisoner Reentry.* Washington, D.C.: The Urban Institute Press. Travis, J. and C. Visher, eds. 2005. *Prisoner Reentry and Public Safety in America.* New York: Cambridge University Press.

[2] Wilkinson, R. A., G. A. Buckholtz, and G. M. Seigfried. 2004. Prison Reform through Offender Reentry: A Partnership between the Courts and Corrections. *Pace Law Review.* 24 (Spring): 609-629. Travis, J. and C. Visher, eds. 2005.

[3] Mauer, M. and M. Chesney-Lind, 2002. *Invisible Punishment: The Collateral Consequences of Mass Imprisonment.* New York: The New Press.

Reginald A. Wilkinson, Ed.D., is the former director of the Ohio Department of Rehabilitation and Correction, and president and executive director of the International Association of Reentry. Edward E. Rhine, Ph.D., is deputy director of the Ohio Department of Rehabilitation and Correction Office of Policy and Offender Reentry.

Presidential Support Is a Start but Still Not Enough

Joey R. Weedon

First printed in *Corrections Today*, a publication of the American Correctional Association, April 2004

Each year, Americans eagerly look to the president to provide a report on the nation's state of affairs. The tradition of the State of the Union address, which is required by the U.S. Constitution (and until the advent of mass media, was delivered in writing and read by a clerk to each house of Congress), provides the president the opportunity to highlight his accomplishments during the past year and outline his priorities for the coming year.

In 2005, given the impending election, the State of the Union took on added significance as President Bush highlighted programs that are sure to become centerpieces of his reelection campaign. Given this context, the following passage taken from Bush's speech on January 2005, is important to everyone in corrections and law enforcement:

> In the past, we have worked together to bring mentors to the children of prisoners and provide treatment for the addicted and help for the homeless. Tonight, I ask you to consider another group of Americans in need of help. This year, some 600,000 inmates will be released from prison back into society. We know from experience that if they can't find work or a home or help, they are much more likely to commit more crimes and return to prison. So tonight, I propose a four-year, $300 million prisoner reentry initiative to expand job training and placement services, to provide transitional housing, and to help newly released prisoners get mentoring, including from faith-based groups. America is the land of the second chance and when the gates of the prison open, the path ahead should lead to a better life.

During the 2004 State of the Union address, Bush called for a new $600 million program to help an additional 300,000 Americans receive substance abuse treatment over three years as well as a $450 million initiative to pair up mentors with more than 1 million disadvantaged junior high school students and children of inmates. These proposals and the use of the State of the Union address clearly indicate that the president and his administration are receptive to initiatives that are targeted at inmate populations and their families.

However, corrections' and law enforcement's work does not end with getting these issues on the president's agenda; in fact, this is where the real work begins. The president's call for action during his State of the Union address and corrections' and law enforcement's priorities must be impressed upon our representatives in Congress. This is of great importance because although Bush called for additional substance abuse treatment last year, the Residential Substance Abuse and Treatment program, the one major federal program that provides funding for substance abuse programs to incarcerated populations, went unfunded in the fiscal year 2004 federal budget. In fact, Congress passed the budget and sent it to the president for his signature just days after the most recent State of the Union address was delivered.

Despite Bush's plea last year for additional federal funding to help provide mentors to disadvantaged youths, the fiscal year 2004 federal budget included significant cuts to several juvenile justice programs. Even offender reentry programs—highlighted just days before the president signed the fiscal year 2004 budget—saw funding reduced from nearly $15 million in fiscal year 2003 to $5 million in fiscal year 2004.

The president's last two State of the Union addresses provide hope that corrections and law enforcement will receive the federal resources that are needed to have a true impact on the nation's communities by helping to reduce drug abuse, decrease juvenile crime, and reduce recidivism. However, it is up to the members of the American Correctional Association and all those in corrections and law enforcement to ensure that Congress makes these programs a priority and that the infrastructure is built at the local level to ensure that the federal aid will be effective.

Joey R. Weedon is former director of governmental affairs for the American Correctional Association.

Hard Time: Ex-Offenders Returning Home after Prison

Joan Petersilia, Ph.D.

First printed in *Corrections Today*, a publication of the American Correctional Association, August 2005

Never before in U.S. history have so many individuals been released from prison. More than 600,000 people—1,600 a day—were released in 2003, a number nearly equal to the population of Washington, D.C., and greater than the state of Wyoming. The number is expected to grow in future years as more inmates complete long prison terms. Just 7 percent of all inmates are serving sentences of death or life without parole, and only a fraction of inmates—about 3,000 each year—die in prison. Thus, 93 percent of all inmates eventually return home.

Society has always struggled with how best to help inmates reintegrate once released, but the current situation is unprecedented. The number of returning offenders dwarfs anything in America's history. The needs of offenders appear more serious, the parole system retains few rehabilitation programs, and the housing and employment barriers offenders face upon return are more daunting. It is now time to design effective reentry programs. To do so, corrections professionals must better understand the characteristics of inmates coming home, the needs and risks offenders represent, and society's legal and practical barriers to reintegration.

Who Is Coming Home?

Most of those released from prison today have serious social and medical problems. More than three-fourths of the inmates scheduled for release in the next year report a history of drug and/or alcohol abuse. One-fourth have histories of injection drug use and 16 percent report a mental condition.

Yet, less than one-third of exiting inmates received substance abuse or mental health treatment in prison. And while some states have provided more funding for prison drug treatment, the percentage of state inmates participating in such programs has been declining, from 25 percent a decade ago to about 10 percent today, according to *Prisoner Reentry in Perspective*.[1]

Few inmates have marketable skills or sufficient literacy to become gainfully employed. According to the Bureau of Justice Statistics, one-third of all U.S. inmates were unemployed at their most recent arrest, and only 60 percent of inmates have a GED or high school diploma (compared with 85 percent of the U.S. adult population). The National Adult Literacy Survey established that 11 percent of inmates, compared with 3 percent of the general U.S. population, have a learning disability, and 3 percent are mentally retarded.

Again, despite evidence that inmates' literacy and job readiness has declined in the past decade, fewer inmates are participating in prison education or vocational programs. Today, only 25 percent of all those released from prison will have participated in vocational training programs, and about one-third of exiting inmates will have participated in education programs—both figures down from a decade ago, *Prisoner Reentry in Perspective* indicates.

Preparing Inmates for Release

If inmate needs are more serious than in the past, why have the programs to meet those needs declined? Part of the problem is money, which is even more of a problem now with a declining economy. The nation now spends about $31 billion a year to operate the nation's prisons. By adding in jail, probation and parole, the nation spends nearly $50 billion annually on corrections.

These dollars have not funded more treatment and work programs, but rather prison staff, construction, and rising prison health care costs. Inmates are the only U.S. citizens who have a constitutional right to receive free medical care because they are not able to seek care on their own. As the inmate population has gotten older and sicker, data from the American Correctional Association indicate that inmate health care costs have risen from an annual average of $880 per inmate in 1982 to nearly $3,300 per inmate in 2003.

According to the 2003 *Corrections Yearbook* by the Criminal Justice Institute Inc., medical budgets make-up, on average, 10 percent to 12 percent of a state's total correctional operating budget, and that percentage is increasing each year. Prison treatment programs, on the other hand, make-up 1 percent to 5 percent of state prison budgets, and that percentage is decreasing each year. At least 25 states report having made cuts in vocational and technical training, the areas most likely to provide inmates with an alternative career when they leave prison.

Ironically, as inmate needs have increased and in-prison programs decreased, parole supervision and services also have decreased for most reentering inmates. In 1977, just 4 percent of all inmates released "maxed out" or served the maximum amount of time allowed by law for their criminal conviction. But today, 18 percent—or nearly one in five of all exiting inmates—max out, having no obligation to report to a parole officer or abide by any other conditions of release.[2] That is about 150,000 inmates a year, or about the same number of total parole releases in 1980.

This all results in higher-risk inmates going into prison, fewer programs, and more idle time while in prison, and a greater number getting out of prison without the benefits and control of parole supervision. Some worry that inmate reentry equates to inmate recidivism and may lead to increased crime rates. FBI statistics show that murder increased 1.7 percent in 2003, the only crime type to show an increase from 2002. Already, crime increases in Boston, Chicago, Oakland, California, and Los Angeles are being blamed on inmate returns.

Inmates who do not max out are released to parole supervision, but what does that mean for most inmates? Most of them will be given a bus ticket and told to report to the parole office in their home community. National statistics also show that 10 percent of all state parolees who are required to report to parole offices after release fail to do so. They abscond supervision and their whereabouts remain unknown to parole authorities. In California, which supervises one out of five parolees nationwide, the abscond rate is a staggering 22 percent.

By adding the number of parole absconders (about 44,000), to the number who were not required to report to parole in the first place (150,000), this comes to nearly 200,000 parolees coming out of prison each year who remain unsupervised, or their whereabouts unknown on a daily basis—this equates to one-third of all exiting inmates. Clearly this should be a cause for public concern, particularly for the inner-city communities to which most ex-offenders return.

Employment and Workplace Restrictions

While prisons were reducing services to inmates behind bars and after release, Congress and many state legislatures were independently passing dozens of laws restricting the kinds of jobs ex-inmates could be hired for, easing the requirements for their parental rights to be terminated, limiting their right to vote, and restricting their access to public welfare and housing subsidies. Jeremy Travis, author of the article "Invisible Punishment: An Instrument of Social Exclusion,"[3] writes that these new laws have remained rather unnoticed and undebated, but their effects on inmate reintegration are profound.

Most experts believe that finding a job is critical to successful reintegration. Employment helps ex-offenders be productive, take care of their families, develop valuable life skills, and strengthen their self-esteem and social connectedness. Research has empirically established a positive link between job stability and reduced criminal offending. Despite this critical link, the number of occupations ex-offenders are barred from has increased dramatically since 1985, and former inmates face an explicit unwillingness of many employers to hire them for jobs from which they are not legally barred.

Figure 1

Number and Percentage of U.S. Adult Population with Criminal Records of Various Types, 2000

Type of Criminal Record	Total	Percent of Population		
		All Adults	Adult Males	Adult Black Males
Inmates (includes current or former inmates and parolees; federal and state)	5 million	2.5%	5%	15-19%
Felons (includes prison, parole, felony probation, and convicted felony jail populations)	13 million	6.5%	11%	29-37%

Source: Uggen et al. 2002.

* The lower-bound estimates assume a 25 percent higher recidivism rate for black inmates, probationers, and parolees.

It is generally illegal for an employer to impose a flat ban on hiring ex-offenders. However, employers are increasingly forbidden from hiring them for certain jobs and are mandated to perform background checks before hiring an applicant for many others. Ex-offenders are now commonly barred from working in the fields of child care, education, security, nursing and home heath care—exactly the jobs that labor economists say are growing the fastest. More jobs are also now unionized, and many unions flatly exclude ex-offenders. Even a prior arrest as a juvenile is an absolute bar to employment in certain occupations in many states.

Even if ex-offenders legally can qualify for some jobs, a recent employer survey conducted by Worthlin Worldwide[4] in five major U.S. cities for unskilled jobs found that roughly 65 percent of all employers would not knowingly hire an ex-offender (regardless of the offense), and between 30 percent and 40 percent actually checked the criminal history records of their most recently hired employees (*see* Figure 1). Therefore, the number of jobs for ex-offenders is declining rapidly.

No state or federal prison tracks the number of inmates employed after release, but the few available statistics continue to reveal high rates of joblessness among this group. Unemployment among ex-offenders has been estimated at between 25 and 40 percent. In California, it has been estimated that as many as 80 percent of ex-offenders remain jobless a year after being released from prison.

Clearly, the bias and stigma arising from having a criminal record limit the job prospects of ex-inmates. Civil disabilities and other legal restrictions limit the jobs for which they can apply, and in jobs for which they are legally eligible, there is stiff competition for a declining number of them. If parolees are truthful about their backgrounds, many employers will not hire them. If they are not truthful, they can be fired for lying if the employer learns about their conviction.

Publicly Available Criminal Records

The expansion of legal barriers has been accompanied by an increase in the ease of checking criminal records due to new technologies and expanded public access to criminal records through the Internet. Historically, criminal records were restricted to law enforcement and those with a "need to know." Today, those restrictions have been lifted and, for all practical purposes, one's criminal past is public. In twenty-nine states, "anyone" can obtain at least some type of criminal record information on anyone they wish. In twenty-five states, that information can be publicly accessed through the Internet.[5]

Expanded restrictions now apply to a greater percentage of the U.S. population simply because of the explosion in the number of people convicted and imprisoned during the past decade. The Department of Justice reports that more than 59 million Americans have a criminal arrest record on file with state repositories—or 29 of the nation's entire adult population—the number of records more than doubling in the past decade.

Further, researchers estimate that more than 13 million Americans are ex-felons, that is, they had been convicted of a felony and served or are currently serving a felony probation, parole, prison or jail sentence. This equals about 6 percent of the entire adult population, 11 percent of the adult male population and an astounding 29 to 37 percent of the adult black male population (*see* Figure 2).

Certainly, the public safety benefits of sharing criminal record information are undeniable, but there are inherent dangers as well. Some of the criminal record information in the FBI and state registries has been shown to be inaccurate, yet it is shared with landlords, financial institutions, and employers as if it were valid. Eric Johnson, of SEARCH Group Inc., conducted a review in 2002 for the Department of Justice, and he found that about 60 percent of all arrest entries failed to record final disposition data.[6] Yet, ten states provide members of the general public with this arrest-without-disposition information.

Of course, access to criminal records is tremendously useful in protecting victims, community members, and employers. This value cannot be overstated. However, the detrimental effects on returning inmates must be considered, given that these records—some of them inaccurate—will be used to make decisions about them for the rest of their lives. As the number of people and kinds of crimes that get people sentenced to prison has expanded, more first-time drug offenders have these restrictions applied to them—often for life. These people, who would not have gone to prison just twenty years ago, would not go to prison in other countries and are now forever labeled an ex-offender. Once someone's record gets posted on the Internet, there is no pulling it back.

Figure 2: Employer Survey on Hiring of Ex-Offenders

Category	Percentage
Would Never Hire Anyone With a Criminal Record	8%
Would Never Hire Anyone With a Criminal Record Within Five Years	17%
Would Never Hire Anyone With a Felony White Collar Conviction	38%
Would Never Hire Anyone With a Felony Drug Conviction	40%
Would Never Hire Anyone With a Violent Felony Conviction	43%

Source: Wirthlin Wordwide, 2000.

Housing and Homelessness

Parole officials say finding housing for parolees is by far their biggest challenge, even more difficult and important than finding a job. State inmates are often incarcerated in facilities far away from their return destination, and have no opportunity to secure housing prior to discharge. Parole conditions also can prevent parolees from living or associating with others who are criminally involved. This restriction includes family and friends who may be willing to take this person in. And since ex-inmates are usually unable to amass the funds required to move into an apartment (for example, first and last month's rent, security deposit), the private housing market, which represents 97 percent of the total housing stock in the United States, is usually cost-prohibitive. Even if they can afford it, landlords conducting background checks or requiring credible work histories usually pass over an ex-offender applicant.

Ex-inmates attempt to locate suitable public housing, but recently passed public housing laws now require public housing agencies and providers to deny housing to certain felons (for example, drug and sex offenders). Even if they qualify, waiting lists can be as long as two-to-three years for subsidized housing. What results is that former inmates show up at crowded shelters with long waiting lists and limits on the number of days they can remain in residence.

Inmates returning to their families in subsidized public housing complexes are often no longer welcome. Due to the U.S. Department of Housing and Urban Development's "one strike and you're out" policy, the Public Housing Authority may evict all members of the household for criminal activities committed by any one member of a household. In addition, federal regulations grant the Public Housing Authority the discretion to prohibit admission of all other criminally involved individuals. These restrictions, combined with the fact that the inventory of U.S. public housing continues to shrink, means that parolees are seldom allowed to live in public housing.

Housing and homelessness certainly affect an individual's chances of recidivism. However, analysts say there are broader implications and parolee homelessness influences overall crime rates in the community. Large numbers of transients, panhandling and vagrants increase citizen fear, and that fear ultimately contributes to increased crime and violence.

Reforming Parole and Reentry Practices

For most offenders, corrections does not mean correct. Indeed, the conditions under which many inmates are handled are detrimental to successful reintegration, and many of the restrictions placed on returning inmates proved deeply counterproductive. Clearly, policies are needed that reflect the states' legitimate interests in public protection, but do not simultaneously, in and of themselves, diminish an individual's motivation and ability to change, which produces more crime in the long run. The following recommendations should receive priority in parole reform efforts.

Reinvest in prison work, education and substance abuse programs. The corrections field simply cannot reduce recidivism without funding programs that open up more treatment and work programs for ex-offenders. Today, there is ample evidence that treatment can reduce recidivism if the programs are well-designed, well-implemented, and targeted appropriately.

Effective programs include therapeutic communities for drug addicts, substance abuse programs with aftercare for alcoholics and drug addicts, cognitive-behavioral programs for sex offenders, and adult vocational education and prison industries for the general prison population. Steve Aos and his colleagues[7] found that each of these programs has been shown to reduce the recidivism rates of program participants by 8 to 15 percent. Even with these relatively modest reductions in subsequent recidivism, these programs pay for themselves in terms of reducing future justice expenditures.

Discretionary parole should be reinstituted in the sixteen states that have abolished it. Abolishing parole was a politically expedient way to appease the public who wrongly equated parole with letting inmates out early. However, the public was misinformed when it labeled parole as *lenient*. On the contrary, recent research shows that inmates who are released through discretionary parole actually serve longer prison terms, on average, than those released mandatorily, and the difference is most pronounced for violent offenders. Inmates released by a discretionary parole board also have higher success rates. Both of these results hold true even after statistically controlling for crime type, prior criminal history, and other demographics.

These data suggest that having to earn and demonstrate readiness for release, and being supervised post-prison, may have some deterrent or rehabilitation benefits—particularly for the most dangerous offenders. Discretionary parole systems also provide a means by which inmates who represent continuing public safety risks can be kept in prison. And discretionary parole also serves to refocus prison staff and correctional budgets on planning for release, not just opening the door at release.

Front-load post-prison services during the first six months after release.

Recidivism data show that return to crime happens very quickly; 30 percent of all released inmates are rearrested for a serious crime in the first six months. On the other hand, recidivism declines dramatically after three years, and after five years of arrest-free behavior, recidivism is extremely low. These data suggest that the first three to six months after release are critical to success, and the limited resources available should concentrate on that time period. At the same time, parole terms of longer than five years for all but the most serious offenders should be eliminated for parolees who have remained arrest free during that time.

It makes no sense to spend $23,000 a year on an inmate—even three times that amount if he or she were in maximum security—and then on the day of the inmate's release, spend from zero dollars (for unconditional releases) to about $2,500 a year for the average parolee. What if corrections spent that same amount of money per month during the first three months after release as is done for the three months prior to release? This would cost about $7,000 for every inmate returning home. This money would support transitional housing, employment if no other job could be found, drug treatment, medical attention, family counseling—in short, whatever was required to increase the odds of successful transition.

Implement a "goal parole" or earned discharge system. Factors such as work, education and treatment incentives would be built into the system, and parolees could earn time off their parole term by succeeding in pro-social activities. There is little public risk in such a system since research shows that informal social controls—those interpersonal bonds that link ex-inmates to churches, jobs, law-abiding neighbors, families and communities — are strong predictors of reduced recidivism.

Recognize the vital role crime victims have to play in managing the offender's return. Most states now have statutes authorizing the victim to be notified of parole hearings and of parole eligibility dates. Unfortunately, this is a hollow victory; victims have increasingly gained the right to appear and testify at parole hearings, but fewer states are holding such hearings. Crime victims often have the most detailed knowledge of the offender and the risks he or she poses to public safety. They are ideally suited to assist correctional authorities in assigning parole conditions. Even if most parole boards no longer retain the discretion to set the date of release, all of them set the conditions of release. Of course, authorities must balance the victim's need for vengeance and safety with the true risks posed by the returning inmate.

It is not just that the victim could provide information to parole officials, but parole officials could help reduce victims' fears if they were more communicative. They might tell the victim that the parolee has completed a substance abuse program, is employed full time, or will be monitored on an intensive supervision caseload, all of which might serve to increase the victim's sense of safety.

Establish procedures by which some ex-offenders can put their criminal offending entirely in the past. The United States has the highest incarceration rate of industrial democracies, but unlike all other democracies, it has virtually no practical means of sealing or expunging adult criminal records. A criminal conviction, no matter how trivial or how long ago it occurred, scars a person for life. In terms of this issue, the United States has the worst of both worlds: higher rates of application of the criminal process combined with no way to move legally beyond its stigmatizing effects. Establishing some procedure by which some ex-offenders can move beyond their criminal records is critically important.

Nearly all other countries have recognized the value in doing this. For example, England's Rehabilitation of Offenders Act allows some adult criminal convictions to become "spent" or ignored after a significant period of time (usually seven to ten years) has elapsed from the date of conviction, if no felony convictions occur during this time. For those ex-offenders who meet the criteria, when asked, "Have you ever been convicted of a crime?" the law allows them to say no. England's act is actually more stringent than those of most other countries, where all criminal offenses become spent after specified time periods.

These and other reforms discussed in this author's book, *When Prisoners Come Home: Parole and Prisoner Reentry*, will help to create a more finely tailored system—where those who are dangerous will remain in prison through discretionary decision making, and those who are not will have an opportunity to participate in proven treatment and work programs both in prison and on parole. Procedures will be adopted so that society will not continue to impede, for a lifetime, the efforts of those ex-offenders who wish to go straight, but often are prevented from doing so because barriers are put up that even nonoffenders would not be able to overcome.

The nation faces enormous challenges in managing the reintegration of increasing numbers of individuals who are leaving state and federal prisons. It is time to do the hard work of developing more effective responses to these challenges. This should be done not only because it will be good for offenders returning home, but because it will ultimately be good for their children, their neighbors, and the community at large.

ENDNOTES

[1] Lynch, J. P. and W. J. Sabol. 2001. *Prisoner Reentry in Perspective*. Washington, D.C.: Urban Institute.

[2] Petersilia, J. 2003. *When Prisoners Come Home: Parole and Prisoner Reentry*. New York: Oxford University Press.

[3] Travis, J. 2002. Invisible Punishment: An Instrument of Social Exclusion. In M. Mauer and M. Chesney-Lind, eds. *Invisible Punishment: The Collateral Consequences of Mass Imprisonment*, pp. 15-36. Washington, D.C.: Urban Institute.

[4] Wirthlin Worldwide. 2000. *Member Survey: Taking the Next Step: Welfare to Work Partnership*, Vol. 1. McLean, Virginia. Available at www.welfaretowork.org.

[5] *See* Petersilia J. 2003. *When Prisoners Come Home: Parole and Prisoner Reentry:*New York: Oxford University Press for tables indicating each state's policies.

[6] Johnson, E. 2002. U.S. *Survey of Access to Criminal Records: Update.* Unpublished tables. Sacramento, California: SEARCH Group, Inc..

[7] Aos, S., P. Phipps, R. Barnoski and R. Lieb. 2001. *The Comparative Costs and Benefits of Programs to Reduce Crime.* Seattle: Washington State Institute for Public Policy.

Joan Petersilia, Ph.D., is a professor of criminology at the University of California, Irvine. She is the author of Reforming Probation and Parole in the 21st Century, *available from ACA.*

Reentry/ Reintegration Survey, 2004

First printed in *Corrections Compendium*, a publication of the American Correctional Association, March/April 2004

As evidenced by this *Corrections Compendium* survey on reentry/reintegration, many correctional systems find value in programs that prepare inmates for release. In fact, New Jersey is the only statewide adult correctional system among the forty-five U.S. correctional systems that responded to this survey that does not have a formal reentry program in place. However, it is in the planning stages of implementing a formalized program. Four jurisdictions in Canada also submitted completed surveys, and all but Newfoundland reported having reentry programs.

Schedules

Attendance in planned programs is required in 27 percent of the U.S. reporting systems and in none of the Canadian reporting systems. In Minnesota, participation is mandatory in facilities that have sufficient transition staffing. Some inmates are exempted from the requirements, including those serving time for misdemeanant convictions in Alaska; those with medical, mental health, discipline and/or attitude issues in Colorado; those sentenced to less than 120 days in Washington, D.C.; those not in certain facilities in the metropolitan Baltimore area; those having no felony or immigration holds in Nevada; or those serving a life or death sentence or more than five years away from a possible release date in South Dakota. Attendance is voluntary in nine U.S. reporting systems.

Nineteen of the U.S. reporting systems indicated that their planned programs were created to last at least six months, while Colorado, Kansas, Mississippi, and Nebraska have one-year programs. Programs in New York, South Dakota, and Vermont begin with an inmate's arrival at the facility and last throughout the inmates' time in prison. The length of scheduled programs varies in all other reporting systems. Formal class schedules vary by the type of class or by the facility, and no consensus is offered.

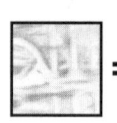

Class Components

The U.S. reporting systems offer the following classes through their reentry/reintegration programs: education, 84 percent; job readiness, 98 percent; community resources, 95 percent; substance abuse, 93 percent; housing, 77 percent; rules of post supervision, 91 percent; family reunification, 77 percent; and cognitive behavior, 82 percent. Other formal sessions mentioned by the reporting systems include general life skills, motor vehicle training, health matters, money management, victim awareness, career assessment, faith-based resources, citizenship, and character development, the impact of crime, and anger management. In Canada, two of the four reporting systems hold sessions in all stated program areas except substance abuse and family reunification, and three of them offer sessions on housing. Numerous informal sessions are also noted in Table 2.

Staffing Patterns

Each of the four Canadian reporting systems assigns staff specifically to the reentry program, while 91 percent of the U.S. reporting systems do so. Credentials for the teaching staff vary from a bachelor's degree to a degree plus some experience or demonstrated skill in curriculum development and working with inmates. In Indiana, requirements include philosophy and credits in theory of corrections, general legal knowledge, specialized knowledge of work/study release procedures, and communication skills. Staff are contracted through local community colleges in Maryland and Nebraska and are certified by the technical college system in Wisconsin. In Nevada and New Mexico, staff must have a master's degree.

Volunteers are actively pursued to assist with reentry/reintegration programs in 64 percent of the U.S. reporting systems and by two of the Canadian reporting systems. Primarily, job-specific credentials are required in most of the systems as well as the completion of orientation and the departmental training series. California, Maryland, South Carolina and Wyoming require volunteers to pass a security clearance. Formal ties with the local communities are maintained by all the Canadian reporting systems and by 89 percent of the U.S. reporting systems. A new parole model provides a contracted social worker in each California district. An extensive community participation effort is conducted in Kansas in the areas of housing, employment, job training, mental health care, substance abuse treatment, mentoring, medical care, hygiene packet distribution, batterer intervention, victim safety planning, family counseling, and financial/ credit counseling. To most of those liaisons, Nevada adds mental health treatment, clothing, food, veterans' services, family reunification, and other services. Formal community participation in reentry/reintegration occurs prior to discharge in 70 percent of the U.S. reporting systems and three of the Canadian reporting systems.

Transition Detention

Separate units within facilities are provided to those preparing for reentry in 18 percent of the U.S. reporting systems. Community halfway houses are used by 33 percent of the U.S. reporting systems. Other methods of transition detention include prerelease facilities in 31 percent of the U.S. reporting systems (for the last thirty days of confinement in South Carolina), day reporting centers in 29 percent of the systems, and community agencies in 29 percent of the systems. Substance-abuse transitional housing is available in Florida on a voluntary basis and includes 400 faith-based beds and 400 general beds. The percentage range of those placed in transition detention is 3.5 percent in West Virginia to 90 percent in New Hampshire, while placements are made for 100 percent of the inmates in the North Dakota reentry program. Except for a halfway house in Newfoundland, the Canadian reporting systems do not offer transition detention.

Discharge

The types of personal effects provided to exiting inmates were itemized by forty-two of the reporting systems, including the four Canadian reporting systems, while the items were not specified in six other systems. In Mississippi, inmates are not provided with anything upon their release. Ninety-three percent of the U.S. and Canadian reporting systems return personal property to inmates and 40 percent return their account balances. Gate money is offered in 33 percent of the reporting systems and ranges from $50 to $200. Airplane or bus fare (if needed) is provided by 31 percent of the U.S. and Canadian systems; clothing is provided by 48 percent; medications by 12 percent; and identification materials by 17 percent. Oregon also supplies a referral letter for social assistance, as well as a hygiene packet to females and a Smart Start kit to males, which includes a ten-minute calling card, personal hygiene products, and information on sexually transmitted diseases.

Eleven U.S. reporting systems and one in Canada do not conduct any formal follow-up on released offenders. A wide variety of follow-up procedures are being conducted by the remaining forty-four systems and three Canadian systems. These procedures include: parole and probation supervision, when applicable, throughout the mandated release-from-parole date or from six to twelve months in Colorado, depending on employment and other support system status; follow-up by case manager advocates for six months in Kansas for those on special location releases; one-year monitoring by Mississippi prerelease counselors or until employment is secured; and at intervals of six, twelve, and eighteen months for participants of the reentry program in North Dakota. Recidivism rates are calculated for up to three years following release in Pennsylvania and recidivism interviews are conducted for those who return to prison in South Dakota.

Evolving Programs

The results of a similar survey conducted in 2000 indicated that many respondents had prerelease programs in place but they were not nearly as formalized as those noted in the current survey. In addition, the majority did not conduct any type of formal follow-up service—a far cry from today's efforts to thwart recidivism.

REENTRY / REINTEGRATION — TABLE 1: SCHEDULE

SYSTEM	PLANNED PROGRAM			FORMAL CLASS SCHEDULE
	Yes/No	Required	Exempted	Length	
ALABAMA	No response				
ALASKA	Yes	No	Inmates being released after serving time for misdemeanant convictions	6 months	Schedule varies depending on the individual need of the inmate
ARIZONA	Yes	Yes		6 months	Eight-hour classes that include a video presentation and related workbook
ARKANSAS	Yes	No	Voluntary	2 months, approximately	Half-day classes for the 62-day program
CALIFORNIA	Yes	Yes	Some inmates due to custody classification and limitation of available program space based on security requirements	240 days	
COLORADO	Yes	No	Inmates with medical, mental health, discipline and/or attitude problems	1 year	120-180 hours
CONNECTICUT	Yes	No	Voluntary	Varies, depending on the facility	Varies, depending on the facility
DELAWARE	Yes	Yes		6 months	Varies by type of class
DISTRICT OF COLUMBIA	Yes	No	All inmates being held for pretrial or those sentenced to under 120 days	3 months	Four days per month; 2½ hours per class
FLORIDA	Yes	Yes		6 months	120 hours
GEORGIA	Yes	No	Due to a small number of transitional center beds, acceptance is based on parole board requirements or facility recommendations	6 months	Varies by site but usually based on 10-20 hours per class
HAWAII	Yes	No	Inmates sentenced to less than nine months	Varies	Varies from 2 to 6 hours per day for 12 to 20 days per month, depending on program
IDAHO	Yes	No	Voluntary	6 months	15 days per month; 3 hours per class
ILLINOIS	No response				
INDIANA	Yes	Yes		6 months	Varies, but the standard program is 80 hours
IOWA	No response				
KANSAS	Yes	No	Program 1, which focuses on life skills, cognitive change, and job preparedness, is available to minimum-custody inmates; Program 2 is for high-risk inmates ages 18-35 returning to the Topeka area; and Program 3 is for inmates with disabilities, including mental illness	10 weeks; 1 year for first-time releasees of programs 2 or 3; scaled-back program for condition/parole violators serving 90 days	6 hours per day for 10 weeks for Program 1; 2 hours twice each week for 6-8 weeks for Program 2, depending on the topic
KENTUCKY	Yes	No	Inmates housed in area jails	30 days	Single class for 3 hours
LOUISIANA	Yes	Yes		6 months but can begin as early as 1½ years prior to release	Each institution is required to provide 100 hours but there is no established number of days or hours; 6 components with a minimum of 16 hours per component are provided
MAINE	No response				
MARYLAND	Yes	No	Those inmates not targeted in five zip codes within the Baltimore metropolitan area	18 months	20 days per month; 2-hour classes
MASSACHUSETTS	No response				
MICHIGAN	No response				
MINNESOTA	Yes[1]			4-6 months	18 classroom hours
MISSISSIPPI	Yes	No	Inmates who do not meet eligibility requirements	1 year	23 days per month; 6-hour classes
MISSOURI	Yes	No	Target population through a grant	Varies based on needs identified in a transition accountability plan	Linkage to services in the community prior to release based on identified needs
MONTANA	Yes	No	Inmates who do not meet eligibility requirements	7-8 months on average	None
NEBRASKA	Yes[2]	No	Voluntary	1 year	38 hours after development of a personalized plan indicating needs (substance abuse, mental health issues, education, and so forth.)

[1] MINNESOTA: Participation is mandatory at facilities with sufficient transition staffing.
[2] NEBRASKA: The department is developing a pilot reentry program specifically for violent offenders at risk of recidivating upon discharge.

REENTRY / REINTEGRATION — TABLE 1: SCHEDULE

PLANNED PROGRAM

SYSTEM	Yes/No	Required	Exempted	Length	FORMAL CLASS SCHEDULE
NEVADA	Yes	No	Inmates who do not meet specific requirements (those paroling to areas other than southern Nevada), no felony/immigration holds, and no violent offenders with weapons, gang, or multiple violent felonies, present or past	6 months prior to parole and 1 year post release	15-20 days per month; 1- to 4-hour classes
NEW HAMPSHIRE	Yes[3]	Yes		Approximately 2 months prior to parole date	None
NEW JERSEY	No[4]				
NEW MEXICO	Yes	No	Voluntary	Varies by type of program	Varies by type of program and includes homework
NEW YORK	Yes	Yes		Phase 1: upon arrival, Phase 2: during term of incarceration, Phase 3: 6 to 9 months prior to release	20 days per month; 2½-hour classes
NORTH CAROLINA	Yes	No	Voluntary	Varies, based on length of sentence	2 hours per class
NORTH DAKOTA	Yes	No	Inmates not participating in the reentry program or transitional housing programs	4 weeks	30 hours overall
OHIO	Yes	Yes	Inmates with serious mental health or medical problems or for security issues	6 months but varies at institutions housing short-term inmates	Varies per month; 2½-hour workshops
OKLAHOMA	Yes	No	Inmates who do not require program services	6 months	Generally, a minimum of 40 hours per class that varies by facility
OREGON	Yes	No	Program is not offered at all institutions	6 months	Varies by institution
PENNSYLVANIA	Yes	No	Optional for inmates completing their maximum sentence date	1 month	10 days per month; 7½-hour classes
RHODE ISLAND	Yes	No	Voluntary	From 18 months to 60 days[5]	Varies by the vendors
SOUTH CAROLINA	Yes	No	All inmates not targeted for the Serious and Violent Offender Reentry Initiative or inmates at prerelease centers	12 to 18 months	15 to 20 days per month; 1 to 1½-hour classes
SOUTH DAKOTA	Yes	No	Inmates serving a life sentence or death sentence or those more than five years away from possible release date	Begun at sentencing	Varies by type of program
TENNESSEE	Yes	No	Voluntary	90 days	20 days per month; 4- to 6-hour classes, varying by institution
TEXAS	Yes	No	Inmates as a result of custody classification or those not targeted for specific-needs programs; some programs may be limited in capacity	6 months for most programs (sex offender treatment and faith-based programs are 18 months in length)	20 days per month; 3-hour classes
UTAH	Yes	Yes		6 months	1 hour per class, one day per month
VERMONT	Yes	No	Inmates who max out	Begun at sentencing	N/A
VIRGINIA	Yes	Yes[6]		40 hours	Varies
WASHINGTON	Yes	No	All inmates with post-release supervision requirements who do not develop plans	6 months	Varies
WEST VIRGINIA	Yes	No	Inmates discharging their sentences	6 months	2 hours
WISCONSIN	Yes	No	Inmates not required to participate in specific programs	3 to 6 months; some phased programs begin prior to 6 months	Varies depending on the type of session
WYOMING	Yes	No	Voluntary	6 months	2 to 4 days per week depending on the facility
FEDERAL BUREAU OF PRISONS	No response				

[3] NEW HAMPSHIRE: The program relates only to the writing of an inmate's parole plan.
[4] NEW JERSEY: A formalized program is in the planning stages.
[5] RHODE ISLAND: Ten discharge planning vendors establish their own protocols.
[6] VIRGINIA: The program is required when space is available.

REENTRY / REINTEGRATION — TABLE 1: SCHEDULE

SYSTEM	Yes/No	Required	PLANNED PROGRAM Exempted	Length	FORMAL CLASS SCHEDULE
CANADIAN SYSTEMS					
NEWFOUNDLAND	No				
NOVA SCOTIA	Yes	No	All juveniles ages 12-17 and certain adults determined on a case-by-case basis	60 to 90 days	Varies
ONTARIO	Yes	No	Voluntary	Varies by institution and, in some cases, is by inmate request only	N/A
CORRECTIONAL SERVICE CANADA	Yes	No	Inmates who do not meet the criteria of the program	6 months	1 to 5 days per week; 2½-hour classes based upon need

REENTRY / REINTEGRATION — TABLE 2: PROGRAM COMPONENTS

SYSTEM	Education	Job Readiness	Community Resources	Substance Abuse	Housing	Rules of Post Supervision	Family Reunification	Cognitive Behavior	Other	INFORMAL SESSIONS
ALABAMA	No response									
ALASKA	X	X	X	X	X	X	X	X	General life skills	Incorporated into all general classes offered by the department (in other words substance abuse education, basic literacy, GED preparation, and vocational education)
ARIZONA	X	X	X	X	X	X	X			
ARKANSAS		X	X	X		X	X	X		
CALIFORNIA	X	X	X	X	X	X	X	X	Extensive services to parolees	
COLORADO	X	X	X	X	X	X	X	X		Personal development, life skills, employability skills, and transition planning in a modular format
CONNECTICUT	X	X	X	X	X	X	X	X	Motor vehicle training	
DELAWARE	X	X	X	X	X	X	X			
DISTRICT OF COLUMBIA	X	X	X	X	X	X	X		Health matters	Employment program for males; Our Place (employment, housing and clothing); ex-offenders' support group
FLORIDA	X	X	X	X	X	X	X	X		A video and related workbook
GEORGIA	X	X	X	X	X	X	X	X		AA/NA, motivational speakers and ex-offender speakers
HAWAII	X	X	X	X	X	X	X	X		Work, electronic monitoring and education furloughs, AA/NA, family counseling and domestic violence classes
IDAHO	X	X	X	X	X	X		X		
ILLINOIS	No response									
INDIANA	X	X	X	X	X	X	X		Establishing social identity	Due to time or other constraints, some inmates receive an individual workbook rather than a classroom-based program
IOWA	No response									
KANSAS		X				X	X		Money management, human relations, living in today's world, thinking for a change, communications and the law, and situational response [1]	Case manager advocates work individually with Program 2 inmates; individualized work also is done with Program 3 inmates, with a focus on the disability
KENTUCKY						X				
LOUISIANA	X	X	X	X	X	X	X	X	Money management and victim awareness	
MAINE	No response									
MARYLAND		X	X			X		X		Exit orientation fairs for inmates unable to participate in the formal classes
MASSACHUSETTS	No response									
MICHIGAN	No response									
MINNESOTA	X	X	X	X	X	X	X	X	Personal ID documentation, transportation, personal health and money management	Transition resource centers for self-service access by inmates
MISSISSIPPI	X	X	X	X	X	X	X			
MISSOURI	X	X	X	X		X	X	X		
MONTANA	X	X	X	X		X	X	X		Anger management, chemical dependency counseling, employment skills, self-help skills, parenting, and GED preparation

[1] KANSAS: Components for the Shawnee County Reentry Program include additional subjects such as life skills, budgeting, transportation, diversity and tolerance, resume building, and women's health and nutrition.

REENTRY / REINTEGRATION — TABLE 2: PROGRAM COMPONENTS

SYSTEM	Education	Job Readiness	Community Resources	Substance Abuse	Housing	Rules of Post Supervision	Family Reunification	Cognitive Behavior	Other	INFORMAL SESSIONS
NEBRASKA	X	X	X		X	X	X	X	Career assessment and money management	
NEVADA	X	X	X	X	X	X	X	X	Mental health evaluation and counseling	Parenting skills, Project Metamorphosis, anger management, money management, job development skills, AA and NA
NEW HAMPSHIRE		X	X	X	X	X	X	X		Parole plan preparation
NEW JERSEY [2]										
NEW MEXICO	X	X	X	X	X	X	X		Health and social services	
NEW YORK	X	X	X	X	X	X	X	X	Various enrichment and life skills activities	
NORTH CAROLINA	X	X	X	X	X	X				
NORTH DAKOTA	X	X	X	X	X	X		X	Faith-based resources, mental health workshop, and community justice	
OHIO		X	X	X	X	X		X		
OKLAHOMA	X	X	X	X				X		
OREGON	X	X	X	X	X	X	X	X		
PENNSYLVANIA	X	X	X	X		X	X	X	Spiritual, victim awareness, citizenship, and character development	Bridging the Gap for 25 inmates returning to the south/central region of the state; Forensic Reentry Development for 30 females with mental health/mental retardation and co-occurring substance abuse disorders; and Erie Reentry for 270 inmates
RHODE ISLAND	X	X	X	X	X	X	X	X	Infectious diseases and life skills by one vendor	Other agencies offer individual case management for discharge planning
SOUTH CAROLINA	X	X	X	X	X	X	X	X	Impact of crime	
SOUTH DAKOTA	X	X	X	X	X	X	X	X		
TENNESSEE	X	X	X	X	X	X	X	X	Community service projects	Outside agency speakers participate in sessions with inmates on the inside
TEXAS	X	X	X	X		X	X	X	Anger management	At Windham Unit: Project RIO (Reintegration of Offenders) documents job history and vocational training and provides information to the Texas Workforce Commission to help secure employment.
UTAH	X	X	X	X	X	X	X	X		
VERMONT	X	X	X	X	X	X	X	X	Sex offender treatment	An Offender Responsibility Plan is in effect for the duration of an inmate's incarceration
VIRGINIA	X	X	X	X	X	X	X	X		Some inmates are returned to local jails for programming and transition planning and often work release; transitional housing in community contract facilities for inmates in the substance abuse therapeutic community programs; and VASAVOR where violent inmates are returned to local jails for special programming and transition planning by a team of local agencies
WASHINGTON	X		X	X	X	X	X	X		Establishment of community collaborators for high-risk inmates offering assistance in locating a residence and family friendly activities
WEST VIRGINIA	X	X	X	X	X	X		X	Infectious disease education	

[2] NEW JERSEY: A formalized program is being developed.

REENTRY / REINTEGRATION — TABLE 2: PROGRAM COMPONENTS

SYSTEM	FORMAL SESSIONS									INFORMAL SESSIONS
	Education	Job Readiness	Community Resources	Substance Abuse	Housing	Rules of Post Supervision	Family Reunification	Cognitive Behavior	Other	
WISCONSIN	X	X	X	X	X	X	X	X	Financial literacy, vocational training and work experience	Individual meetings between social workers and inmates for planning purposes
WYOMING	X	X	X	X				X		
FEDERAL BUREAU OF PRISONS	No response									
CANADIAN SYSTEMS										
NEWFOUNDLAND	X				X			X		Case management staff assist in programming
NOVA SCOTIA	X	X	X	X	X	X	X	X	Leisure activities	Individual case management conferences
ONTARIO									Core rehabilitative programs that address substance abuse, anger management, and anti-criminal thinking	Discharge assistance is available to all inmates by ministry program staff, community-based organizations under contract with the ministry and by volunteer organizations
CORRECTIONAL SERVICE CANADA		X	X		X	X			Substance abuse, education, cognitive behavior, and so forth, are offered separately from the formal prerelease program	

REENTRY / REINTEGRATION — TABLE 3: STAFFING PATTERNS

SYSTEM	INTERNAL STAFF Assigned	INTERNAL STAFF Credentials; Training	VOLUNTEERS Pursued	VOLUNTEERS Credentials; Training	FORMAL COMMUNITY PARTICIPATION Pursued	FORMAL COMMUNITY PARTICIPATION Type of Service	FORMAL COMMUNITY PARTICIPATION Prior to Discharge
ALABAMA	No response						
ALASKA	Yes	Job-specific credentials, depending on the particular program involved	No		Yes	Many of the planned programs offered	Yes
ARIZONA	Yes	Must be CO-III level or parole officers; academy graduates	Yes	Secular and/or faith-based acting as mentors; orientation training	Yes	Substance abuse treatment and follow-up, mental health and medical services, job development and housing	Victim notification and pre-home investigations
ARKANSAS	Yes	Bachelor's degree	No		No		
CALIFORNIA	Yes	Must meet minimum qualifications prior to hiring; contracts identifying accepted experience are required	No	Must pass security clearance	Yes	New parole model provides a contracted social worker in each district	No
COLORADO	Yes	Bachelor's degree and some experience; training developed by program staff	No		Yes	Work closely with various state, local and private agencies	No
CONNECTICUT	Yes	Varies	Yes	Not specified	Yes	All planned programs	Sometimes
DELAWARE	Yes	Counseling credentials	Yes	Established by state and specific agency standards	Yes	Varies	Not specified
DISTRICT OF COLUMBIA	No		Yes	Complete 16 hours of in-service training	No		
FLORIDA	No		Yes	Some experience; complete basic volunteer orientation and training	Yes	Employment, housing, transportation, continuing education, and so forth.	Yes
GEORGIA	Yes	Bachelor's degree	Yes	Complete orientation and training	Yes	Physical placement, vocational rehabilitation, educational upgrading	Yes
HAWAII	Yes	University degree; certified social workers, education instructors or substance abuse counselors'	Yes	Complete departmental training program	Yes	Vocational rehabilitation, employment, housing, drug treatment and educational, work or sex offender programs	Yes
IDAHO	Yes	Job-specific credentials; on-the-job training	Yes	Job-specific credentials; on-the-job training	Yes	Not specified	Yes
ILLINOIS	No response						
INDIANA	Yes	Extensive[1]	Yes	Job-specific credentials; orientation for frequent volunteers	Yes	Housing, employment, education, vocational training, mental health issues, and addictions	Yes
IOWA	No response						
KANSAS	Yes	Bachelor's degree and demonstrated skill in curriculum development and working with inmates	Yes	Job-specific credentials; complete orientation and specific training	Yes	Housing, employment, job training, mental health care, substance abuse treatment, mentoring, medical care, hygiene packet distribution, batterer intervention, victim safety planning, family counseling, and financial/credit counseling	Yes
KENTUCKY	Yes	Institutional parole officers	No		No		

[1] INDIANA: Requirements include philosophy and theory of corrections, general legal knowledge, specialized knowledge of work/study release procedures and communication skills.

REENTRY / REINTEGRATION — TABLE 3: STAFFING PATTERNS

SYSTEM	INTERNAL STAFF Assigned	INTERNAL STAFF Credentials; Training	VOLUNTEERS Pursued	VOLUNTEERS Credentials; Training	FORMAL COMMUNITY PARTICIPATION Pursued	FORMAL COMMUNITY PARTICIPATION Type of Service	FORMAL COMMUNITY PARTICIPATION Prior to Discharge
LOUISIANA	Yes	Varies by facility	Yes	Orientation/training session for all faith-based volunteers; proper credentials of professionals requiring legal licensure or certification; a volunteer services manual is provided [2]	Yes	Substance abuse, religious, parenting/family relations, character education, victim awareness, job search, job skills, mental health, and housing	Yes
MAINE	No response						
MARYLAND	Yes	Contracted through local community college and must pass security screening/clearance	Yes	Contracted through local community college and must pass security screening/clearance	Yes	Transitional housing, education, employment, and substance abuse treatment	Yes
MASSACHUSETTS	No response						
MICHIGAN	No response						
MINNESOTA	Yes	College experience with social science emphasis for both casework and transition staff	Yes	Must be specialized presenters	Yes	Collaborate with state employment agency, human services, legal assistance, health, and so forth, and network with community nonprofit organizations	No
MISSISSIPPI	Yes	Bachelor's degree in a related subject	No		Yes	Social Security Administration and the state's Job WIN Centers	Yes
MISSOURI	Yes	Training, as appropriate	Yes	One day of corrections training; credentials depend on representation	Yes	All social service agencies, faith-based, and state and local government	Yes
MONTANA	Yes	Job-specific training	No		Yes	Chemical dependency and mental health services	Yes
NEBRASKA	Yes	Contracted through local community college; inmates are assigned to a unit case manager who assists	No	Guest speakers from various community, state, and nonprofit agencies present classes	Yes	As information sources for housing, college prep, job service, lending and financial institutions, county health department, and parole officers	Yes
NEVADA	Yes	Master's degree for psychologist and reentry coordinator, bachelor's degree with corrections experience for caseworkers and an associate's degree for caseworker with lengthy experience	Yes	Professionals in the areas of banking and finance, community health care, community mediation, and job development; a clinical social worker who is an expert in dual diagnosis and treatment	Yes	Substance abuse treatment and counseling, mental health and medical treatment, employment, housing, clothing, food, transportation, welfare, Social Security, veterans' services, Workforce Investment Act services, education, victim's impact panel, reentry court, family reunification, financial management, and job skills	Yes
NEW HAMPSHIRE	No		No		No		
NEW JERSEY	No		No		No		
NEW MEXICO	Yes	Master's degree or above	No		Yes	Departments of Labor and Healths	Yes
NEW YORK	Yes	Four-year degree or equivalent	Yes	Certified credentials by agency of employment and/or experienced community individuals	Yes	HIV/AIDS, family reintegration, community health, AA/NA, Alanon, employment counseling	Yes

[2] LOUISIANA: A criminal history check is conducted on all volunteers who have direct contact with inmates.

REENTRY / REINTEGRATION — TABLE 3: STAFFING PATTERNS

SYSTEM	INTERNAL STAFF			VOLUNTEERS			FORMAL COMMUNITY PARTICIPATION	
	Assigned	Credentials; Training	Pursued	Credentials; Training	Pursued	Type of Service	Prior to Discharge
NORTH CAROLINA	No		Yes	Not specified	Yes	Department of Health and Human Services, Division of Alcohol and Chemical Dependency, Employment Security Commission, Vocational Rehabilitation, Division of Veterans Affairs and community colleges	Yes
NORTH DAKOTA	Yes	Licensed teacher or career counselor	No		Yes	Job Service, adult learning center human service center, faith-based programming, mental health services, case management and aid services, aftercare programming and cognitive programming	Yes
OHIO	Yes	Job-specific credentials (education staff for resume/applications and recovery services staff for substance abuse program workshops)	Yes in some facilities	Speakers/workshop leaders trained in specialized areas	Yes	Ohio Job and Family Services, Adult Parole Authority, Bureau of Motor Vehicles, Community Connection	Yes
OKLAHOMA	Yes	Department reentry process training	No		Yes	Varies, according to facility	Yes
OREGON	Yes	Varies, depending on class and/or institution	Yes	Varies, depending on the institution	Yes	Disability services, faith-based organizations with housing options, recovery treatments and mentors, area community college, and so forth.	Not specified
PENNSYLVANIA	Yes	Job-specific credentials and training	No		Yes	Career Link, Salvation Army, faith-based, alcohol and other drug community service programs	Yes
RHODE ISLAND	Yes	Counseling staff with counseling degrees or equivalent experience assist with identifying high-risk cases for discharge planning[3]	Yes	Mentors who must attend departmental volunteer training and mentor training conducted by the departmental mentor program manager	Yes	Case management/discharge planning services	Yes
SOUTH CAROLINA	Yes	Bachelor's degree plus experience in social services	Yes	Volunteer application screening, background checks; must attend orientation and training session	Yes	Alston Wilkes Society, faith-based organizations, nonprofit groups, vocational rehabilitation, Veterans' Administration, and so forth.	Yes, in some cases
SOUTH DAKOTA	Yes	Not specified	Yes	Not specified	Yes	Treatment, child support enforcement, domestic violence, and so forth.	Yes
TENNESSEE	Yes	Meet requirements for Counselor III	Yes	NIC training for cognitive-behavior classes and an annual departmental volunteer training program	Yes	Employment, education, health, transitional housing, and mentors	Yes
TEXAS	Yes	Varies, depending on the level of the program; licensure as a substance abuse counselor or a bachelor's or master's degree in psychology or social work often are required	Yes	Complete agency volunteer training program	Yes	Some programs work with local probation offices and aftercare providers	Yes
UTAH	Yes	Probation and parole staff	No		Yes	Prison Information Network, departments of work force services and motor vehicles and ID provision	Not specified
VERMONT	Yes	Member of the caseworker staff	Yes	Caring demeanor; must attend eight hours of training	Yes	Housing, employment, alcohol and drug treatment, community mental health, transportation and education	Yes

[3] RHODE ISLAND: Vendors also are asked to provide staff with equivalent case management experience.

REENTRY / REINTEGRATION — TABLE 3: STAFFING PATTERNS

SYSTEM	INTERNAL STAFF Assigned	INTERNAL STAFF Credentials; Training	VOLUNTEERS Pursued	VOLUNTEERS Credentials; Training	FORMAL COMMUNITY PARTICIPATION Pursued	FORMAL COMMUNITY PARTICIPATION Type of Service	FORMAL COMMUNITY PARTICIPATION Prior to Discharge
VIRGINIA	Yes	Bachelor's or graduate degree in human services field plus related experience	No		Yes	Substance abuse, mental health, HIV/AIDS, employment, emergency shelter	Yes
WASHINGTON	Yes	State-accredited teachers for classroom settings, complete an adult services academy (classification/transition counselors), on-site training	Yes	Academic or experience levels are not a requirement; must attend an orientation class	Yes	Employment transition, housing, financial assistance, transportation and identification cards	Yes
WEST VIRGINIA	Yes	Skilled and trained for program facilitation	No		No		No
WISCONSIN	Yes	Licensed social workers; certification for teachers and guidance counselors through the Wisconsin Technical College System[4]	Yes	Orientation programs developed in each institution to include the correctional climate and safety/security policies of the institution; volunteers assist with programs and no specific credentials are normally required	Yes	Housing, employment, treatment or aftercare and family support	Yes
WYOMING	Yes	Appropriate to instructors or case managers	Yes	Background check must show a clean record	Yes	Employment and a grant for providing services to serious and violent inmates	Yes
FEDERAL BUREAU OF PRISONS	No response						

CANADIAN SYSTEMS

SYSTEM	Assigned	Credentials; Training	Pursued	Credentials; Training	Pursued	Type of Service	Prior to Discharge
NEWFOUNDLAND	Yes	Case managers	No		Yes	John Howard Society, pastoral care, probation services, human resources and employment	Not specified
NOVA SCOTIA	Yes	Officers with additional training in conferencing	No		Yes	Children and Family Services, local school boards	Yes
ONTARIO	Yes	Professional service staff and/or discharge planners/rehabilitation officers	Yes	No specific credentials; training is provided by the local institution in consultation with community agencies and the Bell Cairn Staff Development Center	Yes	Employment, housing, financial assistance and identifying appropriate community support	Yes, when volunteer agencies are involved
CORRECTIONAL SERVICE CANADA	Yes	University degree, plus language proficiency (depending on location) and experience-specific requirements, as well as a reliability check	Yes	Screened and trained; however, there is no standard identified for credentials	Yes	Numerous agencies, varies among regions	Yes

[4] WISCONSIN: In situations where a program is provided through a contract with an outside agency, the vendor must provide staff whose credentials meet specific state requirements.

REENTRY / REINTEGRATION
TABLE 4: TRANSITION DETENTION

SYSTEM	Separate Within Facility	Community Halfway House	Prerelease Facility	Day Reporting Centers	Community Agency or Other	Percentage Placed in Transition Detention
ALABAMA	No response					
ALASKA	No	Yes	No	No	No	15%
ARIZONA	No	No	No	No	No	N/A
ARKANSAS	No	No	No	No	No	N/A
CALIFORNIA	No	No	No	No	Yes[1]	100%
COLORADO	Yes	No	No	Yes	Yes	4.9%
CONNECTICUT	Yes	Yes	No	No	Yes	N/A
DELAWARE	No	Yes	Yes	Yes	No	Unknown
DISTRICT OF COLUMBIA	No	No	No	No	No	N/A
FLORIDA	No	Yes	No	No	Yes[2]	<10%
GEORGIA	No	Yes	No	Yes[3]	No	15%
HAWAII	Yes	Yes	Yes	Yes	Yes[4]	3%-30%
IDAHO	Yes	No	Yes	Yes	No	10%
ILLINOIS	No response					
INDIANA	No	No	No	No	No	N/A
KANSAS	No	Yes	No	Yes	Yes	25%-30%
KENTUCKY	No	No	No	No	No	N/A
LOUISIANA	Yes	No	Yes	Yes	No	12%
MAINE	No response					
MARYLAND	No	No	No	No	No	N/A
MASSACHUSETTS	No response					
MICHIGAN	No response					
MINNESOTA	No	No	No	No	No	N/A
MISSISSIPPI	No	No	No	No	No	N/A
MISSOURI	No	No	No	No	No	N/A
MONTANA	No	No	No	No	Yes	Unknown
NEBRASKA	No	No	No	No	Yes	10%
NEVADA	No	No	No	No	No	N/A
NEW HAMPSHIRE	No	Yes	No	No	No	90%

SYSTEM	Separate Within Facility	Community Halfway House	Prerelease Facility	Day Reporting Centers	Community Agency or Other	Percentage Placed in Transition Detention
NEW JERSEY	No	No	No	No	No	N/A
NEW MEXICO	No	No	No	No	No	N/A
NEW YORK	No	Yes	Yes	No	Yes	20%
NORTH CAROLINA	No	No	No	No	No	N/A
NORTH DAKOTA	No	Yes	No	No	No	5%[5]
OHIO	No	No	No	Yes	Yes[6]	4.8%
OKLAHOMA	No	No	No	No	No	N/A
OREGON	No	No	Yes	No	Yes	70%
PENNSYLVANIA	Yes	Yes	Yes	Yes	Yes[7]	70%, est.
RHODE ISLAND	No	No	No	No	No	N/A
SOUTH CAROLINA	No	No	Yes[8]	No	No	16%
SOUTH DAKOTA	No	No	No	No	No	N/A
TENNESSEE	No	No	No	No	No	N/A
TEXAS	No	No	Yes	No	No	13%
UTAH	Yes	Yes	Yes	Yes	No	Unknown
VERMONT	No	Yes	No	Yes	No	95%
VIRGINIA	No	No	Yes	Yes	No	50%
WASHINGTON	Yes	Yes	Yes	No	No	30%[9]
WEST VIRGINIA	No	No	Yes	No	No	3.5%
WISCONSIN	No	Yes	Yes	Yes	No	66%, est.
WYOMING	No	No	No	No	Yes	20%
FEDERAL BUREAU OF PRISONS	No response					

CANADIAN SYSTEMS

SYSTEM	Separate Within Facility	Community Halfway House	Prerelease Facility	Day Reporting Centers	Community Agency or Other	Percentage Placed in Transition Detention
NEWFOUNDLAND	No	Yes	No	No	No	Unknown
NOVA SCOTIA	No	No	No	No	No	N/A
ONTARIO	No	No	No	No	No	N/A
CORRECTIONAL SERVICE CANADA	No	No	No	No	No	N/A

---

[1] CALIFORNIA: Residential community correction reentry centers or Half-Way Back programs are used. Substance abuse treatment control units and aftercare components also are available by contracted community or county organizations; targeted population for such referrals are for 40 to 60,000 offenders.

[2] FLORIDA: Substance abuse transitional housing is available on a voluntary basis (400 faith-based beds and 400 general beds).

[3] GEORGIA: Day reporting centers are used only for those on probation.

[4] HAWAII: Transition detention information is based on responses from four of five facilities. A work furlough residential community also is used.

[5] NORTH DAKOTA: placements in detention facilities are made for 100% of those inmates in the reentry program.

[6] OHIO: Release under strict supervision to a licensed halfway house until released onto parole or post-release control status.

[7] PENNSYLVANIA: Private vendor community corrections centers.

[8] SOUTH CAROLINA: Prerelease program is used for last 30 days of sentence.

[9] WASHINGTON: Approximately 7% are housed at one time.

REENTRY / REINTEGRATION — TABLE 5: DISCHARGE PROCEDURES

SYSTEM	DISCHARGE PROCEDURES	AUTHORIZING AGENCY	PERSONAL EFFECTS PROVIDED	FORMAL FOLLOW-UP
ALABAMA	No response			
ALASKA	Follows a pre-signed condition-of-release form	Booking office at the releasing facility	All personal property and plane fare to home community, if applicable	Probation or parole supervision for most felony offenders
ARIZONA	Housing development for selected inmates before approval and proposed inmate placement investigation	Community Corrections Division in concert with prison operations	$50 plus account balance, shirt, jeans and tennis shoes or boots	Parole supervision if statutorily mandated until sentence expiration
ARKANSAS	Conditions are determined by the Post Prison Transfer Board with final discharge by the parole officer	Facility records office	All personal property that is not state-issued, gate money and, if necessary, clothing and bus ticket	Parole supervision is provided by the Department of Community Correction
CALIFORNIA	All offenders are placed on parole by statute for one, three or five years	Bureau of Prison Terms determination	Personal property and $200	Information and statistics are collected to analyze effectiveness of the New Parole Model
COLORADO	Extensive review of required forms, including the taking of a DNA test and being photographed	Offender Case Management	Personal property, account balance, $100, a bus ticket, full set of clothing and medically approved medications	Regular follow-up for parole and optional follow-up by Community Reintegration for six to 12 months, depending on employment and other support system status
CONNECTICUT	Varies by facility	Facility counselors	Varies by facility	No
DELAWARE	Paperwork is checked and verified by the shift commander	Records department	Personal property and account balance plus gate money and clothing, if necessary	Parole/probation supervision by Community Corrections
DISTRICT OF COLUMBIA	By May 2004, all inmates will be dismissed with referrals to community programs and for free medical services, if applicable	Deputy warden for operations/programs	Personal property; clothing for inmates sentenced to 15 days or more	No
FLORIDA	Currently being redrafted	Bureau of Classification and Records	Personal property	No
GEORGIA	An attempt is made for all discharges to have a residence and job; if parole, must have verified residence	Division of Inmate Administration and the parole board	Clothing, if requested	Yes, for those on parole or probation
HAWAII	Inmate signs a release form and a property release form	Hawaii Paroling Authority	Personal property	Strong networking between ex-inmates, parole and police, etc.
IDAHO	Parole commission sets a firm release date; an aftercare plan is prepared and monitored	Transition parole officer	Personal property	Evaluations are conducted and reported to a review and analysis division
ILLINOIS	No response			
INDIANA	Housing approval and completed verification if parole; progress report completion if probation	Classification division	$75 plus clothing and shoes, if needed	Written stipulations and follow-ups throughout parole period
KANSAS	Plans are developed and forwarded from the facilities for approval four months prior to release and inmates are given release documents; community connections are made with programs and mentors in specialized location releases	Institutional parole officers or general program officers under supervision of the Director of Release Planning	$100 if first release or $40 for subsequent releases, inmate's account balance,[1] clothing and a demagnetized ID card for use in the community	Case manager advocates follow up for six months with special location releasees; some tracking to determine impact on recidivism
KENTUCKY	Parolees must have verified housing and job before release	Offender Records, Probation and Parole	Bus ticket to a destination within the state	No

---

[1] KANSAS: No gate money is given to inmates upon release if their account balance is over a certain amount.

REENTRY / REINTEGRATION — TABLE 5: DISCHARGE PROCEDURES

SYSTEM	DISCHARGE PROCEDURES	AUTHORIZING AGENCY	PERSONAL EFFECTS PROVIDED	FORMAL FOLLOW-UP
LOUISIANA	Coordination with medical, pharmacy, warehouse, security, classification, mental health, and mailroom for applicable services	Business office	Personal property, clothing if needed, five-day supply of medication if applicable, transportation to bus station or airport and a bus ticket, if approved by the warden	Regular parole division follow-up and formal case manager and community resource staff follow-up for inmates participating in a grant program
MAINE	No response			
MARYLAND	Not specified	Not specified	Personal property and account balance	No
MASSACHUSETTS	No response			
MICHIGAN	No response			
MINNESOTA	Established by the departmental hearings and release unit	Departmental hearings and release unit	Personal property and ID documents, clothing, account balance, and $100	No
MISSISSIPPI	Established procedures followed by case managers and paperwork acknowledged and signed by the inmate	Copies are distributed to applicable DOC offices	None	Prerelease counselors follow up for one year or until employment is secured
MISSOURI	A re-entry team meets with the inmates within one year prior to release and transitions the inmate to a community team upon release	Reentry team	Not specified	The reentry program continues for one year after release
MONTANA	Policies and procedures are coordinated through the Community Corrections Division and the institutions	Community Corrections Division and Board of Parole and Probation	Personal property	If court-ordered, plus counseling and treatment, if needed
NEBRASKA	An exit interview is conducted and an explanation of restoration of rights is provided	Records office and parole office	Personal property, a photo ID card, account balance, and a bus ticket	No
NEVADA	After plan approval by the prerelease unit and by a local investigator who consider suitable housing and job prospects, inmate is segregated for one day prior to release and must attend a parole orientation	State Department of Public Safety, parole and probation division, and prerelease coordinator at the facility	Personal property, including appliances purchased through the state by the inmate or his/her family, gate money and account balance and transportation to Las Vegas	Monitored monthly for those in the reentry program and daily by social workers[2]
NEW HAMPSHIRE	Inmates become eligible halfway through their sentence and placement in halfway houses approximately four months prior to discharge; some nonviolent offenders may transition to electronic monitoring	Classification office	Personal street clothing for parolees; prison uniform and jacket, purchased shoes and personal property for inmates released directly from the prison	No
NEW JERSEY	Not specified	Not specified	Not specified	No
NEW MEXICO	Not specified	Adult prisons	Not specified	Two-year follow-up for inmates enrolled in special reentry programs
NEW YORK	Parole release, conditional release, presumptive release and presumptive work release	Department of Correctional Services for inmates completing sentences; state division of parole for other release	Personal property and ID documents	No
NORTH CAROLINA	Inmates are interviewed several days prior to release or transfer and given a transition packet including all pertinent documents	Program staff	Personal property	No
NORTH DAKOTA	Probation and counseling appointments for reentry participants	Division of Field Services	Personal property	Regular monitoring of reentry participants and at six, 12 and 18 months after completion of the program

[2] NEVADA: After nine months to a year on parole, a Community Accountability and Support Committee, composed of local and state partners, determines future needs for service.

REENTRY / REINTEGRATION — TABLE 5: DISCHARGE PROCEDURES

SYSTEM	DISCHARGE PROCEDURES	AUTHORIZING AGENCY	PERSONAL EFFECTS PROVIDED	FORMAL FOLLOW-UP
OHIO	Master file review checklist, including a DNA screening	Records office	Personal property, set of clothing, jacket appropriate to weather, account balance and prorated gate money based on length of incarceration	Adult Parole Authority for those released under supervision
OKLAHOMA	Receive a certificate of discharge	Office of Sentence Administration	$50 or personal savings, plus a two-week medication supply	No
OREGON	A release plan is jointly prepared two months prior to release by counselors, community corrections offices, and board of parole, and an ID card with a photo is issued	Institutions division	Personal property, bus voucher, if needed, sweatpants and shirt, if needed, DOC-issued medication and (for women) a backpack filled with hygiene products, plus an Oregon Trail Offender Debit Card or check and a Smart Start packet[3]	A post-release assessment of inmates participating in the serious and violent offender reentry initiative
PENNSYLVANIA	Discharge papers are approved and signed before being released to either a community corrections center or to a home plan	Security staff	Personal property	Recidivism rates are calculated for up to three years following release
RHODE ISLAND	Discharge planning is offered prior to a general release	Rehabilitative services	Personal property	Discharge planning vendors are required to follow up for at least 60 days after release
SOUTH CAROLINA	Records are reviewed and calls to community contacts are made, via classification and operations	Records are reviewed and calls to community contacts are made, via classification and operations	Personal property, account balance and transportation to the bus station, if needed	Reentry-grant program inmates are followed up by referred agencies and organizations; informal follow-up is conducted by prerelease centers
SOUTH DAKOTA	Release dates are reviewed and checked for any new holds or warrants as well as a check for victim notification	Unit staff and central records	Personal property, bus ticket or transportation to county of commitment and account balance	Recidivism is tracked and interviews are conducted for those who return
TENNESSEE	Completion of assigned program in accordance with established policies	Board of Parole	Not specified	Follow up for at least one year for inmates participating in an enhanced federal grant, prerelease program
TEXAS	Sentence time calculations are verified and most offenders are transported to a centralized release site, via correctional institutions division	Parole, programs and services divisions	Personal property, a change of clothing, a bus ticket voucher, and gate money	Parolees must report to their supervising parole officer within 24 hours of release
UTAH	Not specified	Institutional parole office	Not specified	Follow-up by parole division
VERMONT	All inmates are placed on furlough status, via community correctional service centers; 40% of the sentenced population is on community release status	All inmates are placed on furlough status prior to parole, via community correctional service centers	Personal property and clothing	Monitored throughout furlough and by parole division when applicable
VIRGINIA	A home plan is determined before release	Offender management section and local prison records office	Account balance and ID documents	Formal evaluation to determine recidivism for selected transition and therapeutic community residents; post-release supervision by a parole officer

[3] OREGON: The debit card provides access to the inmate's trust account, for those with a valid social security number; the Smart Start packet contains over-the-counter birth control products, a 10-minute calling card, personal hygiene products and information on sexually transmitted diseases

REENTRY / REINTEGRATION — TABLE 5: DISCHARGE PROCEDURES

SYSTEM	DISCHARGE PROCEDURES	AUTHORIZING AGENCY	PERSONAL EFFECTS PROVIDED	FORMAL FOLLOW-UP
WASHINGTON	Development of an approved transition plan for high-risk offenders; assignment of case to community corrections and completion of scheduling of court-ordered condition obligations	Operations and administrative staff, caseworkers and records office	Personal property, clothing (if needed), account balance, transportation, ID documents and predetermined gate money	Reporting for a predetermined period to a community corrections officer for offenders with post-release requirements
WEST VIRGINIA	Not specified	Records office in conjunction with unit management	Personal property, clothing, 10-day supply of prescribed medication and account balance	Specialized housing programs (i.e., Second Chance Unit for parole violators and long-term mental health unit)
WISCONSIN	Varies by type of release established by a social worker and a supervising agent	Divisions of Adult Institutions or Division of Community Corrections	Personal property, clothing (if indigent) and funds according to the instructions of the supervising agent	Formal process if involved in a formal follow-up program
WYOMING	Preparation of discharge papers	Business offices	Personal property, account balance, ID documents and bus ticket (end-of-sentence inmates, only)	Follow-up phone calls by probation or parole agents
FEDERAL BUREAU OF PRISONS	No response			
CANADIAN SYSTEMS				
NEWFOUNDLAND	Inmates may apply for a temporary absence for addiction treatment, or for release to a residential facility	Corrections and Community Services, sentence administration and/or classification services	Personal property, clothing, and account balance	No
NOVA SCOTIA	Not specified	Community corrections	Personal property	Supervised by community corrections staff
ONTARIO	Inmates are advised on admission of the availability of discharge planning assistance and attempts to interview the inmates are made prior to release	Professional staff and discharge planners	Personal property and a letter of incarceration for help in obtaining social assistance	Follow-up reporting, if a condition of probation, parole, conditional sentence or temporary absence
CORRECTIONAL SERVICE CANADA	A notice of discharge/release is prepared giving the inmate's date/time/mode of travel/release type, etc.	Admission/Discharge Unit under the security wing of operations and reports directly to the correctional operations coordinator for the institution	Clothing (shoes, socks, pair of jeans, underwear, shirt, duffel bag and a choice of a jean jacket or winter jacket, depending on the season)	Parole officers monitor offenders' current circumstances and apply interventions, where required

Reentry Survey, 2005

First printed in *Corrections Compendium,*
a publication of the American Correctional Association,
March/April 2005

Reentry Survey, 2005

As this Survey Summary was being written, the Nebraska Legislature was debating the issue of removing restrictions on voting rights for its population of former felons. Offenders incarcerated on felony convictions may not vote in elections until they have waited for a period not less than ten years after their release and petitioned for and received a full pardon. The legislature is sitting in short session with many bills to debate while the public is filling the airwaves questioning the importance of this one issue over the many others. Twenty-four out of forty-two U.S. reporting systems that have not previously eliminated their restrictions to voting rights are wrestling with this same issue, as are three of the six Canadian reporting systems. The outcomes will be interesting to watch as part of the reentry process reported in the current survey tables.

Voting Rights and Restrictions

Fifty-five percent of the U.S. reporting systems previously have removed voting restrictions. Four reporting U.S. systems are considering legislation for elimination of the restrictions—Delaware, Nebraska (previously mentioned), Rhode Island, and Virginia. Seven other U.S. reporting systems are unaware of any actions being considered for removing voting restrictions. Restrictions that are in place include: inmates must reinstate themselves and receive the governor's approval; voting rights are automatically restored after completion of parole; the inmate's case must be reviewed and approved by the clemency board; and others may request reinstatement after five years following the termination of supervision.

In New Jersey, a current court case was dismissed at the trial court level and now is being heard on appeal. In Pennsylvania, voter registration information and applications are provided to inmates just prior to their release. And in Vermont, voting rights have never been removed, and all inmates may vote even while incarcerated.

Planned Programs

Components of planned programs in anticipation of release from incarceration are in effect in all the United States and three of the Canadian reporting systems. Inmates, however, are required to attend the sessions in only 33 percent of the U.S. reporting systems, while three reporting systems in Canada do not have formal reentry programs in effect. There is a wide range of exemptions for participating in the planned programs such as inadequate time allowed prior to release; physical limitations of the facilities for holding classes; inmates with medical, mental or custody status issues; inmates housed in local jails due to population growth; felony or immigration holds; or violent offenders with weapons, gang or multiple, violent felonies. The only restriction in the Canadian reporting systems is in Nova Scotia for those already having appropriate outside resources.

The length of the planned programs ranges from one month in Pennsylvania to five years in South Dakota. Louisiana, New York, and Oklahoma begin their programs at intake. Formal class schedules also vary. Examples indicated by the systems are Arkansas that holds classes for half a day for sixty-two days, Louisiana's program is conducted for 100 hours with no mandate for the number of days or hours per class, and Nebraska holds classes for twenty-five days per month. In Canada, there is virtually no formal class schedule in its reporting systems.

Optional courses are often added to the formal class schedules. For example, California uses distance learning for those unable to attend classes and uses reentry video sessions on television systems in some facilities and most forestry boot camps; Minnesota holds mock job fairs, transition resource fairs, child support workshops and library transition resource centers; and other systems include optional courses for inmates requiring specialized programs such as Alcoholics or Narcotics Anonymous, or mental health services.

Formal Program Components

The following sessions and the percentage of the U.S. reporting systems that include the classes in their programs are the following: education (86 percent); job readiness (90 percent); community resources (93 percent); housing (76 percent); substance abuse (90 percent); rules of supervision (88 percent); family reunification (81 percent); cognitive behavior (93 percent); health care (86 percent);

mental health (86 percent); and personal identification issues (70 percent). Percentages for these programs are much lower in the Canadian reporting systems, from a high of 67 percent for education and cognitive behavior to a low of 17 percent for family reunification. Other classes are shown in Table 2.

Staffing

Internal staff are assigned to lead program sessions in 93 percent of the U.S. reporting systems and each of the reporting Canadian systems. Florida requires that the staff be high school graduates with no felony convictions; California, Louisiana, and Washington require state licenses for staff teaching academics; Kansas staff must have experience with specialty groups of inmates, such as those who are disabled; Nevada's coordinator must have a master's degree; New Jersey requires that its program supervisor be a social worker with a master's degree; and Ohio requires that its staff have college degrees, be licensed social workers, and have a certificate in chemical dependency for that target population.

The use of volunteers is pursued in 67 percent of all the U.S. and Canadian reporting systems. Colorado requires that volunteers attend eight hours of general training plus four hours of aftercare sessions, volunteers in New York must be established and recognized representatives of their agencies, faith-based volunteers are sought in New Mexico, and the pursuit of volunteers varies by institution in Pennsylvania. Background checks of the potential volunteers are required in eight of the reporting systems.

Community participation is formal in 95 percent of the U.S. reporting systems and in 100 percent of those in the Canadian reporting systems. Agencies providing services include Social Security and the departments of motor vehicles, education, employment development, human services, labor, parole, vocational rehabilitation, health and welfare, and housing and urban development. Among other community liaisons are Alcoholics/Narcotics Anonymous, Volunteers in Probation, and one-stop centers in Florida. There is also a wide variety of nonprofit organizations and faith-based agencies included in the responses.

Transition Detention

Separate facilities within the institutions are used by 49 percent of the reporting U.S. systems, while 63 percent send their reentry candidates to community halfway houses. Twenty-nine percent of the systems maintain prerelease facilities, and 46 percent use day reporting centers. Other forms of transition detention noted are work centers, a sanction and assessment center in Montana, and transition centers and private vendor centers in Pennsylvania. In addition, Manitoba, Canada, uses day reporting centers for its reentry candidates.

Discharge Procedures

All of the U.S. and Canadian reporting systems return an account balance to their reentry inmates. Inmates in New Mexico also are given the balance they have in their forced savings accounts. There are very few restrictions that apply and those primarily are the requirements that checks be issued rather than cash or that money be mailed to the inmate's home destination. Alabama, Missouri, Montana, New Hampshire, North Dakota, Wisconsin and Wyoming do not provide gate money upon release. All other reporting systems do offer gate money, ranging from $10 in Louisiana and Manitoba, Canada, to California that provides up to $200.

Nearly all reporting U.S. and Canadian systems provide at the very least bus transportation to most approved destinations—residence or county within the state—or to the parole office for those not on general release status. Louisiana provides transportation to an airport if approved by the warden. Minnesota offers its high-risk offenders transportation to halfway houses or the agent office, or for humanitarian reasons. Transportation is not provided in Montana, Nebraska, Utah, or Vermont.

Utah does not provide clothing to its releases, but inmates may receive items from faith-based organizations or through the Prisoners Information Network. Other U.S. reporting systems that do not provide clothing are Hawaii, Idaho, Massachusetts, Montana, Pennsylvania and Wyoming. When clothing is provided by the remaining reporting systems, it usually consists of one set (pants, shirt, shoes, socks, underwear, and a jacket appropriate to the season). In Canada, community agencies offer a supply of used garments.

Medications and Prescriptions

No medications are offered to reentering inmates in North Carolina or New Hampshire, while a five-day supply is provided in Louisiana, and medications for 30 days are provided in California. For inmates with mental health disorders, 90 days of medications are provided in Alabama. In general, a supply of medications for at least 30 days is offered in 40 percent of the reporting U.S. systems and that amount can be increased to 60 days in Pennsylvania and Wisconsin in certain circumstances.

Twenty-nine percent of the reporting U.S. systems do not provide prescriptions upon release. Again, Alabama provides a prescription for 90 days to its offenders with mental health disorders. A prescription for just two to three days is offered in New Mexico and British Columbia in Canada and up to 60 days in Wisconsin. The length of a prescription varies by Correctional Service Canada and is determined by the expectation of the length of time for the offender to relocate and find proper access to medical care.

Formal Follow-Up and Employment Restrictions

Including parole reporting, 69 percent of the reporting systems conduct formal follow-up programs, usually for a specific element of the reentry population. They face numerous employment restrictions in 86 percent of the reporting U.S. systems and 33 percent of the reporting Canadian systems. No employment restrictions are on record in Indiana, Montana, Nebraska, New Hampshire, North Dakota or Utah. Primarily, the systems that do restrict employment attach statutes to sex offenders wishing to work with children (schools or day care centers), drug-related offenders who wish to work in hospitals or bars, those convicted of fraud or forgery wishing to work in money-handling positions and those in systems that simply follow federal guidelines.

REENTRY — TABLE 1: PROGRAM SCHEDULE

SYSTEM	PLANNED PROGRAM - Required	PLANNED PROGRAM - Exempted	Length Prior to Release	FORMAL CLASS SCHEDULE	OPTIONAL PROGRAMS
ALABAMA	Yes	Judges, pardon and parole circumstances often don't allow time	Three months	Hourly and unlimited, as assigned	None
ALASKA	No response				
ARIZONA	No response				
ARKANSAS	No		Two months, approximately	Half a day for 62 days	None
CALIFORNIA	No		Up to 120 days	Fifteen days per month; 6.5 hours per class	Distance learning program for those unable to attend classes; reentry video series on television system in some facilities and most fire camps
COLORADO	No		Six months	Life Skills for Transition curriculum, 240 hours	
CONNECTICUT	No		Varies by facility	Varies by facility	
DELAWARE	No	Space limitations and length of remaining sentence govern program	Twelve to 18 months	Twenty days per month; three hours per class	
DISTRICT OF COLUMBIA	No response				
FLORIDA	Yes	Emergency releases	Six months, 100-hour course	Twenty days per month; three hours per class—offered five days per week, excluding weekends and holidays	
GEORGIA	Yes		Six months	Not established	Social Security applications
HAWAII	Yes		Two years	Nine hours per week at minimum-security facility	
IDAHO	No	Inmates who choose to complete their sentences and refuse to participate	Up to one year	Ten days per month; 1.5 to two hours per class	
ILLINOIS	No response				
INDIANA	Yes		Six months	Eighty hours	A workbook-based, individual program for those who cannot attend classes
IOWA	No	All inmates outside of Polk County	Eleven weeks	One-week assessment; 210 hours of classes; 60 hours of vocational training; 45 hours of computer skills; a minimum of three to four individualized sessions	Varied levels within counseling and/or education programs at most institutions
KANSAS	No		Six months is standard; eight months for mentally ill inmates and 12 months for those in reentry programs	Varies from daily classes to six hours per week	Transitional and discharge planning and family services
KENTUCKY	No response				
LOUISIANA	Yes	Inmates with medical, mental health, or custody status issues	From entry into reception and diagnostic centers through release and community supervision	One hundred hours with no mandate on number of days or hours per class	
MAINE	No	Inmates can self-select program options; caseworkers are required to offer release planning for all inmates transitioning to the community	Six months	No; employability readiness classes are limited to some facilities	Community teams; substance abuse, sex offender, or other treatment needs; links to community agencies and resources
MARYLAND	No response				
MASSACHUSETTS	No		Six months but planning starts at intake	Five days per month; six hours per class; eligible to take classes when within one month of release	Case management for those who do not participate in the program

REENTRY — TABLE 1: PROGRAM SCHEDULE

SYSTEM	PLANNED PROGRAM - Required	PLANNED PROGRAM - Exempted	Length Prior to Release	FORMAL CLASS SCHEDULE	OPTIONAL PROGRAMS
MICHIGAN	Yes		Three months or six months	Varies by institution, but core curriculum is 36 hours	
MINNESOTA	No	Inmates housed in facilities with very low release volume; inmates housed in local jails due to population pressure	Four months	Eighteen class hours	Mock job fairs, transition resource fairs, child support workshops, library transition resource centers and individualized assistance from transition and caseworker staff
MISSISSIPPI	No	Inmates who do not meet established criteria	Up to 12 months	Up to 28 hours per week	
MISSOURI	No		Six months	Varies	
MONTANA	No	Inmates who do not meet established criteria	Six to seven months on average	No	Anger management, chemical dependency counseling, employment skills, GED preparation, parenting classes, and self-help skills
NEBRASKA	No	Inmates not in the Reentry Pilot Program within two facilities	Six months	Twenty-five days per month on an individualized hourly schedule	
NEVADA	No	Going Home Prepared Reentry federal grant program; not available for felony/immigration holds or violent offenders with weapons, gang or multiple, violent felonies	At least six months prior to parole release and 12 months thereafter	Five to six weeks, 2.5 hours per week	Parenting, Project Metamorphosis, anger management, money management, job development, Narcotics Anonymous, and Alcoholics Anonymous
NEW HAMPSHIRE	No	Pilot project restricted to specific geographic area and other qualifications such as age	Six months	No	Case management offered to eligible offenders
NEW JERSEY	No		Varies by individual needs	Varies by institution according to resources and population size	Pilot programs in effect for selected inmates to assess programs; comprehensive programs for special populations, such as mentally ill inmates, for those who max out and for serious and violent inmates
NEW MEXICO	Yes		Six months	Based on SOAR (Success for Offenders After Release) program	Classification and parole officers work with inmates to identify community programs
NEW YORK	Yes		Begins at intake — three-phase program (Phase 1 for one to two weeks, Phase 2 usually for three months, and Phase 3 for one month	Varies by facility—Phase 2 lasts 180 hours for teaching cognitive and social skills, and Phase 3 lasts approximately 65 hours for inmates within one year of release	
NORTH CAROLINA	No		Six to 12 months, depending on needs	Up to two two-hour sessions depending on release plans	
NORTH DAKOTA	No		Three months	Varies	
OHIO	Yes		Six months, with planning starting at intake	Five days per week; 1.5 to two hours per session; conducted every day	
OKLAHOMA	Yes	Inmates serving life without parole or death sentences	Begins at intake	Scheduled based on individual needs after being assessed at reception	
OREGON	Yes	Not available for inmates who are not transferred to release institutions, but all inmates are released with formal release plans	Six months	Twelve months; 2.5 hours per session, but may vary by institution	Parole officers and community partners are encouraged to work within the institutions

REENTRY — TABLE 1: PROGRAM SCHEDULE

SYSTEM	PLANNED PROGRAM - Required	PLANNED PROGRAM - Exempted	Length Prior to Release	FORMAL CLASS SCHEDULE	OPTIONAL PROGRAMS
PENNSYLVANIA	No	Optional for inmates not planning to serve their maximum sentences	One month	Ten days (five days of classes and five days of refresher courses of treat women programs)	Parenting and alcohol counseling
RHODE ISLAND	No		Between 60 days and 18 months[1]	Eight weeks (40 hours); two hours per class by two discharge vendors	Case management, infectious diseases and life skills
SOUTH CAROLINA	No response				
SOUTH DAKOTA	No	Inmates serving life or death sentences, U.S. Marshals holds and those more than five years from possible release date	Five years prior to release	Varies	
TENNESSEE	No	Inmates who accept a certain limited program of activity	Three months when within six months of release	Varies by institution: two to four days per month; four to six hours per class	
TEXAS	No	Inmates under some custody classification	Six months; 18 months for sex offender treatment program and for faith-based program	Twenty days per month; three hours per class, taught by the Windham School District; may be limited in capacity	Specific needs offenders (substance abuse, sex offenders, juveniles, and so forth)[2]
UTAH	No	Inmates who will be terminating their sentences have the option to participate	Five to six months, unless an emergency or early release is pending	No	
VERMONT	Yes[3]		Commences on Day 5 of incarceration	Individualized plan that is continually updated by the inmate, case team and community team	
VIRGINIA	Yes	Space permitting	Three months	Forty hours per class (one session or broken into individual sessions over several months)	
WASHINGTON	No	Inmates completing their sentences and also those participating in the Serious Violent Offender Reentry Initiative program	Six months beginning 18 months prior to release	Varies	Establishment of community collaborators for high-risk inmates, assistance in locating housing, and family-friendly activities; work release
WEST VIRGINIA	No response				
WISCONSIN	No		Varies	Varies	Work release, family reintegration, parenting, treatment programs, education, vocational, and so forth.
WYOMING	No	Those participating in the Serious Violent Offender Reentry Initiative three-month program	From six to 12 months	Eight days per month; hours vary from one to two depending on the facility	
FEDERAL BUREAU OF PRISONS	No response				

[1] RHODE ISLAND: Programs are offered by sixteen discharge vendors that include varying protocols.
[2] TEXAS: In 2004, a new prerelease program for administrative segregation inmates classified as serious and violent offenders.
[3] VERMONT: Inmates who choose not to participate will not be recommended for release.

REENTRY — TABLE 1: PROGRAM SCHEDULE

SYSTEM	PLANNED PROGRAM — Required	PLANNED PROGRAM — Exempted	PLANNED PROGRAM — Length Prior to Release	FORMAL CLASS SCHEDULE	OPTIONAL PROGRAMS
CANADIAN SYSTEMS					
BRITISH COLUMBIA	No		No formal program	No	Individualized plans
MANITOBA	No		No formal program; inmates are eligible for program based on established criteria [4]	Varies from one-sixth to one-third of completed sentence based on inmate's needs and offense profile	Case management
NEWFOUNDLAND	No		No formal program; case managers work with inmates starting at intake	No	Case managers, staff, and community agencies work on individualized plans
NOVA SCOTIA	No	Inmates who already have appropriate resources available based on their case plan	Three months	No	People skills, housing options, transportation funds, health care, clothing/food agencies, substance abuse programs and Respectful Relationships
ONTARIO	No		Varies by institution and in some cases by inmate request only	No	Assistance provided by ministry program staff and by community organizations under contract
CORRECTIONAL SERVICE CANADA	No		Varies	Varies	

---

[4] MANITOBA: Specific program attendance is required to earn good time benefits and receive approval for reentry privileges.

REENTRY — TABLE 2: PROGRAM COMPONENTS

System	Education	Job Readiness	Community Resources	Housing	Substance Abuse	Rules of Supervision	Family Reunification	Cognitive Behavior	Health Care	Mental Health	Personal Identification	OTHER
ALABAMA	X	X			X	X	X		X	X	X	
ALASKA	No response											
ARIZONA	No response											
ARKANSAS		X	X		X	X	X	X				
CALIFORNIA	X	X	X	X	X	X	X	X	X	X		
COLORADO	X	X	X	X	X	X	X	X	X	X	X	
CONNECTICUT	X	X	X	X	X	X	X	X	X	X	X	Motor vehicle registration, vocational education, Social Security cards and benefits, and veteran benefits
DELAWARE		X	X	X	X	X	X	X	X	X	X	
DISTRICT OF COLUMBIA												
FLORIDA	X	X	X	X	X	X	X	X	X	X	X	Domestic violence, goal setting, sexual responsibility, money management, values clarification, problem solving, and social situations
GEORGIA											X	
HAWAII	X	X	X		X		X	X	X	X		
IDAHO	X	X	X	X	X	X	X	X				
ILLINOIS	No response											
INDIANA		X			X	X	X	X	X	X	X	Academic and vocational education
IOWA	X	X	X	X		X	X	X	X		X	
KANSAS	X	X	X	X	X	X	X	X	X	X	X	Money management and release planning
KENTUCKY	No response											
LOUISIANA	X	X	X	X		X	X	X	X	X	X	
MAINE	X				X	X	X	X	X			
MARYLAND	No response											
MASSACHUSETTS	X	X	X	X	X				X	X	X	
MICHIGAN	X	X	X	X	X	X	X	X	X	X	X	Budgeting and fiscal management
MINNESOTA		X	X	X		X	X	X	X	X	X	Transportation and fiscal management
MISSISSIPPI	X	X	X		X	X		X		X	X	Reintegration, job placement assistance, and residence verification
MISSOURI	X	X	X	X	X	X	X	X	X	X	X	
MONTANA	X	X	X		X	X	X	X				
NEBRASKA	X	X	X	X	X	X	X	X	X	X	X	Life skills and faith-based organizations
NEVADA	X	X	X	X	X	X	X	X	X	X		
NEW HAMPSHIRE[1]	X	X	X	X	X	X	X	X	X	X		
NEW JERSEY		X	X	X	X	X	X	X	X	X	X	Restorative justice
NEW MEXICO	X		X	X	X		X	X		X		
NEW YORK	X	X	X	X	X		X	X	X	X	X	
NORTH CAROLINA	X	X	X	X	X			X		X		
NORTH DAKOTA	X	X	X	X	X	X		X	X	X	X	
OHIO	X	X	X	X	X	X	X		X	X	X	Faith-based, victim awareness, and skills identification
OKLAHOMA	X	X	X		X			X	X	X	X	
OREGON	X	X	X	X	X	X	X	X	X	X	X	
PENNSYLVANIA	X	X	X		X	X	X	X	X	X		
RHODE ISLAND	X	X	X	X	X	X	X	X	X	X	X	
SOUTH CAROLINA	No response											
SOUTH DAKOTA	X	X	X	X	X	X	X	X	X		X	
TENNESSEE		X	X	X	X	X	X	X	X		X	Life skills, budgeting, fiscal management, dealing with stress, and emergency relief sources
TEXAS	X	X	X		X	X	X	X	X	X	X	Anger management
UTAH	X	X	X	X	X	X	X	X	X	X	X	
VERMONT	X	X	X	X	X	X	X	X	X	X	X	Specific criminogenic treatment
VIRGINIA	X	X	X	X	X		X	X	X	X		
WASHINGTON	X	X	X	X	X	X	X	X	X	X	X	Financial assistance
WEST VIRGINIA	No response											
WISCONSIN	X	X	X	X	X	X	X	X	X			

[1] NEW HAMPSHIRE: A pilot project currently is being developed with components not yet determined.

REENTRY — TABLE 2: PROGRAM COMPONENTS

System	Education	Job Readiness	Community Resources	Housing	Substance Abuse	Rules of Supervision	Family Reunification	Cognitive Behavior	Health Care	Mental Health	Personal Identification	OTHER
WYOMING	X		X	X	X	X			X	X		
FEDERAL BUREAU OF PRISONS	No response											
CANADIAN SYSTEMS												
BRITISH COLUMBIA	X		X		X			X	X	X		Violence prevention and respectful relationships
MANITOBA												Individualized plans may include any number of all of the noted program options
NEWFOUNDLAND	X			X				X		X		Family violence intervention and sex offender programming
NOVA SCOTIA	X	X	X	X	X	X		X	X			
ONTARIO												Individualized plans may include any number of all of the noted program options [2]
CORRECTIONAL SERVICE CANADA	X	X	X	X	X	X	X	X	X	X	X	Sex offender, Aboriginal, female offenders, ethnocultural, inmate pay, special needs, and violent offender programs

---

[2] ONTARIO: A Core Rehabilitation Program is being developed to include substance abuse, anger management, anti-criminal thinking, partner abuse and sexual offending.

REENTRY — TABLE 3: STAFFING PATTERNS

SYSTEM	INTERNAL STAFF		VOLUNTEERS		FORMAL COMMUNITY PARTICIPATION	
	Assigned	Credentials; Training	Pursued	Credentials; Training	Pursued	Type of Service
ALABAMA	Yes	Specialized assignments such as for mental health treatment	No	Volunteers from halfway houses run by individuals or charities that approach us	Yes	Social Security, food stamps through Family Services, and the License Bureau
ALASKA	No response					
ARIZONA	No response					
ARKANSAS	Yes	Bachelor's degree	No		No	
CALIFORNIA	Yes	Credentialed teachers by the state for academics only	Yes	Community speakers visit on a regular basis	Yes	Departments of Employment Development and Motor Vehicles, parole agents, Alcoholics Anonymous, Friends Outside, child support services, office of substance abuse programs Volunteers in Probation or motivational speakers
COLORADO	Yes	Teaching/vocational certificates	Yes	Eight hours of training and four hours of volunteer aftercare training	Yes	Reentry barriers and needs services noted in program components
CONNECTICUT	Yes	Varies	Yes	Varies	Yes	All needs services noted in program components
DELAWARE			Yes	None specified	Yes	Health and social service agencies, public defenders and departments of Labor and Housing
DISTRICT OF COLUMBIA	No response					
FLORIDA	Yes	High school diplomas or above for transition facilitators and no prior felony convictions	Yes	Expertise in the subject and passing a background check	Yes	One-stop centers that include assistance for employment, health, food stamps, etc., as well as contracts with local community support agencies
GEORGIA	No		No		Yes	Department of Labor
HAWAII	Yes	Case managers primarily have a bachelor's degree and some have a master's degree in social work	No		Yes	Job placement and substance abuse services
IDAHO	Yes	Must be educators, probation and parole officers or social workers	Yes	Two days of training and must be credentialed in their area of expertise	Yes	Divisions of Vocational Rehabilitation and Health and Welfare
ILLINOIS	No response					
INDIANA	Yes	Bachelor's degree	Yes	Representatives of community or work force agencies	Yes	Varies and often faith-based support services
IOWA	Yes	Licensed teachers	Yes	Expertise in subject matter	Yes	All-encompassing services formally in conjunction with the Special Violent Offender Reentry Initiative program and with case manager and probation/parole officer teams after release
KANSAS	Yes	Corrections and case management experience; experience with specialty populations for disabled inmates	Yes	Corrections and case management experience; experience with specialty populations for disabled inmates	Yes	Mental health, substance abuse, housing, benefits (SSI and general assistance), job readiness, job search, family services and education
KENTUCKY	No response					
LOUISIANA	Yes	Varies by facility, but primarily classification or educational staff or social workers	Yes	An orientation/training session is required as well as a criminal history check; proper credentials of professionals needing legal licensure or certification also is required	Yes	Motor Vehicles, Social Security and departments of Health and Hospitals
MAINE	Yes	Licensed social workers; in-house training, in some cases within facilities	Yes	Depends on professional expertise; security and mentoring training are provided	Yes	MaineCare (Medicaid); Social Security, mental health, substance abuse and cognitive-behavior treatment, housing, employment, transportation, and areas related to 12-life domains
MARYLAND	No response					
MASSACHUSETTS	Yes	Correctional program officers and vendor staff who offer a five-day workshop	Yes	Screening process	Yes	Mental health, substance abuse treatment, housing and employment

REENTRY — TABLE 3: STAFFING PATTERNS

SYSTEM	INTERNAL STAFF Assigned	INTERNAL STAFF Credentials; Training	VOLUNTEERS Pursued	VOLUNTEERS Credentials; Training	FORMAL COMMUNITY PARTICIPATION Pursued	FORMAL COMMUNITY PARTICIPATION Type of Service
MICHIGAN	Yes	Bachelor's degree and attendance at curriculum training sessions	Yes	Must pass security clearances and attend sessions on departmental policies	Yes	Departments of Human Services, Health, and Workforce Development
MINNESOTA	Yes	A four-year degree is preferred and must attend training and orientation sessions	Yes	Training and credentials are required in program-specific areas in addition to regular agency training	Yes	State housing, human services and employment agencies and a wide variety of community, nonprofit and faith-based agencies
MISSISSIPPI	Yes	College education and/or experience related to duties for officers and clerical staff	No		Yes	Collaboration of state and local agencies for re-entry component (no, for prerelease component)
MISSOURI	Yes	Cognitive changes and transition accountability/issues training	No		Yes	Employment security, mental health, substance abuse, medical, vocational/college/ABE
MONTANA	No		No		Yes	Chemical dependency and mental health services
NEBRASKA	Yes	Transition manager designation	Yes	Depends on the individual needs of each participant	Yes	Mental health, substance abuse, family reunification, faith-based support, housing, life skills and employment
NEVADA	Yes	Master's level for coordinator; other positions vary from an associate's degree to a bachelor's degree, each with corrections experience	Yes	Professionals in banking and finance, community health care, community mediation, job development, and clinical social workers who are experts in dual diagnosis and treatment	Yes	Substance abuse treatment and counseling, mental health and medical treatment, employment, housing, clothing, food, transportation, Welfare Society security, veterans, Workforce Investment Act, education, training, victim impact panel, reentry court, family reunification, financial management and job skills
NEW HAMPSHIRE	Yes	Bachelor's degree, academy attendance, correctional counselor and four years experience	No		No	
NEW JERSEY	Yes	Social workers with bachelor's degrees, supervised by a master's-level social worker	Yes	Orientations; two-day training for the Threshold program; two-day training for Aftercare Chaplaincy Network program	Yes	Housing, mental health, medical services, counseling, out-patient substance abuse services, spiritual mentorship, food stamps, Social Security, veteran's benefits, education and vocational training, job placement and parenting programs
NEW MEXICO	Yes	Parole officers specifically are assigned	No	Religious groups provide assistance	Yes	Human and social services, Social Security and Motor Vehicles
NEW YORK	Yes	Training provided by the Office of Transitional Services	Yes	Must be established and recognized representative of their agency	Yes	Medicaid, Human Resources Administration in New York City, substance abuse, AIDS Institute, mental health, job developers, departments of Health and Labor, Division of Parole, Temporary Disability Assistance office, Osborne Association and the Fortune Society
NORTH CAROLINA	Yes	Case management and transition training	Yes	Orientation and training	Yes	Employment, housing, transportation, and counseling
NORTH DAKOTA	Yes	Depends on the program	No		Yes	Social services and housing
OHIO	Yes	College degree, social work license and chemical dependency certification	Yes	Not specified	Yes	Mental health, medical, housing, recovery services, citizen circles and faith community
OKLAHOMA	No		Yes	Background investigation and training in subject matter	Yes	Department of Human Services
OREGON	Yes	Standards currently are being developed	Yes	Orientation is mandatory and training varies by the program	Yes	Housing, employment, veteran's assistance, and so forth
PENNSYLVANIA	Yes	Experience in treatment and counseling in the areas they are to teach	No	Varies by institution—some employers conduct job interviews and some banking personnel discuss savings and budgeting	Yes	State and local agencies for inmates with special conditions such as sex offenders, chronically ill, and mental health

REENTRY — TABLE 3: STAFFING PATTERNS

SYSTEM	INTERNAL STAFF		VOLUNTEERS		FORMAL COMMUNITY PARTICIPATION	
	Assigned	Credentials; Training	Pursued	Credentials; Training	Pursued	Type of Service
RHODE ISLAND	Yes	Counseling degrees or equivalent experience; vendors provide staff with equivalent case management experience	Yes	Mandatory training as well as mentor training by the department's staff mentor program manager	Yes	Discharge planning and case management
SOUTH CAROLINA	No response					
SOUTH DAKOTA	Yes	Not specified	Unknown		Yes	Not specified
TENNESSEE	Yes	Prior experience as a member of an institutional unit management team[1]	Yes	Approval by the warden is required and volunteers must undergo an annual certification that includes an orientation and review of policies and procedures; and a background check	Yes	Employment, housing, health care/AIDS-HIV, credit counseling, Social Security/disability assistance, and identification document procurement
TEXAS	Yes	Varies depending on the program — a substance abuse counselor licensure or bachelor's/master's degree in psychology or social work are often required	Yes	Completion of the agency's training program specifically for volunteers	Yes	Local probation officers and aftercare providers
UTAH	Yes	Institutional Parole Office members are required to be the level of "agent" and be peace officer certified	No	An already established Prison Information Network provides volunteer services	Yes	Departments of Workforce Service and Motor Vehicles, Social Security, Medicaid, and so forth
VERMONT	Yes	Classification as a case worker	Yes	Training to be members of Offender Responsibility Panels	Yes	A partnership between the community, Vermont Agency for Human Services and all human service partners—local, community, private, public or NGO
VIRGINIA	Yes	Not specified	Yes	Background checks and an orientation	Yes	Employment, applications for benefits and parenting
WASHINGTON	Yes	Some are state-accredited teachers; classification/transition counselors complete an adult services academy	Yes	An orientation and requirement that they cannot themselves be under supervision	Yes	Employment, housing, financial assistance, transportation and identification documents
WEST VIRGINIA	No response					
WISCONSIN	Yes	Social workers	Unknown		Yes	Community and county social services, mental health, churches and schools
WYOMING	Yes	Education staff for general population inmates; case managers and Department of Workforce Services specialists for SVORI inmates	No		Yes	Faith-based programs, departments of Workforce Services and Health, HUD, mental health centers and (for SVORI inmates) local apartment owners
FEDERAL BUREAU OF PRISONS	No response					

[1] TENNESSEE: Staff must have knowledge and training in interviewing and counseling, individual and group dynamics, classification, sexual harassment, time management, victim-impact awareness, drug and alcohol abuse awareness, cognitive-behavior class presentation, and probation/parole policies.

REENTRY — TABLE 3: STAFFING PATTERNS

SYSTEM	INTERNAL STAFF		VOLUNTEERS		FORMAL COMMUNITY PARTICIPATION	
	Assigned	Credentials; Training	Pursued	Credentials; Training	Pursued	Type of Service
CANADIAN SYSTEMS						
BRITISH COLUMBIA	Yes	Must have received training from the Justice Institute of British Columbia	No		Yes	Financial assistance
MANITOBA	Yes	In-house training in case management and program facilitation	Yes	Must have accredited agency supervision and received appropriate training and workplace orientation	Yes	Community mental health, family services and housing agencies, income security, employment and addiction foundations, etc.
NEWFOUNDLAND	Yes	A social science degree, extensive case management, security and program delivery experience	Yes	Not specified	Yes	John Howard Society and probation, addiction, and housing services
NOVA SCOTIA	Yes	Classification officer designation	No		Yes	Metro Turning Point, Salvation Army, Metro Transit, Metro Food Bank, Elizabeth Fry Society, Coverdale, Rob White Society, Recovery House and community services for drug addictions
ONTARIO	Yes	Social workers, psychologists and discharge planners/rehabilitation officers	Yes	Training provided by the local institution in consultation with community agencies and the ministry's Bell Cairn Staff Development Center	Yes	Employment, housing, financial assistance, community support identification, mental health agencies/hospitals, Aboriginal services, and so forth
CORRECTIONAL SERVICE CANADA	Yes	University degree in a related field and undergo specific training for program delivery	Yes	Must have reached the age of majority, attend an orientation, and undergo a security clearance	Yes[2]	Police, immigration officials, Office of the Correctional Investigator of Canada, nongovernmental agencies (for example, John Howard Society, Elizabeth Fry Society, etc.), citizen advisory committees, and victim advocate groups

[2] CORRECTIONAL SERVICE CANADA: The National Parole Board is an independent administrative body that controls the conditional release of federal offenders (those serving a sentence of two years or more) and of provincial offenders in provinces and territories that do not have their own parole boards.

REENTRY — TABLE 4: TRANSITION DETENTION

SYSTEM	Separate Within Facility	Community Halfway House	Prerelease Facility	Day Reporting Centers	Other
ALABAMA	Yes	Yes	No	Yes	
ALASKA	No response				
ARIZONA	No response				
ARKANSAS	No	No	No	No	
CALIFORNIA	No	Yes	No	Yes	
COLORADO	No	Yes	No	Yes	Work/Family Center
CONNECTICUT	Yes	Yes	Yes	Yes	
DELAWARE	No	Yes	No	Yes	
DISTRICT OF COLUMBIA	No response				
FLORIDA					
GEORGIA	No	Yes	No	Yes	
HAWAII	Yes	Yes	Yes	No	
IDAHO	Yes	Yes	No	No	Work centers
ILLINOIS	No response				
INDIANA	Yes	No	Yes	No	
IOWA	Yes	Yes	No	Yes	Work centers
KANSAS	Yes	Yes	Yes	Yes	
KENTUCKY	No response				
LOUISIANA	No	Yes	No	No	Work centers
MAINE	Yes	No	Yes	No	
MARYLAND	No response				
MASSACHUSETTS	No	No	No	No	
MICHIGAN	Yes	Yes	No	Yes	
MINNESOTA	No	No	No	No	
MISSISSIPPI	Yes	No	Yes	No	
MISSOURI	Yes	Yes	No	No	
MONTANA	Yes	No	No	No	Sanction and Assessment Center
NEBRASKA	Yes	Yes	No	No	Work centers
NEVADA	No	Yes	No	No	
NEW HAMPSHIRE	No	No	No	No	
NEW JERSEY	Yes	Yes	No	Yes	
NEW MEXICO	No	No	No	No	

SYSTEM	Separate Within Facility	Community Halfway House	Prerelease Facility	Day Reporting Centers	Other
NEW YORK	No	No	Yes	Yes	Transitional Service Center
NORTH CAROLINA	No	No	No	No	
NORTH DAKOTA	No	Yes	Yes	No	
OHIO	No	Yes	No	Yes	Transitional control
OKLAHOMA	No	No	No	No	
OREGON	No	Yes	No	No	
PENNSYLVANIA	Yes	Yes	Yes	Yes	Private vendor center
RHODE ISLAND	No	Yes	No	No	
SOUTH CAROLINA	No response				
SOUTH DAKOTA	Yes	No	No	No	
TENNESSEE	No	No	No	No	
TEXAS	No	Yes	Yes	Yes	
UTAH	No	Yes	No	Yes	
VERMONT	Yes	Yes	No	Yes	Transition center
VIRGINIA	Yes	No	Yes	Yes	
WASHINGTON	Yes	Yes	Yes	Yes	
WEST VIRGINIA	No response				
WISCONSIN	Yes	Yes	No	Yes	
WYOMING	No	No	No	No	Work centers
FEDERAL BUREAU OF PRISONS	No response				

CANADIAN SYSTEMS

SYSTEM	Separate Within Facility	Community Halfway House	Prerelease Facility	Day Reporting Centers	Other
BRITISH COLUMBIA	No	No	No	No	
MANITOBA	No	Yes	No	Yes	
NEWFOUNDLAND	No	Yes	No	No	
NOVA SCOTIA	No	No	No	No	
ONTARIO	No	No	No	No	
CORRECTIONAL SERVICE CANADA	No	Yes	No	No	

REENTRY — TABLE 5: DISCHARGE PROCEDURES

SYSTEM	PERSONAL ACCOUNT Balance	PERSONAL ACCOUNT Restrictions	GATE MONEY	TRANSPORTATION	CLOTHING	MEDICATIONS Amount	MEDICATIONS Prescription
ALABAMA	Yes		No	Bus or via relatives; varies based on situation at release	One outfit (jeans or a pullover) unless provided by a relative	90 days for mental health; 10 days for others	90 days for mental health; 10 days for others
ALASKA	No response						
ARIZONA	No response						
ARKANSAS	Yes	Mailed to address provided by the inmate	$100	Bus ticket to parole destination	One complete set that they wear when leaving the facility	Evaluated individually	7 days
CALIFORNIA	Yes		Up to $200	Bus ticket to release destination	Pants, shirt, shoes, socks and underwear, or an inmate can elect to receive a parole package from home	3 days	No
COLORADO	Yes		$100 for first-time release		Pants, shirt, shoes and jacket on a case-specific basis	30 days	30 days
CONNECTICUT	Yes		$75		One set	14 days	No
DELAWARE	Yes		$50, if indigent	Bus ticket or personal transport by facility official to destination	One set	7 to 10 days	One refill
DISTRICT OF COLUMBIA	No response						
FLORIDA	Yes	By check and mailed to address provided by the inmate	$100[1]	Bus ticket to release destination, if not provided by family or friends	Donated items from supplies on hand or purchased locally	30 days or other nonprescription medications if used in chronic clinic treatment	30 days
GEORGIA	Yes		$25	Bus ticket to parole destination or last home county	Pants, shirt, shoes, belt jacket	30 days for mental health; 14 days for others	Varies
HAWAII	Yes		No		No	Up to 30 days	No
IDAHO	Yes		Up to $800	Bus ticket within the state	No	14 days	14 days
ILLINOIS	No response						
INDIANA	Yes		Up to $75	Public transportation to closest stop to residence, when required	One set appropriate for the season	7 days or sufficient to last until follow-up appointment; 30 days for mental health or TB	No
IOWA	Yes	By check	$100	Bus ticket to residence within the state	One set appropriate for the season, if needed	30 days plus 30-day refill, if needed	30 days plus 30-day refill, if needed
KANSAS	Yes		Yes	Ticket to destination county	One outfit accessible from clothing banks in the community	30 days, with a few exceptions	No
KENTUCKY	No response						
LOUISIANA	Yes		$10	Bus station or airport, if approved by the warden	One set	5 days	Appropriate for continuity of care
MAINE	Yes		Yes	Yes	Unknown	Yes	Yes
MARYLAND	No response						
MASSACHUSETTS	Yes	By check	$50 if indigent		No	30 days	To be filled upon release; amount varies by prescription
MICHIGAN	Yes		$75	Bus ticket and transportation to nearest bus station	Yes	30 days	30 days

[1] FLORIDA: The payment is made if the inmate's account balance was below $200 within the last six months prior to release.

REENTRY — TABLE 5: DISCHARGE PROCEDURES

SYSTEM	PERSONAL ACCOUNT Balance	PERSONAL ACCOUNT Restrictions	GATE MONEY	TRANSPORTATION	CLOTHING	MEDICATIONS Amount	MEDICATIONS Prescription
MINNESOTA	Yes		$100	For high-risk offenders to halfway houses or to agent office and for humanitarian reasons; not for general-release offenders	Pants, shirt, shoes, jacket, underwear	Balance of blister card or at least 7 days or to maintain a therapeutically safe level	Depends on the medication
MISSISSIPPI	Yes		$25	Bus ticket to anywhere in the state	Jeans, white t-shirt and tennis shoes	Balance on hand	30 days
MISSOURI	Yes		No	Yes	Yes	Yes	Yes
MONTANA	Yes		No	No	No	30 days	No, but contact is made with local providers
NEBRASKA	Yes		$100, depending on account balance	No	Jeans, shirt, shoes, underwear and coat and hat depending on the weather	14 days, but working to lengthen time and availability	14 days, but working to lengthen time and availability
NEVADA	Yes		$25	Bus ticket to parole/probation office or taken to downtown bus station if expiration of sentence	Jeans, shirt, socks and underwear	7 days	7 to 14 days
NEW HAMPSHIRE	Yes		No	No	No	No	No
NEW JERSEY	Yes		No	To a public transportation station, if needed [2]	Jeans, white pullover, sneakers, jacket, socks and underwear, if needed	14 days	14 days
NEW MEXICO	Yes [3]		Up to $50	Bus ticket; airfare, occasionally	Khaki uniform, occasionally	Balance at time of release	2 to 3 days
NEW YORK	Yes		$40 minimum	Bus or train ticket to home destination	Jeans, brown sweatshirt, sneakers, belt, jacket, unless purchased from the facility or provided by the family	Varies depending on type of release and medical need; 14 days for mental health	Depends on type of release and medical need
NORTH CAROLINA	Yes		$45, if indigent	Bus ticket or transport by staff to local county of release	Whatever is needed, including socks, shoes, underwear and outer garments	No	At least 30 days
NORTH DAKOTA	Yes		No	Back to location where sentenced	One set, including a coat	Up to 7 days	Good for one year
OHIO	N/A		Varies	To a bus station, if needed	Prison issue	14 days	No
OKLAHOMA	Yes		$50, discretionary	Bus ticket with the state	Items that are available at the facility	14 days	14 days
OREGON	Yes		$25 to approved inmates	Bus ticket to approved inmates	Gray sweats, if needed	30 days	No
PENNSYLVANIA	Yes		Yes, if indigent	Bus ticket to destination	No	30 or 60 days	No
RHODE ISLAND	Yes	Up to $50, in cash	By check for balance over $50 in account	Bus ticket generally provided by discharge planning agencies for their clients	Provided on occasion by discharge planning agencies	Varies on an individual basis	No, except for rare situations
SOUTH CAROLINA	No response						
SOUTH DAKOTA	Yes	Yes [4]	$50	Bus ticket voucher or shuttle ride to county of commitment or place of equivalent distance	Pants, shirt, shoes, socks, underwear and coat	14 days	14 days
TENNESSEE	Yes		$75 or $30 [5]	Nontransferable, least expensive ticket to approved residence within the state	Pants and shirts or a skirt and blouse, with a jacket if released between November and March	30 days	No

[2] NEW JERSEY: Inmates may buy prepaid New Jersey Transit bus tickets at a reduced cost through the DOC business office.
[3] NEW MEXICO: Inmates also are given the amount in their forced savings account.
[4] SOUTH DAKOTA: Transportation costs are deducted if there is more than $50 in the account.
[5] TENNESSEE: Inmates at expiration of sentence receive $75; all others receive $30.

REENTRY — TABLE 5: DISCHARGE PROCEDURES

SYSTEM	PERSONAL ACCOUNT Balance	PERSONAL ACCOUNT Restrictions	GATE MONEY	TRANSPORTATION	CLOTHING	MEDICATIONS Amount	MEDICATIONS Prescription
TEXAS	Yes		$50 plus $50 when reporting to parole office	Bus ticket to nearest city to county of residence; often transported in a state vehicle for high-profile cases	Pants, shirt and shoes if necessary	10 days	10 days
UTAH	Yes		Up to $100, depending on account balance and history	No	No (often provided by faith-based organizations or Prisoner Information Network)	30 days, if qualified	30 days, if qualified
VERMONT	Yes		Up to $300	No	Personal clothing is returned to the inmate	Depends on the medication	Varies
VIRGINIA	Yes		$25	Bus voucher	One set	30 days	30 days
WASHINGTON	Yes		$40	Public transportation to county of commitment or county of approved release address	Pants, shirt, shoes or boots, underwear and a coat	Up to 30 days	Up to 30 days
WEST VIRGINIA	No response						
WISCONSIN	Yes		No	To home community, if needed	Institution clothing, if needed	30 to 60 days	30 to 60 days
WYOMING	Yes		No	Public transportation to the city of parole and includes intransit meals	No	14 days, except for narcotics	14 to 30 days[6]
FEDERAL BUREAU OF PRISONS	No response						

CANADIAN SYSTEMS

SYSTEM	Balance	Restrictions	GATE MONEY	TRANSPORTATION	CLOTHING	Amount	Prescription
BRITISH COLUMBIA	Yes		No	Bus fare to location of sentencing	Personal clothing is returned to the inmate	2 to 3 days	2 to 3 days
MANITOBA	Yes		$10	Local transit or ground/air to home community	Footwear and basic clothing from used or donated inventories	Varies	7 days
NEWFOUNDLAND	Yes		Not specified	Bus or taxi voucher to home destination or area of sentencing court	Personal clothing is returned to the inmate	5 to 7 days	Only in exceptional circumstances
NOVA SCOTIA	Yes		No	Bus ticket to address known prior to incarceration	Footwear and winter attire (women are assisted by the Elizabeth Fry organization)	1 to 2 days	No
ONTARIO	Yes		No	Bailiffs[7] or most economic mode of transportation to the home community	No, but community agencies may provide seasonal-appropriate clothing if needed	Up to 2 days at the discretion of the health care staff[8]	No
CORRECTIONAL SERVICE CANADA	Yes		Difference between account balance and $50 maximum	Money for transportation by bus, train or plane to any verified destination within the country	If necessary	Varies on a case-by-case basis	Varies, determined by the expectation of the length of time for the offender to relocate and find proper access to medical care

[6] WYOMING: Prescriptions are provided as noted, depending on the release location/destination and the availability of physician follow-up.
[7] ONTARIO: Correctional bailiffs may transport inmate to the jail/detention center in their home community just prior to release.
[8] ONTARIO: Female inmates receive the packet of birth control pills presently in use to avoid missing doses within the cycle.

REENTRY — TABLE 6: POST RELEASE

SYSTEM	FORMAL FOLLOW-UP	EMPLOYMENT RESTRICTIONS IN EFFECT	STATEWIDE VOTING RESTRICTIONS — Previously removed	Plans for removal	Currently in effect or comments
ALABAMA	No	An explanation of a felony or misdemeanor conviction must be given to an employer	No	Unknown	Inmates must reinstate themselves and obtain governor's approval, depending on the crime
ALASKA	No response				
ARIZONA	No response				
ARKANSAS	No	For law enforcement and for some board certification and licensing for attorneys, medical, etc.	No	No	Voting is restricted
CALIFORNIA	Yes, on parole	Varies, depending on the commitment offense	No	No	Restored after completion of parole or upon discharge
COLORADO	No	Felonies preclude certification for certain fields such as medical	No	No	Restored after completion of parole or upon discharge
CONNECTICUT	No	Casino gaming board and insurance companies	Yes	N/A	
DELAWARE	Yes	Division of Professional Regulation will not reissue certain licenses if they expired while incarcerated for a felony	No	Yes	Voting is restricted
DISTRICT OF COLUMBIA	No response				
FLORIDA	Yes, for Project Reconnect job seekers	Sex offenders may not work in child care facilities or in occupations where children are present. Various restrictions apply to inmates with felony convictions.[1]	No	No	Voting rights must be individually reviewed and approved by the clemency board. The executive branch recently removed some of the restrictions on voting rights as part of an overall civil rights restoration process
GEORGIA	No	Unknown	No	No	Restored by the parole board after completion of parole or upon discharge
HAWAII	No				
IDAHO	No	Sex offenders may not work where children are likely to be present; fraud or forgery offenders may not work on jobs that require handling money; injury to a child or the elderly offenders may not work with children or the elderly	No	No	Voting is restricted
ILLINOIS	No response				
INDIANA	Yes, for in-state recidivists	No restrictions	Yes	N/A	
IOWA	Yes, for SVORI offenders	No, unless restricted by supervision officers (e.g., sex offenders to work with children or substance abusers to work in bars, etc.)	Yes, except for felony convictions	No	
KANSAS	Yes[2]	Most health care jobs, various licenses, and some treatment programs, especially those serving juveniles; the department currently is conducting a search for related laws	No	Unknown	Fairly liberal expungement laws are in effect whereby discharging inmates are informed they may pursue expungement for restoration of voting rights
KENTUCKY	No response				
LOUISIANA	Yes, on parole	Sex offenders may not work at a school, in day care, etc.; those under supervision (with history of alcohol abuse) may not work where alcohol beverages are sold or at any place considered disreputable\	No	Unknown	Restored after completion of parole or upon discharge
MAINE	Yes[3]	Follows federal guidelines	Yes	N/A	

[1] FLORIDA: Felony convictions preclude certification as teachers, unless reviewed and approved by the Department of Education; medical professions, unless their civil rights have been restored; serving as correctional, probation or law enforcement officers, or working as barbers, contractors or other licensed professions.
[2] KANSAS: A six-month follow-up for inmates in the SVORI program and periodic follow-up for inmates in the transition/discharge program.

REENTRY — TABLE 6: POST RELEASE

SYSTEM	FORMAL FOLLOW-UP	EMPLOYMENT RESTRICTIONS IN EFFECT	STATEWIDE VOTING RESTRICTIONS — Previously removed	STATEWIDE VOTING RESTRICTIONS — Plans for removal	STATEWIDE VOTING RESTRICTIONS — Currently in effect or comments
MARYLAND	No response				
MASSACHUSETTS	Yes, by phone	Left to employers who have access to criminal records and self-screen potential employees	Yes	N/A	
MICHIGAN	Yes, on parole	Medical professions that require certification or licensing prohibit felony drug convictions	Yes	N/A	
MINNESOTA	Yes, on parole	Depending on the nature of the offense, restrictions exist for professions such as health care, child care, gambling, finance, etc.	No	Unknown	Restored after completion of parole or sentence
MISSISSIPPI	Yes[4]	Some employers conduct extensive background checks and some refuse to hire convicted felons, regardless of the crime	No	No	
MISSOURI	Yes, for SVORI participants	Sex offenders may not work at any job involving children, including bus drivers or for day care, and offenders with drug convictions are prohibited in health care	Yes	N/A	
MONTANA	Yes[5]	No	No	No	
NEBRASKA	Yes, for one year	No	No	Possibly	Legislation has been introduced in the past but has not been well received; legislation will again be introduced in this current session
NEVADA	Yes[6]	Certain companies may require that a potential candidate must possess a clean criminal record; parole agents may screen potential employment opportunities that indicate a risk for the applicant to re-offend	Yes	N/A	
NEW HAMPSHIRE	Yes, on parole		No	Unknown	
NEW JERSEY	No	Approximately 22 categories of jobs for which certain criminal convictions serve as an absolute bar to employment and a number of jobs for which criminal convictions must be disclosed and may serve as a barrier.	No	No	Legislation has been proposed for reinstatement but its support is unknown; also, a current court case was dismissed at the trial court level and is now being heard on appeal
NEW MEXICO	Yes, for SOAR participants	Sex offenders may be restricted	No	Unknown	Offenders may apply for a restoration of voting rights
NEW YORK	Yes[7]	The Division of Parole may set restrictions based on the type of offense such as violence involving weapons, drugs and alcohol use and sex offenders	Unknown	N/A	With a certificate of "Good Conduct," an inmate may apply for restoration
NORTH CAROLINA	No	Employers may determine whether to hire a felon	Yes	N/A	
NORTH DAKOTA	No	No	Yes	N/A	Restored upon release
OHIO	No	Twenty-eight restrictions are on the books	Yes	N/A	
OKLAHOMA	No	Licensing restrictions	Yes	N/A	
OREGON	No	Criminal background checks are required by the Department of Human Services for people planning to work with children, the mentally ill and other vulnerable populations	Yes	N/A	Restored upon release
PENNSYLVANIA	Yes[8]	Restrictions apply, depending on the offense	Yes	N/A	The department provides voter registration information and applications just prior to release

[3] MAINE: Formal follow-up is conducted for those in the SVORI reentry program, and on probation for offenders, when court-ordered.
[4] MISSISSIPPI: Counselors conduct follow-up services for job placement assistance, up to one year after release.
[5] MONTANA: Inmates are tracked when court-ordered and counseling is provided for those needing chemical dependency or other treatments.
[6] NEVADA: Inmates are tracked on parole or when court-ordered.
[7] NEW YORK: An annual three-year follow-up is conducted only to determine issues of recidivism.
[8] PENNSYLVANIA: Inmates are tracked up to three years following release to calculate the rate of recidivism.

REENTRY TODAY: Programs, Problems, and Solutions

REENTRY — TABLE 6: POST RELEASE

SYSTEM	FORMAL FOLLOW-UP	EMPLOYMENT RESTRICTIONS IN EFFECT	STATEWIDE VOTING RESTRICTIONS - Previously removed	STATEWIDE VOTING RESTRICTIONS - Plans for removal	STATEWIDE VOTING RESTRICTIONS - Currently in effect or comments
RHODE ISLAND	Yes[9]	The number of background checks being requested for entry-level jobs is increasing	No	Yes	A nonprofit organization currently is working on this issue and a legislative bill will possibly be offered
SOUTH CAROLINA	No response				
SOUTH DAKOTA	Yes	Sex offenders may not work in schools, day care centers, etc., and offenders on parole are restricted from working where alcohol is served	No	Unknown	Restored upon completion of sentence
TENNESSEE	No	During the application process, employers are allowed to question arrest convictions and incarcerations	No	No	
TEXAS	Yes[10]	Depends on offense and circumstance (e.g., drug offenders cannot work in hospitals; those on electronic monitoring cannot work as long-distance truck drivers)	Yes	N/A	Restored upon completing sentence
UTAH	Yes, on parole	No	Yes	N/A	
VERMONT	Yes[11]	Follows federal guidelines and may include driving restrictions	N/A	N/A	Voting rights have never been removed and all inmates may vote while incarcerated
VIRGINIA	Yes, for evaluating special program participants	Extensive list of restrictions	No	Possibly	Offenders may request a reinstatement after five years following the termination of supervision
WASHINGTON	Yes[12]	The court may apply restrictions for certain jobs, such as drinking establishments or occupations coming into contact with children; the department may apply restrictions if the job subjects the offender or the public to a known risk	No	No	
WEST VIRGINIA	No response				
WISCONSIN	Yes, on parole	Restrictions apply for sexual offenders	No	Unknown	
WYOMING	Yes[13]				
FEDERAL BUREAU OF PRISONS	No response				
CANADIAN SYSTEMS					
BRITISH COLUMBIA	No	No	Yes	N/A	Inmates have full voting rights while incarcerated
MANITOBA	No	No	No	Unknown	Incarcerated inmates may vote in federal or provincial elections but not in municipalities
NEWFOUNDLAND	No	Based on risk factors and community concerns	Yes	N/A	
NOVA SCOTIA	Yes, if court-ordered	No	Yes	N/A	
ONTARIO	Yes, on probation or parole	No	No	Unknown	Sentenced and remand inmates may vote in federal elections and may apply to vote in provincial elections; depending on the municipality, only remand inmates may vote locally
CORRECTIONAL SERVICE CANADA	No	Depends on the type of conviction (e.g., check fraud or robbery convictions may not work in that industry)	No	Yes	

[9] RHODE ISLAND: Discharge vendors are required to follow up for at least 60 days.
[10] TEXAS: Formal follow-up by institutional staff for inmates involved in treatment programs while incarcerated (i.e., sex offenders, mentally ill, those recommended for intensive supervision, therapeutic community offenders, etc.).
[11] VERMONT: All releasing inmates are placed on conditional reentry status that includes intensive pre-parole supervision.
[12] WASHINGTON: Community corrections officers follow up with offenders for a pre-determined period of time, tracking compliance and assisting with needs when possible.
[13] WYOMING: Follow up is conducted for SVORI participants and for offenders with serious mental health issues.

74

REENTRY — TABLE 6: POST RELEASE

SYSTEM	FORMAL FOLLOW-UP	EMPLOYMENT RESTRICTIONS IN EFFECT	STATEWIDE VOTING RESTRICTIONS Previously removed	Plans for removal	Currently in effect or comments
RHODE ISLAND	Yes[9]	The number of background checks being requested for entry-level jobs is increasing	No	Yes	A nonprofit organization currently is working on this issue and a legislative bill will possibly be offered
SOUTH CAROLINA	No response				
SOUTH DAKOTA	Yes	Sex offenders may not work in schools, day care centers, etc., and offenders on parole are restricted from working where alcohol is served	No	Unknown	Restored upon completion of sentence
TENNESSEE	No	During the application process, employers are allowed to question arrest convictions and incarcerations	No	No	
TEXAS	Yes[10]	Depends on offense and circumstance (e.g., drug offenders cannot work in hospitals; those on electronic monitoring cannot work as long-distance truck drivers)	Yes	N/A	Restored upon completing sentence
UTAH	Yes, on parole	No	Yes	N/A	
VERMONT	Yes[11]	Follows federal guidelines and may include driving restrictions	N/A	N/A	Voting rights have never been removed and all inmates may vote while incarcerated
VIRGINIA	Yes, for evaluating special program participants	Extensive list of restrictions	No	Possibly	Offenders may request a reinstatement after five years following the termination of supervision
WASHINGTON	Yes[12]	The court may apply restrictions for certain jobs, such as drinking establishments or occupations coming into contact with children; the department may apply restrictions if the job subjects the offender or the public to a known risk	No	No	
WEST VIRGINIA	No response				
WISCONSIN	Yes, on parole	Restrictions apply for sexual offenders	No	Unknown	
WYOMING	Yes[13]				
FEDERAL BUREAU OF PRISONS	No response				
CANADIAN SYSTEMS					
BRITISH COLUMBIA	No	No	Yes	N/A	Inmates have full voting rights while incarcerated
MANITOBA	No	No	No	Unknown	Incarcerated inmates may vote in federal or provincial elections but not in municipalities
NEWFOUNDLAND	No	Based on risk factors and community concerns	Yes	N/A	
NOVA SCOTIA	Yes, if court-ordered	No	Yes	N/A	
ONTARIO	Yes, on probation or parole	No	No	Unknown	Sentenced and remand inmates may vote in federal elections and may apply to vote in provincial elections; depending on the municipality, only remand inmates may vote locally
CORRECTIONAL SERVICE CANADA	No	Depends on the type of conviction (e.g., check fraud or robbery convictions may not work in that industry)	No	Yes	

---

[9] RHODE ISLAND: Discharge vendors are required to follow up for at least 60 days.
[10] TEXAS: Formal follow-up by institutional staff for inmates involved in treatment programs while incarcerated (i.e., sex offenders, mentally ill, those recommended for intensive supervision, therapeutic community offenders, etc.).
[11] VERMONT: All releasing inmates are placed on conditional reentry status that includes intensive pre-parole supervision.
[12] WASHINGTON: Community corrections officers follow up with offenders for a pre-determined period of time, tracking compliance and assisting with needs when possible.
[13] WYOMING: Follow up is conducted for SVORI participants and for offenders with serious mental health issues.

Inmate Reentry: What Works and What to Do About It

Richard P. Seiter, Ph.D.

*First printed in Corrections Compendium,
a publication of the American Correctional Association,
January/February 2004

The issue of inmate reentry is not new. Inmates have been released from prison and returned to the community since the opening of the Walnut Street Jail in Philadelphia in 1790. During the past two decades, there have been many swings in the philosophy of how prisons were operated, how ex-offenders were supervised in the community, and how programs were offered and services were provided to aid in the transition from prison to community living.

During the 1800s, inmates served determinate sentences, had few rehabilitative programs and did not receive much preparation for release. During much of the 1900s, inmates served indeterminate sentences and prisons accentuated the provision of rehabilitative programs, while parole boards determined when inmates were best prepared to return to the community. During the past two decades, an emphasis on offender accountability has precipitated the reemergence of determinate sentencing as the primary sentencing approach. In addition, there is less emphasis and funding for prison programs geared towards improving offender education, self-esteem, vocational training, and community-based, graduated reentry programs.

These recent changes in sentencing and program offerings have dramatically impacted the situation regarding inmate reentry into the community. Currently, there are many more offenders released from prisons than only a few years ago. With most inmates now released after serving determinate sentences, there are no readiness reviews by parole boards, and some inmates are released without supervision. Inmates are serving significantly longer prison terms and have participated in fewer rehabilitative or prerelease programs. Lynch and Sabol (2000) found that the average time served by inmates released in 1990 was twenty-two months and those released in 1998 served an average of twenty-seven months. In the same study, the authors examined program participation in prison release cohorts between 1991 and 1997. They found that the percentage participating in vocational training decreased from 32 percent in 1991 to 27 percent in 1997, while education participation declined from 42 percent in 1991 to 34 percent in 1997.

Also, the communities to which inmates return do not have the social service resources needed by ex-offenders and their family ties are less solid (Rose, Clear and Scully, 1999). Once on supervision following release, there is less tolerance for violating even the technical conditions of post-release supervision, and a large number of releasees are returned to prison for either commission of new crimes or violating technical conditions of supervision.

This article reviews some of these issues regarding the release of offenders into the community. It also reviews current knowledge regarding the types of programs that have been found to work to improve offender reentry and reduce subsequent recidivism. Finally, it proposes policy implications for improving the successful reentry of inmates based on these research findings. The states and federal government have allocated billions of additional dollars to building and operating prisons during the past twenty-five years with questionable success in returning offenders to the community as productive and law-abiding citizens. Now that information is available to identify the types of program investments that do work in this regard, it is time to allocate dollars to improving success rather than merely allowing the revolving door of incarceration to persist.

The Operation of Current Correctional Systems

The number of people under the supervision of correctional agencies has been increasing during the past twenty years. By the end of the twentieth century, there were more than 6 million offenders either in prison or jail, or under supervision in the community. The Bureau of Justice Statistics correctional surveys (1980-2001) report a 252 percent increase in the number of offenders on probation, a 243 percent increase in the number of offenders in jail, a 316 percent increase in the number of inmates in prison, and a 231 percent increase in the number of offenders on parole between 1980 and 2001.

This growth in the number of offenders under correctional supervision subsequently requires a comparable increase in the funding committed to operate correctional agencies.

During fiscal year 1991, the combined budget for state and federal adult correctional agencies totaled $18.1 billion. By fiscal year 1998, these budgets increased 67 percent to $30.3 billion and represented 4.9 percent of the total budget of state and federal correctional agencies (Camp and Camp, 1999). The Bureau of Justice Statistics reports that from 1982 through 1997, spending for corrections increased by 381 percent, far exceeding the increase in police and judicial spending. Correctional agency spending is expected to continue to increase. In fact, there were 83,000 new prison beds under construction in 1998, 41,368 in 1999 and 47,476 in 2000, with $2.8 billion allocated to new prison construction in 2000 and another $2.7 billion anticipated to be budgeted in 2001 (Camp and Camp, 2001).

This growth has come about for a variety of reasons, many of which impact the process and success of inmate reentry programs. During the 1960s and 1970s, all states used parole boards to determine the release readiness of inmates. In 1977, conditional release reached its peak, as 72 percent of all inmates were released on parole (BJS, 1977). However, since the early 1980s, this approach to release began to change. Partly as a result of the Lipton, Martinson and Wilks (1975) study concluding that rehabilitation does not work, the medical model of corrections lost support and the general public and elected officials demanded offenders be held accountable for their crimes. Funding for prison rehabilitative and transitional programs decreased, and parole supervision changed from a casework (helping) to a surveillance (policing) model (Feeley and Simon, 1992).

The current model of prison operations and inmate reentry is based on incapacitation and deterrence, in contrast with the medical model, which focuses on inmate rehabilitation and preparation for release. Currently, many states have opted to abolish parole, and fifteen states and the federal government have ended the use of indeterminate sentencing with release decisions made by a parole board. Also, twenty states have severely limited the parole-eligible population, and only fifteen states still have full discretionary parole for inmates. In 1997, only 28 percent of prison releasees served an indeterminate sentence and exited prison on parole (BJS, 1997).

As a result of these changes, most offenders serve a determinate sentence that is much longer than in the past, and the prison population grew more rapidly than during any other period of time since prisons were first established, reaching 1.4 million at midyear 2002 (Harrison and Karberg, 2003). As would be expected, the increasing number of inmates results in an increasing number of releasees. Camp and Camp (2002) report that 596,191 inmates were released from prison during 2000. California recently reported that 124,697 offenders were leaving prison after completing their sentences—almost ten times the number twenty years earlier (Petersilia, 2000).

When there were only a few hundred thousand inmates, there were only a few inmates released from prison each year, and the issues surrounding inmate reentry did not seem to seriously challenge community corrections resources or the communities to which inmates returned. However, as the number of inmates increased, the number of offenders returning to their communities skyrocketed and new problems came to the forefront. These problems were clearly presented in a study by the Vera Institute of Justice in New York City, which illustrated issues confronting inmates released from prison, such as finding a job, alcohol and drug abuse, continued involvement in crime, and the impact of parole supervision (Nelson, Deess, and Allen, 1999).

Another critical issue with the large number of inmates being released to their communities is the impact on social cohesion and community stability. The attitudes and behaviors of ex-inmates are often transmitted to those in the community upon release. One study of the impact on communities concluded that "family caretakers and role models disappear or decline in influence, and as unemployment and poverty become more persistent, the community, particularly its children, becomes vulnerable to a variety of social ills, including crime, drugs, family disorganization, generalized demoralization and unemployment" (Anderson, 1990).

In another study, Rose, Clear, and Scully (1999) found that the imprisonment and removal of the offender from a concentrated neighborhood resulted in an increase in crime. The authors question the deterrent and rehabilitative effect of prison, and suggest that not only does the removal of a large number of adult males from a community destabilize it, but the return of a large number of parolees back to the community increasingly destabilizes its ability to exert informal control over its members, as there is little opportunity for integration, increased isolation and anonymity and, ultimately, more crime.

In addition to the challenges mentioned above to both released offenders and their communities, there is also a toughening attitude and expectation regarding their behavior after they return to the community, resulting in an increasing number of inmates being returned as parole and release violators. In 1998, there were 170,253 reported parole violators in the United States, representing more than 23 percent of new prison admissions (Beck and Mumola, 1999). Interestingly, Camp and Camp (1999) report that 76.9 percent of all parole violators are violated for technical violations only, without commission of a new felony.

Research Methodology

In a recent review of the effectiveness of inmate reentry programs, Seiter and Kadela (2003) analyzed all available evaluations of the programs' effectiveness. In that analysis, the authors used the following as a definition of inmate reentry programs: Inmate reentry programs are all correctional programs (United States and Canada) that focus on the "transition" from prison to community (prerelease, work release, halfway houses, or specific reentry programs) or programs that have initiated treatment (substance abuse, life skills, education, cognitive/behavioral, or sex/violent offender) in a prison setting and have linked with a community program to provide continuity of care.

Seiter and Kadela then searched available databases for studies of programs that fit this definition. They identified thirty-two studies that fit their definition of inmate reentry and grouped similar program evaluations into the following categories: vocational training and work, drug rehabilitation, educational programs, sex/violent offender programs, halfway house programs and prison prerelease programs. To determine whether the reentry programs meeting the definition were effective, the authors used the Maryland Scale of Scientific Methods (MSSM) developed by Sherman et al. (1998) to identify crime prevention programs that work. The MSSM ranks studies from 1 (weakest) to 5 (strongest) on overall internal validity.

Generally, the MSSM applies across all settings and includes core criteria, which define the five levels of the scale. The higher the level, the more rigorous the research design and the lower the threat to internal validity. The scale uses the following levels to categorize evaluative studies by their rigor or scientific method:

- Level 1: Correlation between a type or level of reentry program (intervention, for example, substance abuse treatment, violent or sex offender treatment, vocational training, work release, life skills) and an outcome measure at a single point in time (recidivism, return to custody, employment rate, drug use, academic achievement);

- Level 2: Temporal sequence between the program (intervention) and outcome measure clearly observed or the presence of a comparison group without demonstrated comparability to the treatment group;

- Level 3: A comparison between two or more comparable units of analysis, one with and one without the program;

- Level 4: Comparison between multiple units with and without the program, controlling for other factors, or using comparison units that evidence only minor differences; and

- Level 5: Random assignment and analysis of comparable units to program and comparison groups.

Determining the Effectiveness of Inmate Reentry Programs

To determine whether an inmate reentry study worked, the framework created by Sherman et al. (1998) in their evaluation of whether crime prevention programs effectively reduced crime was used. To determine the threshold of scientific evidence answering their question about crime prevention program effectiveness, Sherman and colleagues developed the following criteria.

What works? For a program category to be "working," there must be at least two Level 3 evaluations with significance tests, indicating that the intervention was effective and the preponderance of the remaining evidence must support that conclusion.

What does not work? For a program category to be "not working," there must be at least two Level 3 evaluations with statistical significance, indicating the ineffectiveness of the program and the preponderance of the remaining evidence must support the same conclusion.

What is promising? If there is some empirical basis for predicting that further research could support generalizable conclusions, yet the level of certainty from available evidence is too low to support generalizable conclusions, such as programs are found effective in at least one Level 3 evaluation and the preponderance of the remaining evidence supports that conclusion, then the program category is considered "promising."

What is unknown? Any program category not fitting into one of the above classifications is defined as having unknown effects.

What Works in Inmate Reentry

Seiter and Kadela (2003) analyzed each of the six categories of inmate reentry programs using the Sherman methodology and the MSSM criteria to determine effectiveness. The following represents a summary of the findings of inmate-reentry studies identified within the various reentry categories.

Vocational and Work Programs

Seven programs were evaluated in this area, including two Level 4 studies (Saylor and Gaes, 1992; 1997) and one Level 5 study (Turner and Petersilia, 1996). The Turner and Petersilia study compared recidivism of 218 offenders in Seattle, half of whom participated in a work release program and half of whom completed their sentences in prison. The program achieved its primary goal of preparing inmates for final release and facilitating their adjustment into the community. Offenders who participated in work release were somewhat less likely to be rearrested; however, the results were not statistically significant. The Saylor and Gaes studies evaluated the Post-Release Employment Project for more than 7,000 federal prison system inmates during a four-year period, comparing those participating in training and work programs with similar offenders who did not take part in these programs and with a baseline group of all other inmates. The longitudinal results demonstrated significant and substantive training effects on both in-prison (misconduct reports) and post-prison (employment and arrest rates) outcome measures. There were also three Level 2 studies (Finn, 1999) and one Level 1 study (Finn, 1999) that could have added increased promise for vocational work programs if a pre/post design and comparison control groups were implemented. Conclusions from these studies are that vocational training and/or work release programs are effective in reducing recidivism, as well as improving job-readiness skills for ex-offenders.

Drug Rehabilitation

There were twelve drug rehabilitation programs evaluated, including one Level 5 study (Pelisser et al., 2001) and eight Level 4 studies. Of these eight, three studies evaluated the same program (Texas' Prison-Based Treatment Assessment program) over time (Knight et al., 1997; Hiller, Knight and Simpson, 1999; and Knight, Simpson and Hiller, 1999) and four studies evaluated Delaware's Key-Crest program over time (Martin, Butzin, and Inciardi, 1995; Inciardi et al., 1997; Butzin et al., 1999, and Martin et al., 1999). The other Level 4 program, New York City's Stay 'N Out, was evaluated by Wexler, Falkin, and Lipton (1990).

The Pelisser et al. study examined 2,315 federal inmates: 1,193 treatment subjects, 592 comparison subjects, and 530 control subjects. Findings were that for both measures of outcome—recidivism and relapse to drug use—drug treatment is statistically significant in reducing both outcomes for men, but not for women.

The in-prison therapeutic communities (therapeutic community) evaluated by Knight and colleagues show the effectiveness of intensive treatment when integrated with aftercare. The benefits were most apparent with offenders who have serious crime and drug-related problems, as those who completed the first phase of their aftercare program had lower relapse and recidivism rates than did the parolees in the comparison sample (Knight et al., 1997). A three-year follow-up study based on 291 follow-up eligible parolees showed that those who completed both the therapeutic community program and aftercare are the least likely to be reincarcerated (25 percent) as compared with 64 percent of aftercare dropouts and 42 percent of untreated comparison groups (Knight et al., 1999). Another study of 293 treated inmates and 103 untreated inmates revealed that in-prison therapeutic community programs, especially when followed by residential aftercare, reduce the likelihood of post-release rearrest by 12 percent (Hiller, Knight and Simpson, 1999).

The Key-Crest in-prison therapeutic community and work release program evaluated by Inciardi and colleagues demonstrated marked success in its six-month and three-year follow-ups. In the first evaluation (Martin et al., 1995), baseline data at release from prison and outcome data six months after release were analyzed for 457 offenders in four different evaluative groups. These groups included offenders who participated in neither of the therapeutic communities compared with groups that either participated in the therapeutic community in prison only, the transitional therapeutic community only or both the therapeutic communities. The latter two groups had significantly lower rates of drug relapse and criminal recidivism when adjusted for other risk factors. A second study of eighteen-month follow-up data also indicated that the participants in the two- and three-stage models had significantly lower rates of drug relapse and criminal recidivism (Inciardi et al., 1997).

The third evaluation compared participants in only the Crest Outreach Center in Wilmington, Delaware, (n=334) with a group of drug-involved inmates who entered a traditional work release program (n=250) (Butzin et al., 1999). Results showed that those who complete the program are less likely than those who do not to be incarcerated at eighteen months following release and are also more likely to be employed. Comparing those who completed the program with a similar group of inmates who did not participate finds that not only are they less likely to be incarcerated and more likely to be employed than nonparticipants, but also those who completed the program and are unemployed used fewer drugs less frequently than the unemployed comparison group. This suggests that exposure to a therapeutic community work release environment can moderate expected negative effects (drug use) of unemployment.

The final evaluation examined the success of the therapeutic community outcomes three years after release (Martin et al., 1999). While the program effects declined, they remained significant when program participation, completion and aftercare were taken into account. Clients who completed secondary treatment did better than those with no treatment and those who dropped out, while clients who received aftercare did even better in remaining both drug-free and arrest-free. The authors concluded that the therapeutic community continuum has value in work release and parole settings and that retention in treatment is important in predicting long-term success in reducing the likelihood of recidivism.

The Wexler et al. (1990) evaluation analyzed the Stay 'N Out therapeutic community for more than 1,500 participants in a variety of drug abuse programs. The study compared program participants with inmates who volunteered for the program but never participated, and inmates who participated in other types of in-prison drug abuse treatment programs in different prisons. Results showed that after three years at risk of recidivism, those who completed the therapeutic community program had a significantly lower arrest rate (26.9 percent) than those who had different drug treatment (34.6 percent and 39.8 percent) and those who received no treatment (40.9 percent). In general, the therapeutic community was effective in reducing recidivism, and this positive effect increased as time in program increased but tapered off after twelve months.

The authors also reviewed one additional Level 3 study (Hartman et al., 1997) and two Level 2 studies (Fields, 1985; Knight and Hiller, 1997). While these studies have the potential for selection bias with respect to program completion and participation, their results do not disagree with the findings of the previously cited studies. Drug rehabilitation programs represent the strongest area of quasi-experimental design for evaluations of inmate reentry programs, and it can be concluded that drug treatment programs do work in easing the transition from prison to the community.

Education Programs

There were only two education program evaluations that fit the definition of inmate reentry. Both implemented a quasi-experimental design and measured rearrest and return-to-custody rates, increases in academic achievement after program graduation, and the time the offender was exposed to educational services. The first was a Level 4 study by Vito and Tewksbury (1999) evaluating the LITE program in Kentucky, which was designed to increase the literacy levels of state and local inmates and to reduce recidivism. Results indicate that during a six-week period, graduates increased their reading and math competencies by up to three grade levels; however, the educational component did not seem to have an affect on their recidivism rates when compared with those who did not graduate.

In a Level 3 study, Adams et al. (1994) compared prison behavior and post-release recidivism of more than 14,000 Texas inmates who participated in prison education programs, with others who did not participate. Results showed increases in academic achievement, but recidivism rates were only affected if the offender participated in 200 or more hours of educational programs. As per definitions established by Sherman and colleagues (1998), the mixed results of educational achievement scores increasing while recidivism did not decrease illustrate that educational reentry programs linking prison programs to community-based resources after release are only promising.

Sex and Violent Offenders

One Level 4-, one Level 3- and three Level 2-rated programs were evaluated. All five studies measured recidivism, level of risk of recidivism, and time at risk of recidivism. The Level 4 study by Robinson (1996) randomly assigned 2,125 offenders to either a cognitive-skills training program or a control group and conducted at least a twelve-month follow-up after release. The study indicated that the completion of cognitive-behavioral therapy reduced offenders' return to custody rate by 11 percent and is most effective for offenders with a moderate level of recidivism risk.

The Level 3 study by Barbaree, Seto, and Maric (1996) assessed violent sex offenders' risk of recidivism and suggested treatment alternatives. The results did not indicate a significant difference between recidivism rates of offenders who completed treatment (18 percent) and those who refused treatment (20 percent), yet did indicate that those who refused treatment were at risk of recidivism for a significantly less period of time than those who completed treatment. Therefore, those who refused had a higher failure rate (38.9 percent) than those who completed treatment (22.2 percent).

There were three Level 2 studies (Gordon and Nicholaichuk, 1996; Motuik, Smiley and Blanchette, 1996; and Studer et al., 1996) that simply measured recidivism rates of violent and sex offenders. The weakness of the internal validity of these studies makes it difficult to determine whether sex offender treatment is effective. Additional Level 3 and Level 4 evaluations must be performed before conclusions can be drawn.

Halfway House Programs

Four halfway house programs (one Level 4 study, one Level 3 study and two Level 2 studies) were reviewed. The Level 4 study evaluated Ohio halfway houses, comparing 236 house clients to a 404-parolee comparison group, with statistical controls for selection bias (Seiter, 1975). The study examined outcome both in terms of the frequency and severity of criminal offenses by both groups. The halfway house group committed significantly fewer and less severe offenses during a one-year outcome analysis than the comparison group.

The Level 3 study was an evaluation of a California halfway house for women. Results indicated that the average number of crimes in the treatment group was half that of the control group (Dowell, Klein and Krichmar, 1985), and the severity of the crimes committed by the treatment group was less than two-thirds of the control group. The Level 2 studies examine success rates of participants living in Ohio and Colorado halfway houses (Donnelly and Forschner, 1984; and Department of Criminal Justice, 2001), and findings were not inconsistent with those of the other two halfway house evaluations. While these studies are dated, they still can be included in this analysis, and it was concluded that halfway house programs do work in easing the transition from prison to the community.

Prison Prerelease Programs

There were two prerelease program evaluations reviewed. A Level 3 evaluation of the PreStart program in Illinois was conducted. This is a statewide program to prepare ex-offenders for life in the community through prerelease education and post-release assistance. Rearrest rates within one year of release were 40 percent for participants and 48 percent for the comparison group, and return-to-prison rates were 12 percent for the treatment group and 32 percent for the comparison group (Castellano et al., 1994). Because of a lack of random selection, the possibility of selection bias and other chance factors posing threats to the internal validity of the results, this program only shows promise as a model for other states to use for prerelease programs.

A Level 4 study by LeClair and Guarino-Ghezzi (1991) drew five separate study samples, one which consisted of all males released from Massachusetts Department of Correction facilities in 1974 (n=840) to test the impact of prerelease participation on recidivism rates. One sub-sample consisted of 212 inmates who completed the prerelease program in 1974 and were tracked for twelve months from the date of each individual's release. The researchers used a predictive attribute analysis to calculate base expectancy prediction tables to test for any nonrandom selection effects. The expected recidivism rate for the 212 inmates who participated in prerelease programs was 21.1 percent, yet, the post-discharge behavior only showed that 11.8 percent of the offenders recidivated. While this difference is not significant, it does indicate an intervention effect. When compared with recidivism rates of offenders who did not participate in prerelease programs (29 percent), there is support that the prerelease intervention is effective. In combination, prerelease programs are promising in effectively reducing the recidivism rates of ex-offenders.

Policy Implications of These Findings

From this review of evaluations of inmate reentry programs, there are several positive findings. Vocational training and/or work release programs are effective in reducing recidivism and improving job-readiness skills for ex-offenders. Drug rehabilitation programs are effective in reducing arrests, drug-related offenses, continued drug use, and parole violations. Halfway house programs reduce the frequency and severity of future crimes. In addition, there are promising results for sex and violent offender programs, education programs increase educational achievement scores but do not decrease recidivism, and prerelease programs improve the chance of successful inmate reentry. These findings are extremely useful for correctional policymakers. It can be concluded that to improve reentry success and reduce recidivism, those categories of reentry programs that "work" should be funded and expanded, and those with "promising" findings should be further evaluated.

Unfortunately, it does not appear that there is investment of significant resources in the programs that can now be identified as effective. According to Camp and Camp (2002), on January 1, 2001, state and federal prisons reported that there were only 120,687 inmates (12.9 percent) in drug treatment programs—a decline of more than 50,000 inmates since 2000. On that same date, only 77,380 inmates (6.3

percent) were assigned to prison industries, which have been found to be extremely successful in improving work skills and reducing recidivism. Only 12,149 (3.4 percent) inmates were enrolled in sex offender programs on January 1, 2001. There were only 59,180 inmates placed in halfway houses during 2000—only 9.9 percent of the 596,191 inmates released from state and federal prisons that year. During 2000, there were only 40,164 inmates placed in work or study release. However, it should be noted that these numbers are self-reported by state and federal correctional agencies and have not been validated (Camp and Camp, 2002).

As the prison population climbed during the past two decades, funds to expand opportunities for inmates to participate in programs have not increased proportionately. With information that programs can be effective and reduce recidivism, it is recommended there be increased funding and inmate participation. If expansion of such programs reduces recidivism, crime and taxpayer expenses will decrease. It is further recommended that correctional administrators take note of these programs and use these and other research findings to lobby for additional funds to implement or expand vocational training and prison work programs, work release programs, drug rehabilitation programs, halfway house programs, and prerelease programs that have proved successful, and expand the use of sex and violent offender programs that show promise. Significant program expansion would still represent only a small fraction of the commitment of funds to simply house inmates and operate prisons.

The United States is committing billions of dollars to locking up offenders for increasingly longer periods of time. Yet, proportionally fewer dollars per inmate are directed into rehabilitative programs for inmates and programs that aid in their successful reentry. It must be considered whether such decisions are creating a revolving door of offenders who will be committed to prison time and again as they fail in the community. Identified programs can improve the success of inmate reentry and potentially reduce this revolving door syndrome. Expansion of effective inmate reentry programs deserves a thoughtful policy debate and consideration.

REFERENCES

Adams, K., K. J. Bennett, T.J. Flanagen, J.W. Marquart, S. J. Cuvelier, E. Fritsch, J. Gerber, D.R. Longmire and V. S. Burton. 1994. Large Scale Multidimensional Test of the Effect of Prison Education Programs on Offenders' Behavior. *The Prison Journal*. 74(4): 433-449.

Anderson, E. 1990. *Streetwise: Race, Class and Change in an Urban Community*. Chicago: University of Chicago Press.

Barbaree, H.E., M.T. Seto and A. Maric. 1996. Effective Ex Offender Treatment: The Warkworth Sexual Behavior Clinic. *Forum on Corrections Research*. 8(3): 13-15.

Beck, A. and C. Mumola. 1999. *Prisoners in 1998*. Washington, D.C.: Department of Justice, Bureau of Justice Statistics.

Bureau of Justice Statistics. 1977. *National Prisoner Statistics*. Washington, D.C.: U.S. Department of Justice.

Bureau of Justice Statistics. 1997. *National Prisoner Statistics*. Washington, D.C.: U. S. Department of Justice.

Bureau of Justice Statistics. 2002. Justice Expenditure and Employment Extracts. Available at www.ojp.usdoj.gov/bjs/glance/exptyp.htm.

Bureau of Justice Statistics Correctional Surveys. 1980-2001. The National Probation Survey, National Prisoner Statistics, Survey of Jails and the National Parole Survey. Washington, D.C.: U.S. Department of Justice.

Butzin, C. A., F. R. Scarpetti, A. L. Nielsen, S. S. Martin, and J. A. Inciardi. 1999. Measuring the Impact of Drug Treatment: Beyond Relapse and Recidivism. *Corrections Management Quarterly*. 3(4): 1-7.

Camp, C. G. and G. M. Camp. 1999. *The Corrections Yearbook*, 1998. Middletown, Connecticut: Criminal Justice Institute.

Camp, C. G. and G. M. Camp. 2001. *The 2000 Corrections Yearbook: Adult Corrections*. Middletown, Connecticut: Criminal Justice Institute.

Camp, C. G. and G. M. Camp. 2002. *The 2001 Corrections Yearbook: Adult Corrections*. Middletown, Connecticut: Criminal Justice Institute.

Castellano, T. C., E. L. Cowles, J. M. McDermott, E. B. Cowles, N. Espie, C. Ringel, L. Sharp, I. Soderstrom, and R. Tongsookdee. 1994. *The Implementation of Illinois' PreStart Program: A Final Report*. Carbondale, Illinois: Southern Illinois University Center for the Study of Crime, Delinquency and Corrections.

Department of Criminal Justice, Office of Research and Statistics. 2001. 2000 community corrections study. Manuscript in progress.

Donnelly, P. G. and B. Forschner. 1984. Client Success or Failure in a Halfway House. *Federal Probation*. 48(3): 38-44.

Dowell, D. A., C. Klein and C. Krichmar. 1985. Evaluation of a Halfway House for Women. *Journal of Criminal Justice*. 13(3): 217-226.

Feeley, M. M. and J. Simon. 1992. The New Penology: Notes on the Emerging Strategy of Corrections and Its Implications. *Criminology*. 30(4): 449-479.

Fields, G. 1985. The Cornerstone Program: A Client Outcome Study. *Federal Probation*. 49(3): 51-56.

Finn, P. 1999. Job Placement for Offenders: A Promising Approach to Reducing Recidivism and Correctional Costs. *National Institute of Justice Journal*. July: 1-35.

Gordon, A. and T. Nicholaichuk. 1996. Applying the Risk Principle to Sex Offender Treatment. *Forum on Corrections Research*. 8(2): 36-38.

Harrison, P. M. and J. C. Karberg. 2003. Prison and Jail Inmates at Mid-year 2002. *Bureau of Justice Statistics Bulletin*, April 2003.

Hartmann, D. J., J. L. Wolk, J. S. Johnson and C. J. Coyler. 1997. Recidivism and Substance Abuse Outcomes in a Prison-Based Therapeutic Community. *Federal Probation*. 61(4): 19-25.

Hiller, M. L., K. Knight and D. D. Simpson. 1999. Prison-Based Substance Abuse Treatment, Residential Aftercare and Recidivism. *Addiction*. 94(6): 833-842.

Inciardi, J. A., S. S. Martin, C. A. Butzin, R. M. Hooper and L. D. Harrison. 1997. An Effective Model of Prison-Based Treatment for Drug-Involved Offenders. *Journal of Drug Issues*. 27(2): 261-278.

Knight, K. and M. Hiller. 1997. Community-Based Substance Abuse Treatment: A 1-Year Outcome Evaluation of the Dallas County Judicial Treatment Center. *Federal Probation*. 61(2): 61-68.

Knight, K., D. D. Simpson, L. R. Chatham and L. M. Camacho. 1997. An Assessment of Prison-Based Drug Treatment: Texas' In-Prison Therapeutic Community Program. *Journal of Offender Rehabilitation*. 24(3/4): 75-100.

Knight, K., D. D. Simpson and M. L. Hiller. 1999. Three-Year Reincarceration Outcomes for In-Prison Therapeutic Community Treatment in Texas. *The Prison Journal*. 79(3): 337-351.

LeClair, D. P. and S. Guarino-Ghezzi. 1991. Does Incapacitation Guarantee Public Safety? Lessons from Massachusetts Furlough and Prerelease Programs. *Justice Quarterly*. 8(1): 9-36.

Lipton, D., R. Martinson and J. Wilks. 1975. *The Effectiveness of Correctional Treatment*. New York: Praeger.

Lynch, J. P. and W. J. Sabol. 2000. Prisoner Reentry and the Consequences of Sentencing Reform. Available at www.urban.org/news/tuesdays/12-00/lunch.html.

Martin, S. S., C. A. Butzin and J. A. Inciardi. 1995. The Assessment of Multi-Stage Therapeutic Community for Drug-Involved Offenders. *Journal of Psychoactive Drugs*. 27(1): 109-116.

Martin, S. S., C. A. Butzin, C. A. Saum and J. A. Inciardi. 1999. Three-Year Outcomes of Therapeutic Community Treatment for Drug-Involved Offenders in Delaware: From Prison to Work Release to Aftercare. *The Prison Journal*. 79(3): 294-320.

Motuik, L., C. Smiley and K. Blanchette. 1996. Intensive Programming for Violent Offenders: A Comparative Investigation. *Forum on Corrections Research*. 8(3): 10-12.

Nelson, M., P. Deess and C. Allen. 1999. *The First Month Out: Post-Incarceration Experiences in New York City*. Unpublished monograph, New York: The Vera Institute of Justice.

Pelisser, B., W. Rhodes, W. Saylor, G. Gaes, S. Camp, S. D. Vonyun and S. Wallace. 2001. Triad Drug Treatment Evaluation Project. *Federal Probation*. 65(3): 3-7.

Petersilia, J. R. 2000. The Collateral Consequences of Prisoner Reentry in California: Effects on Children, Public Health and Community. Unpublished monograph.

Robinson, D. 1996. Factors Influencing the Effectiveness of Cognitive Skills Training. *Forum on Corrections Research*. 8(3): 6-9.

Rose, D. R., T. Clear and K. Scully. 1999. Coercive Mobility and Crime: Incarceration and Social Disorganization. Paper presented at the American Society of Criminology meeting, November in Toronto.

Saylor, W. G. and G. G. Gaes. 1992. The Post-Release Employment Project: Prison Work Has Measurable Effects on Post-Release Success. *Federal Prison Journal*. 2(4): 33-36.

Saylor, W. G. and G. G. Gaes. 1997. Training Inmates through Industrial Work Participation and Vocational Apprenticeship Instruction. *Corrections Management Quarterly*. 1(2): 32-43.

Seiter, R. P. 1975. Evaluation Research as a Feedback Mechanism for Criminal Justice Policy Making: A Critical Analysis. Unpublished dissertation. Columbus, Ohio: Ohio State University.

Seiter, R. P. and K. R. Kadela. 2003. Prisoner Reentry: What Works, What Doesn't and What's Promising. *Crime and Delinquency.* 49(3): 360-388.

Sherman, L. W., D. C. Gottfredson, D. L. MacKenzie, J. Eck, P. Reuter and S. D. Bushway. 1998. Preventing Crime: What Works, What Doesn't, What's Promising. *Research in Brief.* Washington, D.C.: U.S. Department of Justice, National Institute of Justice.

Studer, L. H., J. R. Reddon, V. Roper and L. Estrada. 1996. Phoenix: An In-Hospital Treatment Program for Sex Offenders. *Journal of Offender Rehabilitation.* 23(1/2): 91-97.

Turner, S. and J. Petersilia. 1996. Work Release in Washington: Effects on Recidivism and Corrections Costs. *Prison Journal.* 76(2): 138-164.

Vito, G. F. and R. Tewksbury. 1999. Improving the Educational Skills of Inmates: The Results of an Impact Evaluation. *Corrections Compendium.* 24(10): 2-4, 16-17.

Wexler, H. K., G. P. Falkin and D. S. Lipton. 1990. Outcome Evaluation of a Prison Therapeutic Community for Substance Abuser Treatment. *Criminal Justice and Behavior.* 17(1): 71-92.

Richard P. Seiter, Ph.D., is director of the criminal justice program in the Department of Sociology and Criminal Justice at Saint Louis University in Missouri.

Informing Policy and Practice: Prisoner Reentry Research at the Urban Institute

Elizabeth C. McBride,
Christy Visher, Ph.D., and
Nancy G. La Vigne, Ph.D.

First printed in *Corrections Today*, a publication of the American Correctional Association, April 2005

In 2000, the Justice Policy Center at the Urban Institute launched its ongoing investment in prisoner reentry research to address the dearth of studies on this important topic, with the overarching goal of influencing important policy and programming decisions. During the past four years, the Urban Institute's reentry research portfolio has informed a broad set of policy and practice discussions about the challenges facing former prisoners. These research activities were particularly timely given Congress' allocation of $100 million to reentry strategies as part of the Serious and Violent Offender Reentry Initiative. The following describes the Urban Institute's key research projects and publications on prisoner reentry, and highlights findings from Returning Home,[1] a project that has served as the framework for the Urban Institute's ongoing research on the dimensions of prisoner reentry.

Launching a Policy Conversation

In 2000, the Urban Institute introduced the Reentry Roundtable, which has become an ongoing forum that brings together accomplished academics, experienced practitioners, community leaders, policymakers, advocates, and former prisoners twice a year to advance research and practice. Since its inception, the Urban Institute has convened eight meetings of the roundtable. The goal of the roundtable is to sharpen the nation's thinking on prisoner reintegration and criminal justice practice, and to foster policy innovations that will improve outcomes for individuals, families, and communities. The conversations and papers stemming from these roundtables have given shape to policy questions and recommendations, and have served as the foundation for subsequent publications.

Research and Reporting

In addition to fostering dialog about prisoner reentry, the Urban Institute has conducted rigorous research that explores the policy domains of prisoner reentry, its impact at the national, state, and local levels, and programs designed to improve the outcome of prisoners returning to society. The Urban Institute's research portfolio began with *From Prison to Home: Understanding the Dimensions and Consequences of Prisoner Reentry*,[2] a monograph on prisoner reentry that has served as the backbone of research on this topic. *From Prison to Home* provides a broad overview of the key challenges of prisoner reintegration and describes the phenomenon from various policy perspectives. The report's aim is to inform the policy discussions that are under way—from the U.S. Congress, to the community groups that are building networks of support and supervision for those coming out, to former prisoners.

The report *Beyond the Prison Gates: The State of Parole in America*[3] was released shortly thereafter, providing a portrait of the parole process and calling attention to the significant changes in sentencing policies and supervision that have emerged over time. Using national and state-level data, the authors found that the role of parole boards in making release decisions has declined significantly, with parole boards releasing only one in four prisoners. On the other hand, the authors found that the level of parole supervision has increased: four out of five released prisoners are now placed on parole supervision. It was also noted that the number of parole revocations has risen dramatically in the past two decades.

In recent years, the Urban Institute has engaged in more in-depth explorations of unique issues of prisoner reentry. For example, in 2003, the Urban Institute published *Prisoners Once Removed*[4] as well as a policy brief titled *Families Left Behind: The Hidden Consequences of Incarceration and Reentry*.[5] These works investigate the ways in which parental imprisonment disrupts parent-child relationships, alters the networks of familial support, and places new burdens on governmental services such as schools, foster care, adoption agencies, and youth-serving organizations. The *Families Left Behind* policy brief calls attention to the scarcity of studies that have explored the impact of parental incarceration on young children or identified the needs that arise from such circumstances. It also highlights how communities, social service agencies, health care providers, and the criminal justice system can work collaboratively to better meet the needs of the families left behind. In *Prisoners Once Removed*, the authors explore the issue of prisoner reentry—from the psychological impact of imprisonment on prisoners and the difficulty of reentering free society, to the challenges faced by communities that must integrate the prisoners once they return. The authors look at family functioning during a period of imprisonment and how families are affected by the return of an incarcerated parent. Finally, they evaluate the current system and suggest ways to improve interaction between correctional and health and human services to better serve the growing population of children, families, and communities.

Another publication, *From Prison to Work: The Employment Dimensions of Prisoner Reentry*,[6] highlights relevant research and identifies key policy issues surrounding the relationship between employment and reentry. The report describes the current labor market, identifying the gaps that former prisoners could potentially fill when they enter the workforce; describes the prisoner population, including prisoners' skills sets, education levels, work histories and health-related needs; and also examines the past and current involvement of prisoners in work opportunities inside state and federal prisons. Further, it outlines the potential benefits of certain types of prisoner labor and prison programming, as well as the opportunities for and the legal barriers to work on the outside. The report concludes by identifying key considerations needed to meet the goals of enhancing work opportunities available to prisoners and expanding work opportunities after release.

Identifying What Works

Program evaluation is another important element of the Urban Institute's research portfolio on prisoner reentry. During the past four years, the Urban Institute has participated in several rigorous evaluations of reentry programs nationwide. With funding from the National Institute of Justice and in partnership with the Research Triangle Institute International, the Urban Institute is conducting a multiyear comprehensive evaluation of the Serious and Violent Offender Reentry Initiative, a collaborative federal effort to improve reentry outcomes among former prisoners along criminal justice, employment, education, health, and housing dimensions. Sixty-eight state/local sites have received a total of more than $100 million to develop or expand programs that offer integrated supervision and services to offenders. The objective is to promote productive social roles and reduce the likelihood of a return to crime and imprisonment for released offenders. The evaluation consists of two phases: a one-year design and assessment period (Phase 1) and a four-year impact evaluation (Phase 2). The evaluation includes an implementation assessment, impact evaluation and cost-benefit analysis. The project's first report, A *National Portrait of* SVORI, describes the initiative, each grantee's program, and the planned impact evaluation. Additional noteworthy evaluations include the Urban Institute's process evaluation of *Pennsylvania's Community Orientation Reintegration Program*, a reentry pilot program sponsored by the Pennsylvania Department of Corrections. The program's goals are to establish a standard, coordinated release program based on known risk factors and needs, promote effective community linkages, enhance employability, and promote healthy family and interpersonal relationships.

In addition, the Urban Institute recently concluded a study on the effectiveness of supervision. Nationally, very little is known about the behavior and recidivism rates of released prisoners who are under criminal justice supervision compared with those who are not. The goal of this project was to determine whether supervision following release matters, for whom, and under what circumstances. The Urban Institute examined recidivism outcomes for released prisoners, comparing those who are on community supervision with those released unconditionally for a period of three years. The final report, which was released last month, found that overall, parole supervision has little effect on rearrest rates of released prisoners. Mandatory parolees, who account for the largest share of released prisoners, fare no better on supervision than similar prisoners released without supervision. In fact, in some cases they fare worse. The report also stated that while discretionary parolees are somewhat less likely to be rearrested, this difference narrows (to four percentage points) after taking into account personal characteristics and criminal histories. Of the largest groups of released prisoners (male, and drug, property, and violent offenders), only property offenders released to discretionary parole benefit from supervision.

The Cornerstone of the Urban Institute's Reentry Research

The Urban Institute's principal reentry research initiative is *Returning Home: Understanding the Challenges of Prisoner Reentry*, a multistate, three-year study that documents the pathways of prisoner reintegration, examines what factors contribute to a successful or unsuccessful reentry experience, and identifies how those factors can inform policy. The *Returning Home* study is being implemented across four states, including a pilot study in Maryland (completed May 2003) and full research studies in Illinois, Ohio, and Texas. The goal in each state is to collect information on respondents' life circumstances immediately prior to and following their release from prison, as well as up to one year into their reintegration in the community. *Returning Home* documents the challenges of reentry along five dimensions: individual, family, peer, community, and state. Data on these dimensions are collected through interviews with prisoners prior to release and periodically during the year after release, interviews with family members after the prisoners' release, focus groups with residents in communities to which prisoners return, extant data on local indicators of community well-being, interviews with community stakeholders, and a review of state laws and policies. Each study involves surveys and interviews that explore various reentry expectations, needs and experiences such as those related to prerelease preparation, post-release housing and employment, and family reunification.

The intent of the *Returning Home* study is to present the released prisoners' point of view—a perspective not often represented in criminal justice research. Recent findings from *Returning Home* in Illinois, published in *Chicago Prisoners' Experiences Returning Home*,[7] rely on self-reported data from a sample of released male prisoners sentenced to time in state prison and returning to Chicago. Key findings include the following:

- Families are an important source of both emotional and tangible support for released prisoners. When prisoners were interviewed four to eight months after release, respondents cited family as the most important factor in helping them stay out of prison. Predictive analyses confirmed that respondents with family support before prison were less likely to be reincarcerated after release, and those with negative family relationships were more likely to be reconvicted or reincarcerated.

- A significant share of prisoners returned to a small cluster of Chicago neighborhoods characterized by high levels of social and economic disadvantage. Respondents and community residents described these neighborhoods as providing few sources of social support and limited employment opportunities. Respondents who returned to disadvantaged neighborhoods were less likely to find work after release and were more likely to be rearrested.

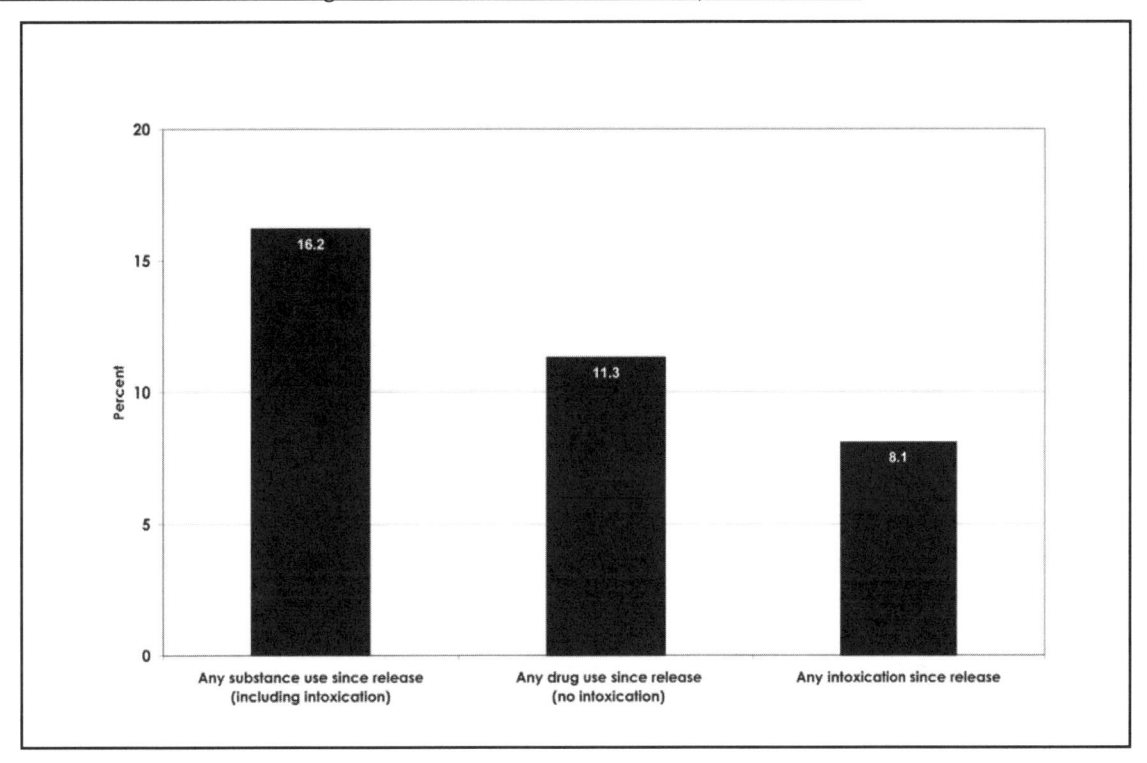

Figure 1. Substance Use at Four to Eight Months After Release (n = 197, 203 and 198)

[Bar chart showing: Any substance use since release (including intoxication): 16.2%; Any drug use since release (no intoxication): 11.3%; Any intoxication since release: 8.1%]

- Although most released prisoners returned to disadvantaged Chicago neighborhoods, these were not necessarily the same communities in which they had lived before prison. In fact, 45 percent of those interviewed after release resided in different neighborhoods, primarily because they wanted to avoid trouble in old neighborhoods or because their families had moved.

- Prior to release, most respondents expressed a strong desire to change and held positive attitudes, especially feelings of high self-esteem and control over life. These positive attitudes further improved after release. Respondents who exhibited negative attitudes, such as negative views about the legal system and dissatisfaction with police, tended to be younger and were less likely to have worked in the six months prior to incarceration.

- Respondents had limited success in finding employment after release. Forty-four percent had worked for at least one week at the time of their post-release interview. Post-release employment, as measured by the number of weeks worked, was significantly higher for respondents who had worked before prison, had a work release job during prison, had an intimate partner (for example, spouse, girlfriend), and/or had not used drugs or been intoxicated after release.

- Though 66 percent of respondents reported some drug use, and 48 percent reported alcohol intoxication prior to prison, only 11 percent and 8 percent, respectively, reported drug use or intoxication after release (*see* Figure 1). Respondents who avoided substance use after release, had higher levels of self-esteem and lower levels of depression, were more likely to have worked

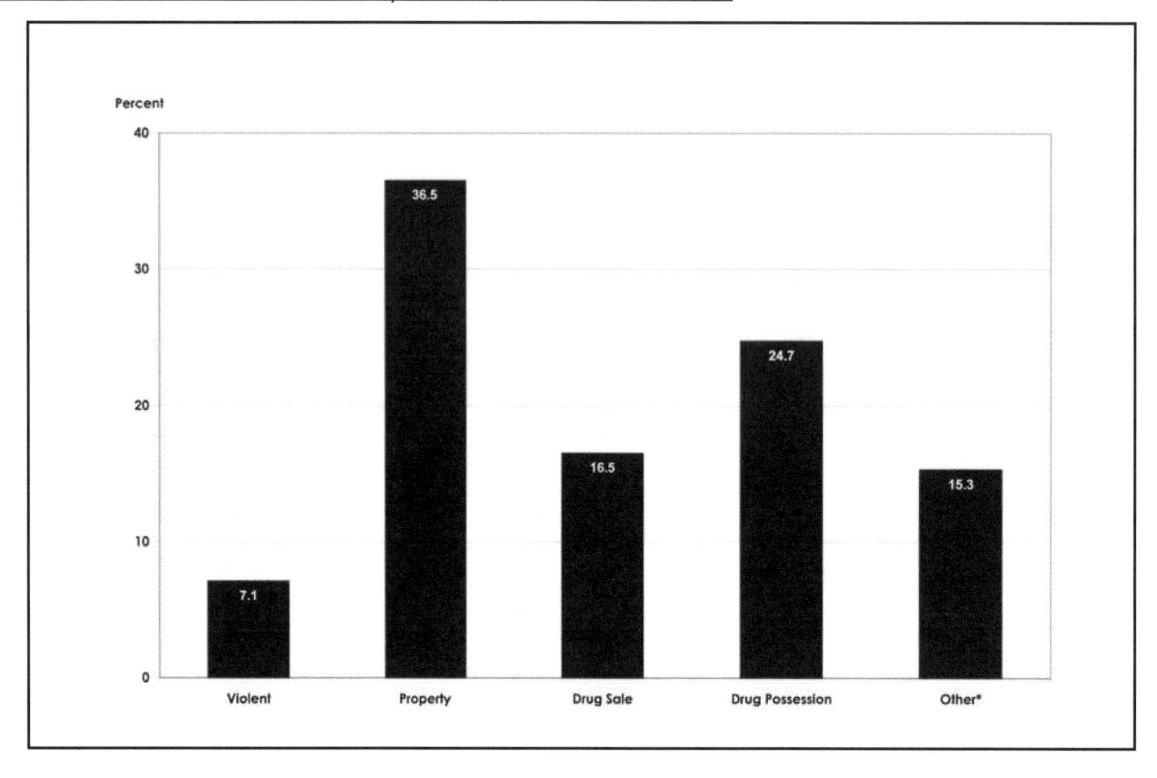

Figure 2. First Post-Release Reconviction by Most Serious Offense (n=85)

[Bar chart showing percentages: Violent 7.1, Property 36.5, Drug Sale 16.5, Drug Possession 24.7, Other* 15.3]

for at least one week after release and tended to live in neighborhoods where drug selling was not a serious problem.

- Three out of ten respondents reported suffering from chronic physical health conditions, and small but important shares showed symptoms of depression (10 percent) and/or post-traumatic stress disorder (4 percent). A total of 81 percent did not have health care coverage after release.

- Finally, to assess respondents' actual success at avoiding criminal involvement after release, information on reconvictions and returns to prison was collected from the Illinois Criminal Justice Informational Authority and the Illinois Department of Corrections. Of the one-fifth (22 percent) who were reconvicted of a new crime within eleven months of release, most were reconvicted for property crimes (37 percent), drug possession (25 percent), and drug sales (17 percent), while a small percentage were for violent crimes (7 percent)(*see* Figure 2).

Chicago Prisoners' Experience Returning Home, like all the publications from the *Returning Home* study, is intended to provide a foundation for policy conversations at the local level on ways to improve reintegration among prisoners returning to these communities. Listening to and documenting the experiences of these prisoners, along with the members of the communities to which they return, will ideally guide policy innovations that are empirically grounded, pragmatic, and reflective of the realities of reentry.

The Urban Institute continues to witness a remarkable level of interest in the issues of prisoner reentry across many sectors of society—from neighborhood organizations to the federal government. At the same time, society must grapple with the paucity of knowledge about the pathways of successful reintegration, the social and fiscal costs of current policies, and the impact of removal, sentencing, and reentry on individuals, families, and communities. To fill this gap in knowledge, and to advance policies and innovations that are rooted in solid research, the Urban Institute's Justice Policy Center plans to continue and expand its portfolio of reentry policy research. For more information on the Urban Institute's reentry research, visit the Urban Institute Web site at http://jpc.urban.org/reentry. To receive monthly e-mail updates of JPC research, e-mail jpc@ui.urban.org.

ENDNOTES

[1] Visher, C., N. La Vigne, and J. Travis. 2004. *Returning Home: Understanding the Challenges of Prisoner Reentry: Maryland Pilot Study: Findings From Baltimore*. Washington, D.C.: The Urban Institute Press.

[2] Travis, J., A. Solomon and M. Waul. 2001. *From Prison To Home: Understanding the Challenges and Dimensions of Prisoner Reentry*. Washington, D.C.: The Urban Institute Press.

[3] Travis, J. and S. Lawrence. 2002. *Beyond the Prison Gates: The State of Parole in America*. Washington, D.C.: Urban Institute Press.

[4] Travis, J. and M. Waul. 2003. *Prisoners Once Removed: The Impact of Incarceration and Reentry on Children, Families and Communities*. Washington, D.C.: Urban Institute Press.

[5] Travis, J., E. Cincotta, and A. Solomon. 2003. *Families Left Behind: The Hidden Cost of Incarceration and Reentry*. Washington, D.C.: The Urban Institute Press.

[6] Solomon, A., K. Johnson, J. Travis and E. Cincotta McBride. 2004. *From Prison To Work: The Employment Dimensions of Prisoner Reentry*. Washington, D.C.: The Urban Institute Press.

[7] La Vigne, N., C. Visher, and J. Castro. 2004. *Chicago Prisoners' Experiences Returning Home*. Washington, D.C.: The Urban Institute Press.

Elizabeth C. McBride is a research associate, Christy Visher, Ph.D., is principal research associate, and Nancy G. La Vigne, Ph.D., is senior research associate at the Urban Institute in Washington, D.C. For more information on the Urban Institute's reentry research activities, contact Elizabeth C. McBride at (202) 261-5709 or emcbride@ui.urban.org.

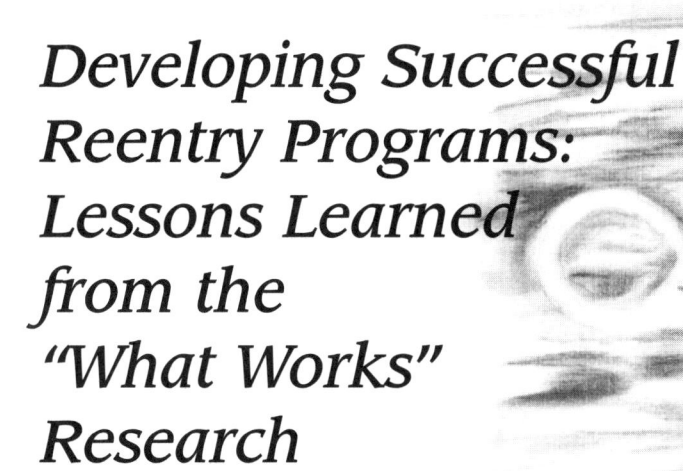

Developing Successful Reentry Programs: Lessons Learned from the "What Works" Research

Christopher T. Lowenkamp, Ph.D.
and Edward Latessa, Ph.D.

First printed in *Corrections Today*, a publication of the American Correctional Association, April 2005

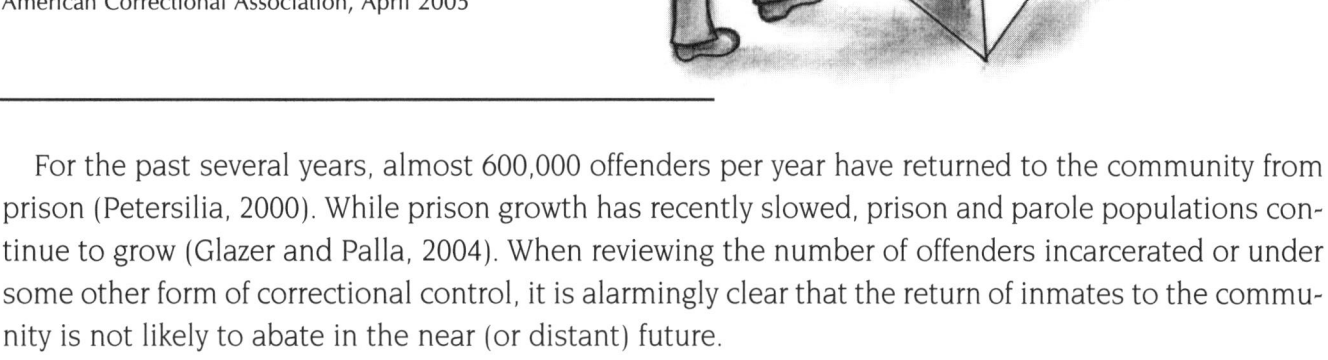

For the past several years, almost 600,000 offenders per year have returned to the community from prison (Petersilia, 2000). While prison growth has recently slowed, prison and parole populations continue to grow (Glazer and Palla, 2004). When reviewing the number of offenders incarcerated or under some other form of correctional control, it is alarmingly clear that the return of inmates to the community is not likely to abate in the near (or distant) future.

While offenders, in some instances, are offered some programming while incarcerated, a good percentage of offenders are returned to the community ill-equipped for reintegration (Petersilia, 2000). For example, of nonviolent offenders returning to the community from prison, 40 percent have less than a high school education, nearly 66 percent indicated they had been using drugs during the month prior to their offense, 25 percent were dependent on alcohol prior to entering prison (Durose and Mumola, 2004), and unemployment is fairly high among this population (Petersilia, 2000). The social costs of inmates returning to the nation's communities are evident, and these social costs are above and beyond those associated with continued criminal behavior.[1]

Given these numbers and the community concerns associated with offender reentry, it is no wonder why federal, state, and local governments have recently been so attentive to this process. One way to facilitate successful offender reintegration is through reentry programming.

Reentry programs are promising for a number of reasons. First, they provide an opportunity to shape offender behavior while offenders are transitioning back to their natural environments, thereby reducing recidivism rates. They also offer the ability to proactively deal with violations of post-release supervision and reduce prison populations—as violators are making up greater percentages of the prison population now than in the past (Cohen, 1995; Travis, 2000). Additionally, such programs can facilitate a successful reentry that, in addition to reducing recidivism, can lead to better and more functional lives for former inmates, their families and communities.

All of this optimism and potential must, however, be tempered with corrections' penchant to do the wrong thing (Gendreau, Goggin, and Smith, 1999; Latessa, Cullen, and Gendreau, 2003). In spite of sound empirical evidence to the contrary, correctional agencies continue to spend good money on the latest and greatest programming and assessment techniques (and the not-so-latest or greatest correctional interventions) in hopes that these novel attempts at correctional interventions will solve all of corrections' problems (panaceaphilia revisited).

The purpose of this chapter is not to rehash failed and botched attempts at implementing correctional programming. Rather, it brings to bear the research on some residential programs that served offenders during reentry, and should shape, to some degree, the development of reentry programs. The question "How should we design a good reentry program?" has been answered already. The components of an effective correctional intervention, including offender reentry programs, have already been enumerated a number of times (Gendreau and Andrews, 1990; Gendreau, 1996; Gendreau and Goggin, 1996; Andrews and Bonta, 1998; Gendreau and Goggin, 2000; Gendreau, French, and Taylor, 2002). And while it is recognized that there may be special issues specific to reentry programs, the core of these programs should follow the basic tenets of effective correctional interventions.

The research discussed in this article, covering thirty-eight residential programs that served parolees and offenders on post-release control in Ohio, can serve as a blueprint in the development or redesign of reentry programs. While the empirical research is limited to programs in Ohio, the results reported here are consistent with research findings from studies conducted during different time periods, in different jurisdictions, in different countries, with male and female offenders, and with adult and juvenile offenders. The amount of evidence on what constitutes an effective correctional intervention is massive. This body of literature is so large and consistent that if operating or designing a reentry program, heed this warning: If the program does not embody a number of the characteristics discussed below, whether residential or not, the likelihood that the program will succeed in reducing recidivism is low. While reading through this chapter and the research findings, assess how well the program performs in these areas.

Prior to discussing the characteristics of effective correctional programs, and thereby the characteristics of effective reentry practices (and these characteristics should start to look familiar), the concept of evidence-based practice will be discussed. There has been a sweeping movement across every jurisdictional level and many disciplines to shift to an evidence-based practice model. Basically, evidence-based practice is a decision-making process that requires a practitioner to make decisions based on empirical evidence (Sackett et al., 1996). For correctional practitioners, that requires assessment and profiling followed by a review of the research to determine the most effective course of action. Evidence-based practice does not seek creativity in developing programs or a reliance upon clinical experience or professional opinion when a large body of empirical literature exists to provide direction. As a matter of fact, by definition, evidence-based practice requires a correctional practitioner to look at what has been done before, determine, based on available evidence, what is effective, and then follow that course of action.[2]

Core Principles of Effective Correctional Interventions

The past thirty years has proved to be very important regarding research on correctional interventions. A substantial number of reviews of the research are available (Gendreau and Ross, 1987; Andrews et al., 1990; Gendreau and Andrews, 1990; Lipsey, 1992; Lipsey and Wilson, 1998; Andrews and Dowden, 1999; Dowden and Andrews, 1999a, 1999b and 2000). And while this research is not being reviewed in detail here, what this research has concluded regarding correctional interventions will be highlighted.

First, correctional programs should focus their resources on higher-risk offenders. The evidence on this is consistent and strong (for a review of this literature, *see* Andrews, Bonta and Hoge, 1990; Lowenkamp and Latessa, 2004 and 2004a). Second, correctional programs must target specific criminogenic needs (for a listing of those needs and their relative impact on recidivism when targeted, *see* Andrews and Dowden, 1999). Next, correctional programs must provide behavioral, cognitive-behavioral, or social-learning- based interventions (Andrews et al., 1990). In addition, correctional agencies must tend to implementation issues, including staff training, evaluation, and support. Finally, correctional programs must have program integrity, which includes the aforementioned principles but also includes quality assurance, evaluation efforts, and overall attention to the intervention's fidelity to the principles of effective interventions. Fortunately, several instruments and processes exist for measuring program integrity, including: the Correctional Program Assessment Inventory (Gendreau and Andrews, 1994), the Correctional Practice Treatment Survey developed by the International Community Corrections Association (2004) and other methods (Lipsey, 1999). All of these processes measure, to some degree, a program's adherence to the aforementioned principles and focus on ensuring that a correctional program has both the content and capacity[3] to deliver a sound correctional intervention.

The study used in this article to illustrate the importance of these characteristics to reentry programs was conducted in 2002. As previously stated, the study involved thirty-eight halfway house programs that provided services to parolees and post-release control offenders. This study included roughly 7,000 offenders with half in the treatment group (those offenders who participated in a halfway house program) and half in the comparison group (those offenders who received regular community supervision). The numbers illustrated in the figures in this article represent the difference in the recidivism rate between the treatment and comparison groups.

Figure 1 shows the reduction in recidivism associated with placement and successful termination from a halfway house. As indicated, participation in one of these halfway house programs by low-risk parolees is associated with an increase in recidivism rates, while participation and successful termination for high-risk offenders has a very different outcome (negative numbers indicate changes in recidivism rates that

Figure 1. Reduction in Recidivism with Placement and Successful Termination from a Halfway House

Figure 2. Reduction in Recidivism Based on Number of Criminogenic Services

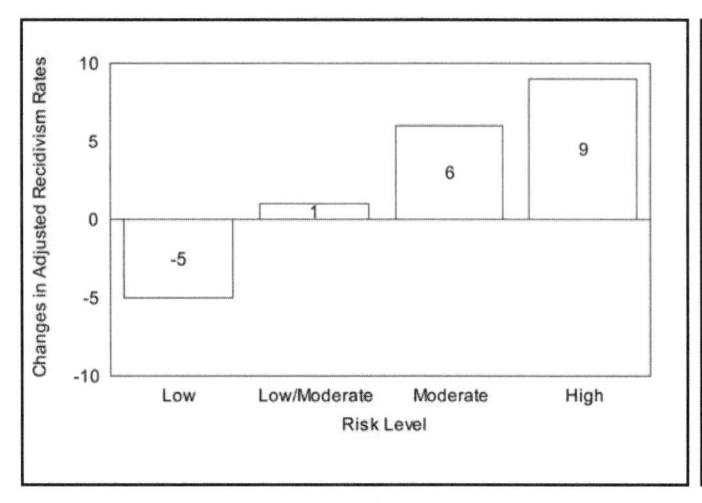

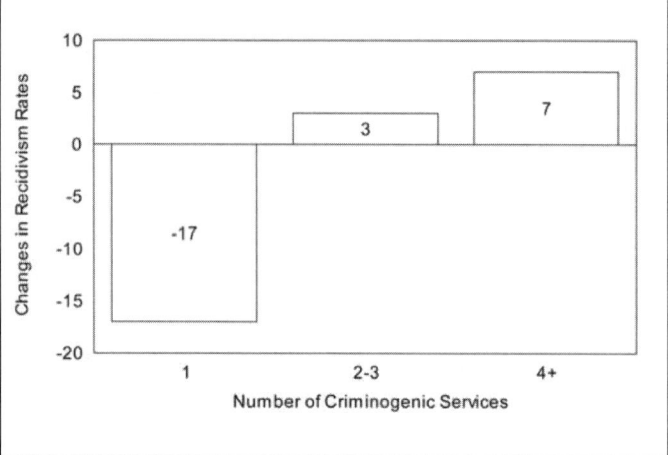

favor the comparison group whereas positive numbers favor the treatment group). This figure indicates that participation in and successful completion of a halfway house program by low-risk offenders is associated with a 5 percent increase in recidivism rates. Conversely, participation in and completion of the same halfway house programs was associated with a 9 percent decrease in recidivism for high-risk offenders. The one exception to this trend is with parole violators: All parole violators, regardless of risk level appeared to have benefited from placement in a residential program compared with similar parolees returned to prison on a parole violation and subsequently released without placement in a residential facility.[4]

Figure 2 illustrates findings regarding the need principle. The number of services each program provided that targeted criminogenic needs was counted. As can be seen in Figure 2, those programs that had one service targeting criminogenic needs were, on average, associated with an increase of 17 percent in recidivism rates whereas those programs that had four or more criminogenic services reduced recidivism, on average, by 7 percent.

The impacts of the key indicators of treatment types are displayed in Figures 3 and 4. First, each program was categorized based on whether it was a cognitive-behavioral or "other" type of program. Figure 3 illustrates the effectiveness of those programs categorized as cognitive behavioral and the relative and absolute ineffectiveness of those programs that were categorized as "other" types of programs (a 10 percent reduction in recidivism for cognitive-behavioral programs versus no change for "other" types of treatment programs). Figure 4 shows the impact of programs that reported regularly using role-playing and regularly having offenders rehearse newly learned skills. As can be seen from Figure 4, programs that do not regularly use these techniques are associated with small (3 percent) reductions in recidivism. Those that regularly use one of these techniques are fairly effective (on average, an 8 percent reduction), while those that regularly use both are the most effective with an average reduction in recidivism of 15 percent.

Figure 3. Effectiveness of Cognitive Behavioral Programs Compared with Other Services

Figure 4. Reduction in Recidivism Based on Group Treatment Activities

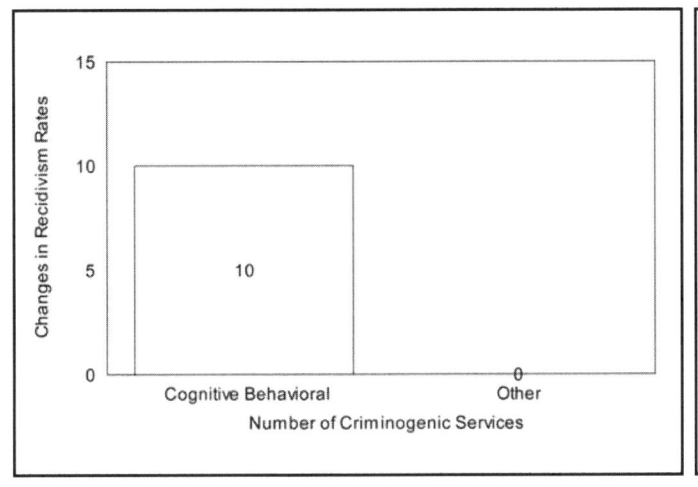

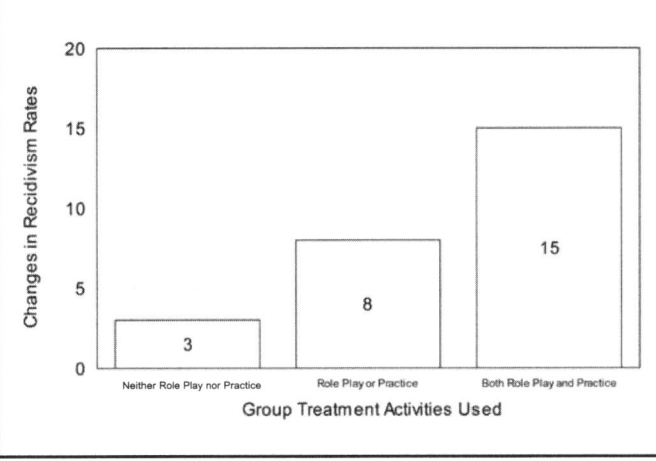

In addition to targeting high-risk offenders and treatment type and targets, implementation is also of significant and substantial importance. Several factors related to program implementation were examined, and it was found that many of these factors were related to program effectiveness. Some of these important factors include: the program director's educational and experiential credentials, the program director's involvement in the program, community support, criminal justice community support, staff training and qualifications, quality assurance, and evaluation. Implementation should not be ignored or thought of as a sterile, one-time process. Failure to monitor implementation of programming can lead an otherwise promising program to failure (*see*, for example, Gendreau and Goggin, 2000; Gendreau, Goggin, and Smith, 2001; Barnosky, 2004).

Finally, a strong relationship between program integrity and program effectiveness (correlation varies between 0.32 to 0.60, depending on the factors used to measure program integrity and the outcome measure used) was found. The highest scoring programs were associated with average reductions in recidivism of 10 percentage points or more (20 percent relative reduction). In contrast, the lowest scoring programs on the measures of program integrity were associated with average increases in recidivism of 19 percentage points.

Summary and Conclusions

The principles and characteristics that previously have been identified as important to correctional interventions in general seem to be applicable and important to programs that serve parolees upon reentry. More specifically, it was found that the residential programs were most effective with parole violators and higher-risk offenders. Further, the residential programs were associated with increases in recidivism for the lower-risk offenders (parole violators exempted). The study also found that services targeting criminogenic needs were related to effectiveness; the most effective programs were those that provided the greatest number of services targeting criminogenic needs. These data also indicated that programs categorized as cognitive behavioral were more effective, as were those programs that engaged in activities associated with theoretically sound programming (role-playing and practicing of newly learned skills). Finally, it was concluded that implementation and other issues captured by measures of program integrity were strongly related to program effectiveness (for a more detailed review, *see* Lowenkamp, 2004) with offenders during the reentry phase. Again, it is stressed that these findings are consistent with previous research on correctional interventions—some of which have been around for more than twenty years now.

There is, and has been, a substantial body of research that investigates the effectiveness of different correctional interventions. While this collection of research is not entirely complete (investigating every detail and nuance of correctional programming and interactions with offender characteristics), it is complete enough to guide the development of correctional interventions. It is time that corrections staff increase the professionalism of the field and begin making evidence-based decisions by relying on, with appropriate consideration, the relevant research rather than spending their efforts refuting the research and continuing to do things that simply do not work.

ENDNOTES

[1] While it is certainly not the case that all inmates re-offend upon reentry, the statistics on the recidivism of inmates released to the community is staggering. For instance, Langan and Levin (2002), after following released inmates for three years, found a 67.5 percent rearrest rate, a 25 percent reincarceration rate for a new crime, and a 26 percent reincarceration rate for a technical violation. These rates are not all that surprising given the increased demand on community supervision resources and the reduced budgets for those same agencies. The expectation to do more with less, where adaptations are not quickly made, can easily lead to higher recidivism rates.

[2] To think, such correctional embarrassments as yoga and tai chi for violent offenders, dressing male offenders in female attire and having them walk around downtown, sentencing an offender to physical fitness for trying to outrun the police, and having offenders write 2,500 times, "I will not do stupid things" all could have been avoided if the judges would have consulted the empirical research rather than be "creative" in their sentencing decisions. Instead, these creative sentences were showcased by USA *Today* in February 2004 and probably served to feed the lack of confidence the general public has for the criminal justice system (for poll results on confidence in U.S. institutions, *see* Saad, 2004).

[3] Content includes the assessment and treatment activities of a program, or what Palmer (1995) refers to as programmatic factors, while capacity is concerned with a program's ability and resources available (staff, implementation, quality assurance) to deliver a correctional intervention (Palmer refers to these as nonprogrammatic factors. For a more detailed discussion and enumeration of these content and capacity factors, *see* Lowenkamp, 2004).

[4] While there may be other explanations for this finding, it is believed that it is because dynamic risk factors were present for the parole violators who were not included in the risk measure.

REFERENCES

Andrews, D. A. and J. Bonta. 1998. *The Psychology of Criminal Conduct*. Cincinnati: Anderson Publishing Co.

Andrews, D. A., J. Bonta, and R. Hoge. 1990. Classification for Effective Rehabilitation: Rediscovering Psychology. *Criminal Justice and Behavior.* 17: 19-52.

Andrews, D. A. and C. Dowden. 1999. A Meta-Analytic Investigation into Effective Correctional Intervention for Female Offenders. *Forum on Corrections Research.* 11(3): 18-21.

Andrews, D. A., I. Zinger, R. D. Hoge, J. Bonta, P. Gendreau, and F. T. Cullen. 1990. Does Correctional Treatment Work? A Clinically Relevant and Psychologically Informed Meta-Analysis. *Criminology.* 28(3): 369-404.

Barnosky, R. 2004. *Outcome Evaluation of Washington State's Research-Based Programs for Juvenile Offenders.* Olympia, Washington: Washington State Institute for Public Policy.

Cohen, R. L. 1995. *Probation and Parole Violators in State Prison. 1991.* Washington, D.C.: U.S. Department of Justice.

Dowden, C. and D. A. Andrews. 1999a. What Works For Female Offenders: A Meta-Analytic Review. *Crime and Delinquency.* 45(4): 438-452.

———. 1999b. What Works In Young Offender Treatment: A Meta-Analysis. *Forum on Corrections Research.* 11(2): 21-24.

———. 2000. Effective Correctional Treatment and Violent Reoffending: A Meta-analysis. *Canadian Journal of Criminology.* 42(4): 449-467.

Durose, M. R. and C. J. Mumola. 2004. *Profile of Nonviolent Offenders Exiting State Prisons.* Washington, D.C.: U.S. Department of Justice Office of Justice Programs.

Gendreau, P. 1996. The Principles of Effective Interventions with Offenders. In A. T. Harland, ed. *Choosing Correctional Options that Work: Defining the Demand and Evaluating the Supply.* Thousand Oaks, California: Sage.

Gendreau, P. and D. A. Andrews. 1990. Tertiary Prevention: What the Meta-Analyses of the Offender Treatment Literature Tell Us About What Works. *Canadian Journal of Criminology.* 32(1): 173-184.

———.1994. *The Correctional Program Assessment Inventory.* Ottawa: Carleton University.

Gendreau, P., S. French, and A. Taylor. 2002. *What Works (What Doesn't Work)-revised 2002: The Principles of Effective Correctional Treatment.* Unpublished manuscript. University of New Brunswick at Saint John.

Gendreau, P. and C. Goggin. 1996. Principles of Effective Correctional Programming. *Forum on Corrections.* 8(3): 38-41.

———. 2000. Correctional Treatment: Accomplishments and Realities. In P. Van Voorhis, M. Braswell, and D. Lester, eds. *Correctional Counseling and Rehabilitation,* 4th ed., pp. 271-280. Cincinnati: Anderson Publishing.

Gendreau, P., C. Goggin and P. Smith. 1999. The Forgotten Issue in Effective Correctional Treatment: Program Implementation. *International Journal of Offender Therapy.* 43(2): 180-187.

———. 2001. Implementation Guidelines for Correctional Programs in the "Real World." In G. A. Bernfeld, D. P. Farrington, and A.W. Leschied, eds. *Offender Rehabilitation and Practice,* pp. 247-268. New York: John Wiley and Sons Ltd.

Gendreau, P. and R. R. Ross. 1987. Revivification of Rehabilitation: Evidence from the 1980s. *Justice Quarterly.* 4(3): 349-407.

Glazer, L. E. and S. Palla. 2004. *Probation and Parole in the United States, 2003*. Washington, D.C.: U.S. Department of Justice.

International Community Corrections Association. 2004. *The Correctional Practice Treatment Survey*. Lacrosse, Wisconsin: International Community Corrections Association.

Langan, P. A. and D. J. Levin. 2002. *Recidivism of Prisoners Released in 1994*. Washington, D.C.: U.S. Department of Justice.

Latessa, E. J., F. T. Cullen, and P. Gendreau. 2003. Beyond Correctional Quackery: Professionalism and the Possibility of Effective Treatment. *Federal Probation*. 66(2): 43-49.

Lipsey, M. W. 1992. Juvenile Delinquency Treatment: A Meta-Analytic Inquiry into the Variable of Effects. In T. D. Cook, H. Cooper, D. S. Cordray, H. Hartmann, L. V. Hedges, R. J. Light, T. A. Lewis, and F. Mosteller, eds. *Meta-Analysis For Explanation: A Casebook*, pp. 83-127. New York: Russell Sage.

Lipsey, M. W. 1999. Can Rehabilitative Programs Reduce the Recidivism of Juvenile Offenders? An Inquiry into the Effectiveness of Practical Programs. *The Virginia Journal of Social Policy and the Law*. 6(3): 611-641.

Lipsey, M. W. and D. B. Wilson. 1998. Effective Intervention for Serious Juvenile Offenders: A Synthesis of Research. In R. Loeber and D. P. Farrington, eds. *Serious and Violent Juvenile Offenders: Risk Factors and Successful Interventions*, pp. 313-345. Thousand Oaks, California: Sage.

Lowenkamp, C. T. 2004. *Correctional Program Integrity and Treatment Effectiveness: A Multi-Site, Program-Level Analysis*. Doctoral dissertation. University of Cincinnati.

Lowenkamp, C. T. and E. J. Latessa. 2004. *Understanding the Risk Principle: How and Why Correctional Interventions Can Harm Low-Risk Offenders. Topics in Community Corrections*, 2004, 3-8. Washington, D.C.: U.S. Department of Justice, National Institute of Corrections.

——. 2004a. Increasing the Effectiveness of Correctional Programming through the Risk Principle: Identifying Offenders for Residential Placement. *Criminology and Public Policy*. 4(1):501-528

Palmer, T. 1995. Programmatic and Nonprogrammatic Aspects of Successful Intervention: New Directions for Research. *Crime and Delinquency*. 41(1): 100-131.

Petersilia, J. 2000. *When Prisoners Return to the Community: Political, Economic and Social Consequences*. Washington, D.C.: U.S. Department of Justice, National Institute of Justice.

Saad, L. 2004. *Military Still American Top-Rated Institution*. Princeton, New Jersey: The Gallup Organization.

Sackett, D. L., W. M. C. Rosenberg, J. A. M. Gray, R. B. Haynes, and W. D. Richardson. 1996. Evidence Based Medicine: What It Is and What It Isn't. *British Medical Journal*. 312: 71-72.

Travis, J. 2000. *But They All Come Back: Rethinking Prisoner Reentry*. Washington, D.C.: U.S. Department of Justice, National Institute of Justice.

Christopher T. Lowenkamp, Ph.D., is assistant director of the Corrections Institute and The Center for Criminal Justice Research at the University of Cincinnati. Edward J. Latessa, Ph.D., is professor and head of the Division of Criminal Justice at the University of Cincinnati.

Evidence-Based Practices in Reentry: Challenges and Opportunities

Arthur J. Lurigio, Ph.D.

First printed in the 2005 *State of Corrections*, published by the American Correctional Association

The number of individuals who are released each year from prison back into the community has reached monumental proportions (Beck, 2000). A total of 600,000 offenders leave prison annually to resume their lives in neighborhoods that are often poor and crime-infested. On average, 1,600 former inmates are confronted daily with the challenge of reintegrating into their communities (Travis, 2005). The difficulties they face include: finding a home and job; reorienting to family life; continuing their education; and accessing treatment for their psychiatric, substance use, and other adjustment problems. The failure to respond adequately to these difficulties perpetuates the revolving door of rearrests and reincarcerations (Austin, 2000). National research shows that two-thirds of former inmates are rearrested within three years of release, suggesting that more efforts should be made to assist them in their attempt to make the transition from prison to the community (Langan and Levin, 2002; Petersilia, 2003).

Today's released inmates encounter many more—and more serious—obstacles to reentry than those in earlier years (Travis, Solomon, and Waul, 2001). Current cohorts of returning inmates are, for example, more likely than their predecessors to be unemployed and unemployable, and to need mental health and drug treatment services (Lynch and Sabol, 2001). In addition, a felony conviction prohibits returning inmates from obtaining a professional license, acquiring a unit in a public housing facility, and receiving Supplemental Security Income or other federal entitlements. All these restrictions bankrupt their futures and limit their chances for successful reentry (Solomon, 2001).

Responding to the Reentry Crisis

The question of how to best facilitate prisoner reentry has gained a lot of attention from several quarters. For example, the federal government recently proposed the allocation of $300 million to support reentry initiatives at the state level (U. S. Department of Labor, 2005). Furthermore, many state governments have convened special task forces to examine the reentry crisis, and several professional associations, such as the American Correctional Association, the National Institute of Corrections, the American Probation and Parole Association, and the National Institute of Justice, have emphasized the importance of identifying the problems and concerns of returning inmates and developing programs and interventions that can effectively alleviate them (Reentry Policy Council, 2005).

Although the issue of prisoner reentry has become a national priority, resources to address the problems have fallen far short of what is actually needed. The mismatch between the programmatic needs of returning inmates and the resources set aside to address those needs begs the question: "How do we respond to former inmates' problems with relatively limited community-based interventions and programs?" In other words, how do correctional officials and administrators decide to invest their relatively scanty dollars to serve returning inmates? The best answer might be: "Decisions about the allocation of reentry resources can be made by identifying and implementing evidence-based practices."

Evidence-Based Practices

Evidence-based practices are never grounded in an agency's traditions, or the experiences or preferences of its staff. Instead, evidence-based practices are supported by independent research that demonstrates their effectiveness in achieving positive, consensual outcomes, which have been broadly endorsed by experts and practitioners in a particular field (for example, Stout and Hayes, 2005). The most compelling evidence of a program's effectiveness stems from research that includes: representative samples of participants; random assignment to treatment and control groups; and baseline and follow-up measures of offender performance that are valid (accurate) and reliable (consistent). Moreover, the most useful results of studies—for the purpose of establishing evidence-based practices—are based on evaluations of programs that are manualized (which means that they can be implemented reliably and at different times by a variety of properly trained staff persons) and implemented by trained staff persons.

Evidence-based practices are methodologically sound. Evidence-based practices in reentry have several common features that apply to different areas of services and cover the various stages of program implementation—from intake to termination. Simply put, evidence-based practices are interventions, programs, and treatments that have withstood the test of the scientific process. Their effectiveness is demonstrated by data that are collected in methodologically rigorous research designs. As this author has suggested above, rigorous studies have examined treatment and control groups that are closely matched on variables that can affect the outcomes being studied. In valid research designs, the only significant difference between the treatment and control group is that the former receives the intervention whereas the latter does not. Random assignment to these groups is the sine qua non of rigorous studies; it is the single most effective means for equating groups on confounding variables. Such factors make it difficult for a researcher to conclude that the treatment—and not preexisting differences between the treatment and controls groups—accounts for significant findings. In short, evidence-based practices must be supported by the results of valid research.

Evidence-based practices must be replicable. Other characteristics also are important in defining evidence-based practices. Specifically, programs are regarded as especially effective when two or more studies have produced consistent or replicable evidence establishing their success in changing offender behaviors. Furthermore, evidence-based programs must be feasible or practicable. Departments must be able to implement programs without a considerable strain on their financial or staff resources. Interventions that are too expensive or difficult to deliver can make no real or sustained contributions to reentry efforts. The most useful evidence-based practices are able to change offenders' behaviors that are linked specifically to the various components of a program and its immediate and long-term goals. For example, an employment-services program for returning inmates, which is intended to enhance their success in obtaining a job, should be evaluated on job starts and not just on rearrests or reincarcerations.

Evidence-based practices must be congruent. Evidence-based practices are most useful when they are consistent with an agency's overall mission, policies, and procedures. They should be congruent with and complementary to other interventions that already are being implemented to respond to offenders' needs and problems. An evidence-based practice that has these characteristics and "looks and feels right" to staff is said to have face validity. Staff will often resist practices that are supported by research but fit poorly into a department's culture or standard operating procedure. In addition, it makes sense to introduce evidence-based practices gradually, giving staff enough time to understand and accept them into their current set of case management tools and strategies. Moreover, evidence-based practices must be sensitive, in their use of language and approaches, to differences in clients' age, gender, race, ethnicity, sexual orientation, and physical and psychiatric disability.

Prison reentry is an ongoing, dynamic practice that begins at intake when a thorough assessment evaluates a new inmate's strengths, deficiencies, and readiness to benefit from services (Taxman, Young, Byrne, Holsinger, and Anspach, 2002). Most inmates are in prison for relatively short periods of time, and should be preparing for release early and often during the period of incarceration. Therefore, evidence-based practices can differ not only on the type of problem being addressed (for example, mental illness, addiction, employment deficits) but also on the point at which an intervention is administered (for example, thirty, sixty, or ninety days before or after release).

Inmates typically enter prison with longstanding problems and a history of failure to meet developmental, educational, and social challenges. Their problems are usually multifarious and interconnected. Educational deficits and housing instability interfere with employment opportunities. Psychiatric disorders impede recovery from substance use disorders and vice versa. Entrenchment in poverty forces released inmates to return to the same criminogenic environments and antisocial companions that initially set them on the pathway to a criminal lifestyle. Successful reentry demands that all their problems be confronted in an integrated action plan that recognizes the holistic nature of offenders' difficulties and the shortcomings of piecemeal or segmented approaches to behavioral change.

The first step in any evidence-based reentry program is a comprehensive evaluation of service needs. In each service domain, historical and current data are elicited on clients' strengths and weaknesses and their treatment histories and responsiveness to different types of interventions. Standardized assessment tools provide accurate and reliable information on problems such as mental illness, developmental disabilities, vocational and educational deficits, and substance use disorders. Such tools often can be self-administered and yield results that can be compared with population norms, which indicate the severity of the client's problems relative to a large number of other individuals who answered the questions or items on the assessment tool. For example, the SCL-90 is a self-administered survey that measures psychiatric symptoms and suggests whether clients should be referred to a mental health professional for an in-depth psychiatric evaluation to determine their treatment needs.

The assessment process should give the case manager enough information to broker services in a case-management plan that refers clients to services and monitors their progress on reaching treatment goals. For the plan to be successful, clients must remain in treatment that is delivered in the proper dose and for a sufficient length of time. For example, clients with substance-use disorders must spend enough time in different levels of care (for example, detoxification, intensive treatment, and relapse prevention) for them to recover successfully from addiction. Returning inmates should be matched to levels and types of programming that correspond to the severity of their needs and take them to the next step in the services gradient. For example, an inmate who has spent 180 days in a therapeutic community should be placed in a relapse-prevention program when released, not in another intensive-treatment program.

Evidence-based reentry programs focus on changing measurable attitudes and behaviors. They use incentives and rewards to increase the frequency of positive responses in clients. Programs should be manualized. As previously noted, this means that they can be implemented reliably at different times by a variety of properly trained staff persons. Manualized programs also are significantly more likely to be administered in accordance with program models and designs; this is an important feature of evidence-based programs, known as fidelity.

In conclusion, the adoption of evidence-based practices is crucial to achieving the overarching goals of reintegrating former inmates into the community and preventing them from being rearrested and reincarcerationed. The evidence-based standard can be a touchstone for program selection and a justification for the continuation of program funding. Because evidence-based practices have manualized operating procedures and measurable outcomes, they also lend themselves to widespread implementation, which might lead to an overall reduction in the recidivism rate of inmates and the size of the prison population.

REFERENCES

Austin, J. 2000. *Prisoner Reentry: Current Trends, Practices, and Issues.* Washington, D.C.: The Institute on Crime, Justice, and Corrections.

Beck, A. J. 2000. *State and Federal Prisoners Returning to the Community: Findings from the Bureau of Justice Statistics.* Paper presented at the First Reentry Courts Initiative Cluster Meeting.

Langan, P. A., and D. J. Levin. 2002. *National Recidivism Study of Released Prisoners: Prisoners Released in 1994.* Washington, D.C.: Bureau of Justice Statistics.

Lynch, J. P. and W. J. Sabol. 2001. *Prisoner Reentry in Perspective.* Washington, D.C.: The Urban Institute.

Petersilia, J. 2003. *When Prisoners Come Home: Parole and Prison Reentry.* New York: Oxford University Press.

Reentry Policy Council. 2005. *Charting the Safe and Successful Return of Prisoners to the Community.* New York: Author.

Solomon, A. L. 2001. *Prison Reentry: A National Overview.* Paper presented at the Annual Meeting of the National Council on Crime Prevention.

Stout, C. E. and R. A. Hayes. 2005. *The Evidence-Based Practice: Methods, Models, and Tools of Mental Health Professionals.* Hoboken, New Jersey: Wiley.

Taxman, F. S., D. Young, J. M. Byrne, A. Holsinger, and D. Anspach. 2002. *From Prison Safety To Public Safety: Innovations in Offender Reentry.* College Park, Maryland: University of Maryland, College Park, Bureau of Governmental Research.

Travis, J. 2005. *But They All Come Back: Facing the Challenges of Prisoner Reentry.* Washington, D.C.: The Urban Institute Press.

Travis, J., A. L Solomon, and M. Waul. 2001. *From Prison To Home: The Dimensions and Consequences of Prisoner Reentry.* Washington, D.C.: The Urban Institute.

United States Department of Labor. 2005. *President Bush's Reentry Initiative: Protecting Communities by Helping Returning Inmates Find Work.* www.dol.gov/cfbci.

Arthur J. Lurigio, Ph.D., is the dean of the College of Arts and Sciences, Departments of Criminal Justice and Psychology, at Loyola University in Chicago.

Making Inmate Reentry Safe and Successful: Using the Report of the Reentry Policy Council

Katherine Brown

First printed in *Corrections Today,* a publication of the American Correctional Association, April 2005

Correctional administrators and practitioners are intimately familiar with the critical need to find ways to keep offenders released to the community from returning to jail and prison. They are now finding powerful allies and new opportunities to promote safe and successful inmate reentry through the Reentry Policy Council. This unprecedented, bipartisan collection of nearly 100 leading elected officials, policymakers and practitioners working in state and local government and community-based organizations—including institutional and community corrections—has developed a comprehensive set of recommendations to reduce recidivism and help ex-offenders to succeed in their communities. These recommendations were released in January 2005 as the landmark *Report of the Reentry Policy Council.*

The commitment of state policymakers of all stripes to the important issue of reentry is demonstrated by the leadership on the Reentry Policy Council. "This isn't a Republican issue or a Democrat issue. It's about keeping our communities safe and saving money—and those are things both parties want to see happen," said Sen. Eric Bogue, R-S.D., who serves as co-chair of the Reentry Policy Council. "Every state in the nation is grappling with the enormous financial burden of incarceration and reincarceration of offenders, which is even more acute in these difficult economic times." Bogue was joined in chairing the Reentry Policy Council by Assemblyman Jeffrion L. Aubry, D-New York, chair of the Assembly Correction Committee, and Rep. John A. Loredo, D-Arizona, minority whip.[1]

Established by the Council of State Governments in 2001, the Reentry Policy Council was organized to develop specific, bipartisan recommendations that would reflect the expertise of a broad spectrum of stakeholders from across the nation. Together, the members of the Reentry Policy Council represent nearly every component of the criminal justice system, as well as those systems that make available education, job training, job placement, housing, health and mental health care, substance abuse treatment, children and family services, victim services, and other forms of support and supervision. These members were organized into three advisory groups—public safety and restorative activities, supportive health and housing, and work force development and employment opportunities—that met both separately and together to identify the key challenges of reentry and to strategize ways for policy makers and practitioners at all levels of government and in private and nonprofit organizations to address them.

To coordinate the contributions from this range of important, highly relevant viewpoints, the Council of State Governments partnered with ten organizations to form a steering committee. The perspective of corrections professionals was represented by the Association of State Correctional Administrators and the American Probation and Parole Association. Other agencies included the following:

- Corporation for Supportive Housing

- National Association of Housing and Redevelopment Officials

- National Association of State Alcohol/Drug Abuse Directors

- National Association of State Mental Health Program Directors

- National Association of Workforce Boards

- National Center for State Courts

- Police Executive Research Forum

- The Urban Institute

Prominent members of the corrections community also participated as members of the policy council, including Reginald Wilkinson, director of the Ohio Department of Rehabilitation and Correction, and past president of the American Correctional Association and the Association of State Correctional Administrators; and Timothy J. Ryan, chief of corrections, Orange County Corrections Department, Orlando, Florida, and past president of the American Jail Association.

In addition to Wilkinson and Ryan, institutional and community corrections executives from Maryland, Texas, Iowa, Missouri, Massachusetts, Pennsylvania, New York, and Utah participated in the advisory group discussions, ensuring that professionals who work closest to inmates and those under community supervision would have a voice alongside community and policymaking partners. Ryan lauded the principles of consensus building embodied by the Reentry Policy Council and articulated in its report: "The recommendations of the Reentry Policy Council provide a powerful basis for collaborative efforts in any jurisdiction. Close coordination between county jails, state and local criminal justice agencies, and housing, health and employment providers in our communities is fundamental to stopping the cycle of recidivism and allowing our corrections system to focus on keeping the most dangerous criminals locked up," Ryan said.

Findings of the Reentry Policy Council

"The Report of the Reentry Policy Council is encyclopedic; corrections administrators and others involved with reentry should have a copy at their fingertips," Wilkinson stated. Available online at www.reentrypolicy.org, the report provides, in a single document, a comprehensive analysis of those elements essential to a successful return to the community, a review of relevant research, and a look at programs and policies that illustrate how policymakers and practitioners in jurisdictions across the country have implemented a particular recommendation. The voluminous material is organized into three parts.

Part 1: *Planning a Reentry Initiative.* This section reviews the steps that policymakers and practitioners need to execute to ensure a solid foundation for new or improved reentry programs, policies or practices. Thus, individuals interested in building a reentry initiative are urged to get started by bringing together the diverse group of state and local government agencies and community-based organizations relevant to inmate reentry, and providing those stakeholders with accurate, jurisdictionally specific information about released inmates such as how they are prepared for their transition to the community, where they go after their release, and the kinds of violations for which they most often return to prison. The rest of this section of the report recommends strategies for overcoming some of the central challenges that will affect those undertaking a reentry initiative, including redefining missions, funding, integrating systems, measuring performance, and educating the public.

Part 2: *Review of the Reentry Process.* This section identifies and describes the opportunities along a person's path from admission to a correctional facility to the completion of supervised release for improving the likelihood that he or she will avoid crime and become a healthy, productive member of his or her family and community. This part is organized into chapters that delineate the key events or decision points during an offender's process of reentry, including admission, institutional programming, release decision-making, transition, and community supervision. This portion of the report particularly emphasizes the need for collaboration among staff inside correctional facilities and those on the outside, including community-based health care and social services providers, relatives, victims and community members. In particular, Part 2 details how a successful reentry effort requires the development of policies and programs that feature smart release and community supervision decisions, support for victims, safe places to live, substance abuse treatment, services for physical and mental illnesses, meaningful relationships (with family, peers, partners and the faith community), access to safe housing, and training, education, and jobs.

Part 3: Elements of Effective Health and Social Service Systems. The final section provides a context for understanding the service systems upon which the successful implementation of reentry programs and practices are predicated. It addresses those systems that provide housing, workforce development, substance abuse treatment, mental health services, children and family supports, and health care to needy communities. Part 3 offers a primer on the main components of each system, including an explanation of the population that the system serves (including, but not limited to, individuals who are reentering), the primary issues and challenges within each system, an explanation of how each system is organized and funded, and recommendations for improvements that should be made within those systems.

Though each part has a different focus, each is divided into a series of "policy statements" (a total of thirty-five throughout the report), which group-specific recommendations to provide policymakers and practitioners with key steps for implementing a particular aspect of a reentry initiative. Taken collectively, the policy statements represent a comprehensive vision for the safe and successful transition of a person from prison or jail to the community. Reading the entire document will help anyone concentrating on one particular aspect of reentry to understand the entire set of activities that reentry contemplates. Reviewing all of the policy statements also helps policymakers and practitioners to appreciate how interdependent these goals are. For example, successfully linking an ex-offender to employment is nearly impossible if he or she is chemically dependent and not engaged in treatment. Engaging someone in treatment is especially hard if he or she does not have a place to live. In sum, the policy statements together provide a context for any focused reentry initiative.

Determining which policy statements to start with will depend on the leadership and resources available in a specific jurisdiction. For instance, a state workforce investment board member seeking to set up a one-stop career center to reach potential workers might review Policy Statement 21, "Creation of Employment Opportunities," and Policy Statement 22, "Workforce Development and Transition Plan," and then, partnering with the state community corrections agency officials, could decide to co-locate the center with a regional parole office, and educate potential employers about financial incentives for hiring people with criminal records. A director of correctional programming, on the other hand, might begin with Policy Statement 9, "Development of Programming Plan," for an overview of matching a person's strengths, needs and risks with programming that will prepare him or her for reentry. What works in one community may not be a perfect fit for its neighbor, let alone for a community halfway across the continent; within the framework provided by the *Reentry Policy Council* report, each jurisdiction should find its own solutions to these complex and interrelated problems.

Using the Reentry Policy Council Report

In the hands of someone committed to effecting change around one of today's most pressing policy issues, this report can be an invaluable tool, backed by the experience and convictions of respected and prominent representatives of the full spectrum of systems relevant to inmate reentry. Any one of the following strategies can serve as the first step towards building meaningful, collaborative solutions to reduce public spending, promote public safety, and ensure the safe and successful return of inmates to the community.

Engage a policymaker or other key official to an inmate reentry initiative. Often there has been at least one person key to a jurisdiction's reentry effort whose investment in the initiative has been tenuous at best. *The Reentry Policy Council* report can be used to demonstrate to a state or local government official that a counterpart in another jurisdiction has been actively involved in thinking about, and addressing, the issue of inmate reentry.

Focus interest in reentry on a particular aspect of the problem. Coalitions or task forces formed to tackle inmate reentry are often overwhelmed by the enormity of the problem. Constant analysis of the issue can become paralyzing. Selecting a particular policy statement on which to concentrate initial attention and energy can help such a group to translate its commitment into tangible action steps.

Determine how to address a particular obstacle that has impeded offenders' safe and successful transition from prison or jail to the community. Whether it involves connecting people in prison to housing before their release or prioritizing the use of limited drug treatment slots, the *Reentry Policy Council* report provides detailed recommendations that can inform efforts to address longstanding roadblocks to successful reentry.

Assess comprehensiveness of an existing reentry effort. Officials in a state or county interested in identifying any shortcomings of current reentry efforts can use the *Reentry Policy Council* report as a checklist to inventory their existing programs, policies, and practices.

Find out what other jurisdictions are doing. Elected or appointed officials presented with a proposal for a new or modified program or policy can learn about other jurisdictions that have successfully implemented the proposed approach.

Learn about relevant research. Although many key research questions regarding inmate reentry remain unanswered, studies and reports analyzing different aspects of reentry abound. With research condensed into easy-to-use highlights, the *Reentry Policy Council* report is an ideal resource for readers wondering what the evidence says about a particular aspect of reentry.

Advocate for change. *The Reentry Policy Council* report provides a bipartisan platform that can be invaluable to advocates who are unanimous in their commitment to make inmate reentry safe and successful, but divided about how best to accomplish that goal in their jurisdiction. Furthermore, the report provides specificity and pragmatism to advocates whose efforts may be undermined by an agenda that is ambiguous or unrealistic.

Respond to public pressure generated by a recent tragedy. Too often, public policy is shaped in the immediate aftermath of a tragedy that has been reported widely in the media. The atmosphere in such situations is typically not conducive to the development of thoughtful policy. *The Reentry Policy Council* report is an ideal resource in such situations, as it provides a menu of hundreds of carefully considered recommendations, each of which has bipartisan support and the backing of public safety officials and service providers alike.

Educate the media. Stakeholders in the reentry process can direct journalists seeking context for a particular event or issue to relevant sections of the *Reentry Policy Council* report; its evidence and conclusions can provide a thoughtful framework for the challenges of a particular community.

Whether the *Reentry Policy Council* report is employed towards one or more of these ends, it provides an unprecedented resource to corrections professionals interested in improving the likelihood that an offender's reentry will be safe and successful. *The Reentry Policy Council* report urges corrections professionals to consider their role in ensuring that when an offender leaves a correctional facility, he or she will not return.

The *Report of the Reentry Policy Council* may be ordered, reviewed or downloaded at www.reentry policy.org, or by calling the Council of State Governments store at 1-800- 800-1910.

ENDNOTE

[1] Term-limited after serving ten years in the House, Loredo has been appointed chair of a blue ribbon committee established by the governor to address inmate reentry.

Katherine Brown is a policy analyst of the Reentry Policy Council for the Council of State Governments in New York.

An Initial Comparison of Graduates and Terminated Clients in America's Largest Reentry Court

Jeffrey B. Spelman, Ph.D.

First printed in the *Corrections Today*, a publication of the American Correctional Association, August 2003

Richland County, Ohio, is located in the north-central region of the state and has a population of 129,000. There are three cities, seven villages, and eighteen townships within the 497-square-mile county. Mansfield, the largest of the three cities, has a population of 57,000 and is the county seat. According to the 2000 census, 89 percent of Richland County's population is white, 10 percent is black, and the remaining are American Indian, Hispanic, Asian or another nationality.

Prior to the reentry court program in Richland County, inmates released from prison received the same supervision as most inmates reentering the community from state prison under parole or post-release control—supervision by state parole officers. When clients violated their supervision conditions, they faced a revocation hearing in front of a parole board hearing officer or a full parole board. The majority ended up back in prison. When inmates were released from prison by the court under split sentencing or judicial release (formerly called shock probation), they also were supervised. If they violated the conditions of supervision, they appeared before a judge and could also be sent back to prison.

Reentry court has changed the way convicted offenders are processed in Richland County. The Richland County Court has teamed up with the Ohio Department of Rehabilitation and Correction. Upon sentencing, the court assesses offenders and recommends specific treatment while in prison. A reentry court treatment coordinator monitors offenders' progress and treatment while in prison. This involves interviewing inmates and communicating with inmates' institutional unit managers and/or case managers to assess the progress. If offenders complete the treatment, they might be recommended for release into the reentry court program. Prior to release into the community, an inmate community treatment plan is prepared and is agreed upon by the judge, treatment coordinator, and the supervision staff.

Upon release, reentry clients must appear in court each month. Clients released by the court appear in front of a judge to discuss their progress while clients released by the State Adult Parole Authority appear in front of a parole board member. Monthly meetings are key elements of the reentry court program (drug court operations also possesses this fundamental component). During this time, clients receive individualized attention and might receive sanctions or incentives. Reentry court supervision throughout this one-year program not only is intensive, but also mandatory for program graduation. Reentry court supervision involves an average of twelve contacts per month. In comparison, 80 percent of U.S. parolees being supervised on a regular, rather than intensive, caseload receive less than two fifteen-minute face-to-face contacts per month.[1]

Client Data and Analysis

Richland County accepted its first reentry court client November 1, 2000. Within the first twenty-two months, 160 clients were placed in the reentry court program. This number includes fifty-six parole and or post-release control clients (state referred) and 104 common pleas court, split sentence, and judicial release clients (county referred). Of the initial 160 reentry clients, 104 (65 percent) were still active in the program as of August 31, 2002. Of the fifty-six clients who no longer were active in the reentry court program on this date, thirty-four had successfully completed the mandatory one-year supervision and graduated. The other twenty-two were terminated from the program. Table 1 conveys information regarding the reentry court's first 160 clients.

One year of successful community supervision is a requirement for graduation from the reentry court program. Sixty-six offenders entered the reentry court program between November 1, 2000, and August 1, 2001. Of the sixty-six clients, thirty-four successfully graduated from the reentry court program, and twenty-two clients failed and were terminated from it prior to one year. Failure in this program occurs as a result of a new arrest, multiple technical violations, or one serious technical violation.

For this chapter, the thirty-four reentry court graduates were placed side by side with the twenty-two terminated reentry court clients for an initial inquiry to observe how these two sets of clients differ. Although Richland County has the largest reentry court in operation today, this reentry court project is relatively new and as such, the statistics are derived from a very limited number of clients. Therefore, absolute conclusions must not be formulated from these percentages. Even so, some important information may emerge from the following figures while other data may cause questions to arise, demanding further investigation. Certainly, this survey of Richland County's reentry court will continue to provide valuable data for analyzing well into the future.

Table 1. Characteristics of the First 160 Clients

Client Origination
- 56 Parole and Post-Release Control clients (State, Parole) (35 percent)
- 104 Judicial release (County Court) (65 percent)

Gender
- 147 Male (92 percent)
- 13 Female (8 percent)

Race and Ethnicity
- 90 White (56 percent)
- 66 Black (41 percent)
- 2 Biracial (1 percent)
- 2 Hispanic (1 percent)

Educational Level
- 1 Bachelor's degree (1 percent)
- 6 Some college or associate's degree (4 percent)
- 48 High school graduate (30 percent)
- 22 GED (14 percent)
- 78 Ninth to 12th grade (no diploma) (49 percent)
- 5 Below ninth grade (3 percent)

Offense Level*
- 10 Felony 1 (6 percent)
- 41 Felony 2 (26 percent)
- 39 Felony 3 (24 percent)
- 37 Felony 4 (23 percent)
- 33 Felony 5 (21 percent)

Employment
- 125 Employed (78 percent)
- 35 Unemployed** (22 percent)

Marital Status**
- 21 Married (13 percent)
- 15 Divorced (9 percent)
- 12 Separated (8 percent)
- 112 Single (70 percent)

Ages
- 2 19 or younger (1 percent)
- 87 20 to 29 (54 percent)
- 42 30 to 39 (26 percent)
- 23 40 to 49 (14 percent)
- 5 50 to 59 (3 percent)
- 1 60 or over (1 percent)

*Some clients may have been convicted of multiple offenses. The most serious felony is recorded.
**The client may be in school, disabled, or caring for dependent children.
***Of the 160 clients, 83 (52 percent) have dependent children.

Table 2. Reentry Court Graduates vs. Terminated Clients

Breakdown of Graduate Origination
- 9 Parole and Post-Release Court clients (State) (26 percent)
- 25 Judicial release clients (Common Pleas Court) (74 percent)

Breakdown of Clients Terminated From Reentry Court Origination
- 7 Parole and PRC clients (3 new arrests, 4 technical violations) (32 percent)
- 15 Judicial release clients (1 new arrest, 14 technical violations) (68 percent)

Table 3. Breakdown of Reentry Court Clients

Reentry Graduates	Terminated Clients
Gender	
29 Males (85 percent)	21 Males (95 percent)
5 Females (15 percent)	1 Female (5 percent)
Race	
15 White (44 percent)	11 White (50 percent)
19 Black (56 percent)	10 Black (45 percent)
	1 Biracial (5 percent)
Educational Level	
2 Some college (6 percent)	0 Some college (0 percent)
15 High school graduate (44 percent)	4 High school graduate (18 percent)
5 GED (15 percent)	3 GED (14 percent)
12 Ninth to 12th grade (no diploma) (35 percent)	15 Ninth to 12th grade (no diploma) (68 percent)
Employment	
34 Employed (100 percent)	10 Employed (45 percent)
0 Unemployed	12 Unemployed (55 percent)
Marital Status	
23 Single (68 percent)	19 Single (86 percent)
5 Married (15 percent)	0 Married (0 percent)
3 Divorced (9 percent)	2 Divorced (9 percent)
3 Separated (9 percent)	1 Separated (5 percent)
Age	
Male Female Age	Male Female Age
10 3 20 to 29 (38 percent)	15 1 20 to 29 (73 percent)
10 1 30 to 39 (27 percent)	6 0 30 to 39 (27 percent)
8 1 40 to 49 (26 percent)	0 0 40 to 49 (0 percent)
1 0 50 to 59 (3 percent)	0 0 50 to 59 (0 percent)
Note: Average age = 42.7	Note: Average age = 26.7
Offense Conviction Level	
Felony 1 3 (9 percent)	Felony 1 2 (9 percent)
Felony 2 11 (32 percent)	Felony 2 3 (14 percent)
Felony 3 4 (12 percent)	Felony 3 5 (23 percent)
Felony 4 9 (26 percent)	Felony 4 7 (32 percent)
Felony 5 7 (21 percent)	Felony 5 5 (23 percent)
Offense Type	
Violent 17 (50 percent)	Violent 14 (64 percent)
Property 8 (24 percent)	Property 7 (32 percent)
Drug 6 (18 percent)	Drug 1 (5 percent)
Sex 3 (9 percent)	Sex 0 (0 percent)

Of the sixty-six clients who had the opportunity to complete one year in reentry court, fifty-six had either graduated or were terminated from the program. The remaining ten continued the program because they either required additional treatment as a precondition for graduation, or received a sanction to a community-based correctional facility or residential treatment facility. When additional time is required in a community-based correctional or residential treatment facility, it does not count as a part of the one-year community supervision requirement. These ten clients continued in reentry court as of August 31, 2002, and consequently are labeled as neither graduates nor terminated clients. However, they are counted as part of the 104 active reentry court participants.

Table 2 compares the thirty-four reentry court graduates with the twenty-two clients who were terminated during the first twenty-two months of the program. It is important to note that since ten of the sixty-six clients (15 percent) are neither graduates nor terminated clients, they were not evaluated below. While it may be accurate to consider them successful because they remained in the program for one year, it is equally possible that they will choose behaviors that could result in their termination prior to successful graduation. Since they have not been terminated from the program, only future evaluation will establish their successes or failures in the reentry court system.

The fifty-six clients who were terminated or graduated by August 31, 2002, are categorized based on their origination into the reentry court system. While the court began placing clients into the reentry court November 1, 2000, the state began placing parole or post-release control cases into reentry court January 1, 2001. Therefore, reentry court planners anticipated that the common pleas court would place more clients into the reentry court program than would the state parole board during its first year of operation.

Of the twenty-two terminated clients, only four were terminated because they were charged with a new criminal law violation. This is a noteworthy detail that seems to shine a promising light on the reentry concept. The other eighteen clients were terminated because of a technical violation. Consequently, the failure is 33 percent for the first sixty-six reentry court clients. Recently released inmates are frequently prone to involve themselves in some type of criminal behavior. The 33 percent initial failure rate for Ohio's first reentry court is favorably lower than the nationwide parole failure rate of 58 percent published by the Bureau of Justice Statistics for parolees discharged from parole in 1999.[2] The rearrest of released offenders often occurs very quickly. The rearrest rate of Ohio's first reentry court clients was 6 percent within the first year. Bureau of Justice Statistics data from a fifteen-state recidivism study in 1994 indicate that nearly 30 percent of released inmates were rearrested within six months and an additional 14 percent were arrested in the subsequent six months. This brings the one-year recidivism rate for the immediate twelve-month period following release to 44 percent.[3] The contrast between the reentry court's 6 percent rearrest rate and the Bureau of Justice Statistics study's 44 percent rearrest rate is remarkable and renders further investigation valuable.

While the vast majority of prison inmates are male, female clients in this reentry program appear to have a high success rate. In fact, five out of the six females in this early program comparison graduated (see Table 3). Fifty-six percent of the first 160 clients were white, while 41 percent were black. Compared with white clients, 12 percent more black clients graduated from the reentry court program, whereas 5 percent more white clients were terminated.

The educational gap between the reentry graduates and those terminated from the program is notable. In fact, a discrepancy of more than 30 percent exists between these two groups regarding the clients holding a high school diploma. While 50 percent of Richland County reentry court graduates completed high school, only 18 percent of terminated clients were high school graduates. Likewise, while 68 percent of those terminated held no high school diploma or GED, only 35 percent of those who graduated from the reentry court program had failed to attain a high school diploma.

While it is well-documented that inmates have a lower educational attainment than those who are not offenders, the results of this study continue to highlight to both prison and community corrections providers the importance of education in ending recidivism.

Like education, employment is another crucial factor in ending recidivism, allowing former inmates to meet financial responsibilities. Data in Table 3 show the role of employment in the successful reintegration of offenders into the community.

Although it appears that reentry court clients are more likely to be single than married, the number of single terminated clients was 18 percent higher than the number of single clients who graduated. Although 15 percent of the graduates were married, not one of the terminated clients was married.

The significance of a client's age is not a revelation to criminal justice officials. This study reinforces the fact that young people are more inclined to commit crimes. However, several interesting facts are worth noting. This data show that 100 percent of the terminated clients were younger than forty, and more than 70 percent were under thirty. In addition, the average terminated client was sixteen years younger than the graduating client.

The offense-conviction levels were relatively similar, with the slight exception of the felony 2 category. Interestingly, there were 18 percent more felony 2 convictions by those who ultimately became graduates of the program than by those who were eventually terminated.

As with other categories, it is difficult to draw definitive conclusions based on this new program's limitations; however, one thing seems to draw initial interest. It appears that the reentry program's drug and sex offenders were generally likely to become graduates. Initial drug and sex offender successes may be related to the excessive supervision contacts averaging twelve per month, their required monthly appearances in reentry court, the frequent drug-testing, and the use of electronic monitoring. As previously stated, further studies are warranted.

Summary

Although time will test the accuracy of these early results, initial data seem to indicate that extensive supervision benefits a client's chance for success. Even so, certain characteristics seem more likely to lead to a client's success in the reentry court program. Initial data indicated that female clients were likely to become graduates. Education was another key indicator; in fact, those clients without a high school diploma were more likely to be among the terminated. Two other important indicators were employment and age. Every successful graduate was employed and sixteen of the twenty-two terminated clients were age twenty-nine or younger. Each client older than thirty-nine graduated.

Though these initial results are of interest and not without merit, the results of future studies will provide a more accurate assessment of the reentry program and its significance in the lives of individuals, communities, and society as a whole.

ENDNOTES

[1] Petersilia, J. and S. Turner. 1993. *Evaluating Intensive Supervision Probation/Parole: Results Of A Nationwide Experiment*. Washington, D.C.: U.S. Department of Justice, National Institute of Justice.

[2] Hughes, T., D. Wilson and A. Beck. 2001. *Trends in State Parole*, 1990-2000. Bureau of Justice Statistics Special Report. Washington, D.C.: U.S. Department of Justice.

[3] Morrison, A. 2002. Inmate Reentry and Post-Release Supervision. *Perspectives*. 26(4): 32-38. Lexington, Kentucky: American Probation and Parole Association.

Jeffrey B. Spelman, Ph.D., is assistant professor of criminal justice at Ashland University in Ashland, Ohio.

Assessing for Success in Offender Reentry

Kathleen A. Gnall
and Gary Zajac, Ph.D.

First printed in *Corrections Today*, a publication of the
American Correctional Association, April 2005

Imagine that a couple goes to the grocery store, fills a cart with their desired items, walks to the checkout lane, and the clerk simply eyeballs their selections and says, "looks like about $200 worth to me." They probably would not be too happy with this approach. Of course, if they felt that it was an underestimate, they might be willing to let it go, but most people would expect a more systematic means of tallying the bill. Indeed, the widespread use of barcode scanners is yet the latest attempt to take human error out of the cashiering process.

As ridiculous as this example may seem, it is a fairly decent analogy for how criminal justice agencies often attempt to determine what is "wrong" with offenders and how best to prepare them for reentry to the community. A large number of evaluations of correctional programs across the country have found that offender assessment is one of the most poorly implemented principles of effective offender intervention.[1] Central to this weakness is a frequent reliance on subjective, clinical assessments of offenders' likelihood of re-offending (risk) and specific risk factors (criminogenic needs), without the aid of standard, objective assessment instruments.

The accurate and objective assessment of offender risk, needs, and responsivity is one of the most important features of an effective correctional treatment system.[2] Providing a criminal justice intervention to an offender absent careful consideration of the offender's risk and need for that intervention is akin to prescribing a drug to a patient without a diagnosis of what is wrong.

Approaches to Offender Assessment

How best to assess offender risk and needs has been an ongoing concern within the field of criminal justice. This question is embedded in the larger discussion in the field of psychology about the most effective approach to conduct any sort of individual assessment. Much of this discussion has focused on the dichotomy of clinical versus actuarial assessment. Clinical assessment refers to the approach that has been used for generations to gain insight into the problems of any individual undergoing treatment. This (usually) involves a trained practitioner, the clinician, sitting down with a client who is being considered for treatment and asking that client a series of questions, or perhaps even having a more open-ended discussion. For corrections' purposes, a clinician may be a psychologist/psychiatrist, social worker, corrections counselor, parole official, and so forth. Clinical assessment, then, is essentially an interpersonal process that occurs between individuals, where one person is charged with making a decision about providing services to the other.

The logic behind the clinical approach to assessment is that the clinician has a basis of experience, expertise, and perhaps even natural insight that allows for an impressionistic interpretation of what is wrong with the client. The key point is that the questions that the clinician asks often will be idiosyncratic, inconsistent, unstructured, and perhaps only tangentially related to the problem under consideration; that is to say, they may or may not be "good" questions. Some clinicians may ask good questions most of the time, some may ask bad questions most of the time. More often than not, clinicians will be hit or miss in their assessments (some studies have found that clinical assessment produces prediction success rates that are worse than flipping a coin).

The actuarial or mechanical approach to assessment attempts to control the subjectivity and inconsistency inherent in the clinical approach by structuring a set of observations based on discovered patterns of behavior across large numbers of cases. The observations (factors) that are recorded are driven by a statistical understanding of the relationship between the factor and the behavior or outcome in question. For example, if lung cancer is found to develop in a large percentage of cigarette smokers, but much less so in nonsmokers, a cancer screening tool would likely ask questions about smoking habits (smoking would be a risk factor), among other things. An actuarial assessment tool asks the same set of questions of each individual, asks them in the same way, and interprets the answers consistently. An actuarial tool may involve an interview or conversation by a clinician, but the content of the interview is grounded on known patterns in the data.

The clinical-actuarial dichotomy is actually a continuum, ranging from purely subjective, unstructured clinical interviewing, to clinical interviewing guided by an empirical understanding of risk factors, to a fully codified assessment tool that in some cases may require little clinical expertise to administer. Most approaches to assessment, however, can be fitted into either the basic clinical or actuarial category, based on their degree of structure and grounding in the literature.

The relative outcomes of these two approaches have been studied for more than fifty years. The seminal work on this topic was done by the psychologist Paul Meehl, who established the general superiority of actuarial approaches to risk prediction.[3] The findings of Meehl's original study have been supported by subsequent research that reports on the findings of more than 130 studies showing actuarial predictions to be more accurate than clinical predictions.[4] Most studies found actuarial methods to outperform clinical methods; approximately 40 percent of the studies found substantially better predictive results for actuarial assessments compared with clinical assessments. These studies included those with criminal justice outcomes (other fields of human services were included) and even studies where the clinician-raters had more information available to them than was available to raters using actuarial tools. It is telling that the clinicians' education, level of experience, and professional backgrounds made little difference to the accuracy of their predictions versus predictions made by actuarial tools; the actuarial predictions excelled under almost all conditions.

In sum, the literature offers a strong consensus that actuarial approaches outperform clinical assessments in most circumstances, even where the clinical assessors are highly trained and experienced.[5] The primary source of superiority of actuarial approaches seems to be their grounding in the behavioral literature and the consistency and objectivity offered by standardized assessment instruments. It is difficult for even the most skilled clinician to maintain a high level of objectivity and consistency when rating large numbers of cases over time. In a sense, an actuarial tool distills the "conventional wisdom" about risk factors that is theoretically present in the clinician community, but imposes the rigors of scientific methods to this wisdom. The judgment of the clinician remains valuable, but more so when informed and guided by an objective assessment tool. In the field of criminal risk prediction, the best tools, such as the Level of Service Inventory-Revised (LSI-R), incorporate the substantial body of literature that finds significant correlations between re-offending and factors such as antisocial attitudes, criminal thinking, criminal history, criminal associates, employment, family stability, and conventional lifestyle.[6] These tools make predictions that take advantage of decades of research into the correlates of criminal behavior. The criminal justice community is well served by the use of such tools. If mechanical rigor is expected when adding up a grocery purchase, no less should be expected when assessing offenders.

A New System for Assessing Inmates

During the past two years, the Pennsylvania Department of Corrections has implemented a rigorous new system for assessing the criminogenic risk and needs of its offenders. This development was spurred in large part by the findings from numerous program evaluations conducted within the department of corrections during the past seven years, pointing to the need for enhanced assessment practices within its programs. The department of corrections began with a careful pilot test of a group of risk and needs tools on several thousand inmates, which informed a decision in 2003 to adopt three tools for administration to all newly committed inmates—the aforementioned LSI-R, the Criminal Sentiments Scale-Modified, and the Hostile Interpretations Questionnaire. The latter two tools provide additional measurement of critical risk factors related to criminal thinking, attitudes, and associations that can serve as useful targets for treatment interventions with offenders. Reducing these risk factors is part of the department's overall efforts to better prepare offenders for positive reentry to society.

In terms of reentry planning, the department of corrections is considering approaches to the systematic reassessment of offenders on these measures. At its best, an offender assessment system periodically assesses offenders as they progress through incarceration and treatment to monitor their need for remedial treatment prior to reentry. Some offenders may show substantial progress after only one treatment exposure; others may need repeated and multiple doses of programming in prison before gains become evident. Similarly, some offenders may have a great need for continuing treatment in the community after release; others may stand to gain little from aftercare. Periodic reassessment can inform decisions about ongoing services.

Options for such reassessment include conducting reassessments annually, doing them after completion of specific programs, and doing them at a fixed time prior to release (six months, for example) to allow the correctional system to address any final remaining needs before the offender returns to the community. Each option has its costs (in terms of staff time and instrument purchase) and benefits. The critical thing is for the reassessment information actually to be used to inform ongoing treatment planning; if it is not used, then there is little point in doing it. Agencies must consider their available assessment resources as well as their ability to actually use the results, when deciding on an approach to reassessment.

Promoting Effective Offender Assessment

Staff training on the purpose, interpretation, and application of assessment systems is critical to ensuring that agencies make treatment decisions based on all important information available. The Pennsylvania Department of Corrections recently began this important training initiative. The first step was to deliver an overview of the principles of effective intervention, with special emphasis on assessment, to the department of corrections' executive staff and superintendents. This helps to promote a common understanding and language throughout the department. The presentation was then expanded to include discussions of the assessment instruments that the department of corrections has already adopted, what they are used to measure and how the results should be used to inform treatment decisions. This presentation was delivered to key treatment and management staff working in the state correctional institutions in a half-day session. A new overview course will be designed and delivered to all new staff entering the department's training academy. A more targeted course on use of assessment information for selected institutional staff is also being considered.

The training initiatives underway in the department of corrections are designed so that all staff who work with the inmate population will be exposed to the latest research on the causes of criminal behavior, what factors can be targeted for change within a prison environment, how assessment tools can be used to measure these factors, and how best to use this information in delivering treatment. The department maintains that every interaction with an inmate is a chance to teach that person something positive, whether it be how to communicate clearly, effectively interact with another person or solve problems constructively. Nontreatment staff such as correctional officers, teachers, and food service instructors have many opportunities to challenge and guide offenders to correct thinking errors that support antisocial behavior; that is why all employees should at least receive a high-level overview of the principles of effective intervention, including the value of assessment.

The internal training of correctional staff is but one step towards better preparing offenders for reentry. It is critical that other agencies engaged in reintegrating offenders understand the relevance of assessment data and how they may be used to plan for a successful transition. In Pennsylvania, the Board of Probation and Parole is vested with the authority to make decisions regarding the release of inmates who have reached their minimum sentences. These decisions are informed, in part, by treatment programs received by the offender in prison, as well as by input from department of corrections institutional staff. It is critical that all parties involved in making decisions about readiness for release share an understanding of the principles of effective intervention and the value of actuarial instruments.

The Pennsylvania Department of Corrections and the Pennsylvania Board of Probation and Parole have taken several steps to ensure that everyone is on the same page. First, the department regularly reviews the research literature on effective offender assessment and intervention. This literature, along with findings from key internal research projects, is summarized in a quarterly publication called *Research in Review*. It is made available on the Department of Corrections' public website (www.cor.state.pa.us) with electronic notification of its posting disseminated to staff, the Pennsylvania Board of Probation and Parole, as well as all other state departments of corrections.

Second, the Department of Corrections and the Pennsylvania Board of Probation and Parole leaders meet at least quarterly. The agenda for these meetings often includes reviews of recent studies and literature. During these meetings, the agencies frequently discuss how to improve the sharing of assessment data, what pieces seem to be missing, and how those areas might be measured. As a result of these discussions, all of the department's assessment data on individual offenders are made available to the Pennsylvania Board of Probation and Parole members reviewing cases for release. The board administers the LSI-R to offenders being considered for parole and re-administers it periodically while the offender is on parole. The two agencies are working toward a seamless system for the sharing and use of such assessment data. Finally, the two agencies continue to work together on training initiatives. The Department of Corrections has delivered an overview session on the principles of effective intervention and the specific instruments it currently is using to the Pennsylvania Board of Probation and Parole members.

The need for a common understanding of assessment goes well beyond the corrections and paroling authority. In fact, the results of selected actuarial instruments could be used at the front end to inform sentencing options. Pennsylvania is further along at the back end with using assessment data to inform placement in community-based programs. For example, approximately 70 percent of the parolee population transitions through community corrections centers, run by the department of corrections, prior to parole on the street. Assessment data are part of the referral packet that travels with an offender from prison to the halfway house. This information is factored into a case manager's decision about appropriate referrals for that offender. The case manager shares with local providers the offender's treatment needs, indicated partly by assessment data, as well as treatment history.

Assessing for Reentry

Another more recent initiative brings together state agencies and local providers engaged in the reintegration of offenders into the community. Pennsylvania's pilot project, called the Erie Pennsylvania Reentry Project, is funded under the federal Serious and Violent Offender Reentry Initiative. The project is designed to offer services in areas the research has deemed as key to success in the community, including but not limited to drug and alcohol treatment, job training and placement, interpersonal relationships, and decision-making skills. Assessment is key to determining the needs of the target population and when and how to best address those critical areas.

The process begins with counselors within the state correctional institutions reviewing and making recommendations on appropriate cases for placement in the Erie program. These recommendations are then forwarded to the Erie project manager who is a department of corrections' employee. The project manager reviews any and all assessment data available from department records and then seeks input from the Pennsylvania Board of Probation and Parole. The board administers the LSI-R to all inmates, including those being considered for parole to the Erie project, a few weeks prior to the parole interview. The board administers additional actuarial tools for sex offenders being considered for parole. All of this information is factored into both the decision on whether to parole and on the specific conditions that will be attached to the individual offender if he or she is granted parole. Once an offenders are accepted into the Erie project, they are assigned a case manager at the Greater Erie Community Action Committee, which is the local umbrella organization providing most of the community-based services for Erie project participants. The case manager considers assessment data as part of a decision to place offenders in particular types and intensity of services within the community. A statewide advisory committee meets regularly to discuss ways to improve the Erie project. An ongoing topic for discussion will be how best to measure criminogenic factors, how to ensure that assessment data travel with the offender along the continuum, how often to reassess offenders, and most important, how to use assessment data to inform placement in programs.

Assessing for Success

For too long, the criminal justice field has made critical decisions about offenders based on subjective impressions. It is now known, after fifty years of research on the topic, that actuarial assessment tools are superior to unaided clinical judgment in making treatment decisions. Reviews of correctional programs often point to weaknesses in assessment. This was a finding from research on several department of corrections' programs. As a result, Pennsylvania adopted several objective instruments.

Pennsylvania has begun the process of training its staff on the broader principles of effective intervention with specific attention to assessment, as well as on the specific tools it has adopted, and how they might be used to inform placement in programs. The department of corrections is likewise working on training with the Pennsylvania Board of Probation and Parole to ensure that the sister agencies share a common understanding and language with respect to assessment. Finally, the department of corrections and the Pennsylvania Board of Probation and Parole are working with local agencies engaged in the re-integration of offenders to share assessment data to provide seamless services from prison to the community.

ENDNOTES

[1] *See*, for example, E. J. Latessa and A. Holsinger. 1998. The Importance of Evaluating Correctional Programs: Assessing Outcome and Quality. *Corrections Management Quarterly.* 2(4): 22-29.

[2] Andrews, D. A. and J. Bonta. 1994. *The Psychology of Criminal Conduct.* Cincinnati: Anderson Publishing.

[3] Meehl, P. E. 1954. *Clinical Versus Statistical Prediction: A Theoretical Analysis and a Review of the Evidence.* Minneapolis: University of Minnesota Press.

[4] Grove, W. M. and P. Meehl. 1996. Comparative Efficiency of Informal (Subjective, Impressionistic) and Formal (Mechanical, Algorithmic) Prediction Procedures: The Clinical-Statistical Controversy. *Psychology, Public Policy and Law.* 2(2): 293-323.

Grove, W. M., D. Zald, B. Lebow, B. Snitz and C. Nelson. 2000. Clinical Versus Mechanical Prediction: A Meta-Analysis. *Psychological Assessment.* 12(1): 19-30.

[5] Jones, P. 1996. Risk Prediction in Criminal Justice. In A. T. Hartland, ed. *Choosing Correctional Options that Work: Defining the Demand and Evaluating the Supply*, pp. 33-68. Thousand Oaks, California: Sage.

[6] Andrews, D. A. and J. Bonta. 2001. *The Level of Service Inventory-Revised: User's Manual.* North Tonawanda, New York: Multi-Health Systems Inc.

Kathleen A. Gnall is director of planning, research, statistics and grants, and Gary Zajac, Ph.D., is research and evaluation manager for the Pennsylvania Department of Corrections.

Engaging Communities: An Essential Ingredient to Offender Reentry

Reginald A. Wilkinson, Ed.D.

First printed in *Corrections Today,* a publication of the American Correctional Association, April 2005

Although it is a widely acknowledged variable to the success of offender reentry, the development, maintenance, and influence of community providers in the reentry process has become more paramount as releases from confinement continue to increase at record levels. In less than a decade alone, communities nationally have witnessed a double-digit percentage increase in the number of adults on parole from 1995 through 2003,[1] with nearly two-thirds of all offenders returning to prison within three years of their release.[2] Therefore, it is an obvious conclusion that more innovative strategies must be undertaken to engage community providers in an effort to establish both a conceptual and operational foundation for offender success.

Given the increasing number of offenders currently being supervised in the community, compounded with stagnant or declining budgets equating to fewer personnel, correctional leaders are being placed in the precarious situation of being almost dependent upon outside providers to jointly take ownership of the reentry process. This is not to say that the linkage between corrections and the community is something new to the field. On the contrary, the use of community providers such as churches, businesses, and social service agencies essentially has been imbedded in the corrections profession. Yet, the field still has a long road to travel to change the ideology of communities into taking a more significant role in the processes involved with re-integrating offenders back into society.

In effect, the burden no longer can be exclusively placed upon corrections to ensure that formerly incarcerated individuals become productive citizens. Correctional agencies should not be the only entity tackling this problem. For reentry to be a success, communities must become engaged and empowered to work collaboratively with corrections to provide guidance and direct assistance to released offenders. Correctional entities also should maintain a primary role in working with each community to facilitate change and to provide technical assistance when necessary. Similarly, corrections professionals must recognize that each community is unique and may expect ideas towards successful offender reentry to reflect that communities' priorities and values. The adage of "one glove fits all" simply will not work across diverse communities.

Dispersing Responsibility

Neither corrections nor communities can view reentry as being the sole responsibility of the other. From a historical perspective, communities by and large have ostensibly been comforted in the knowledge that the post-release supervision of offenders would act as a "safety net" for both the offender and themselves. For it was this point during an offender's supervision that determined whether successful reintegration was occurring.

However, significant increases in the number of released offenders coupled with limited resources clearly have weakened what was, and still is considered to be a vital link to offender rehabilitation. With more offenders also being released without any supervision, the safety net is rapidly diminishing to where the criminal justice system's influence on post-release behavior is tenuous. Because of the inverse nature of this relationship, where more offenders requiring greater need is met with less support and programming, a larger number of offenders are being returned to prison.[3] Thus, it becomes imperative for correctional leaders to work towards the development, maintenance, and influence of community providers to play a larger role than previously sought in reentry initiatives.

It is reasonably safe to portend that the benefits of engaging community entities in the reentry process can far exceed corrections officials' current realities in terms of reentry success. The dilemma that is faced, however, is the question of how to engage the community so that the potential for success is optimized. Though still evolving, the question of community engagement is being confronted across multiple fronts in Ohio that include cooperative efforts with businesses, prosocial support systems, and family reunification initiatives. Similar to the processes currently ongoing within the Ohio Department of Rehabilitation and Correction's thirty-two prisons, a comprehensive reentry plan within Ohio's communities is in place that encompasses a core set of programming focusing on employment opportunities, professional intervention for special needs offenders (for example, substance abuse), and social, familial, and faith-based interactions. Research has suggested that offenders who discontinue crime are socially bonded to family and/or significant others, show characteristics that include those that are embedded in structured routines, are socially bonded to family and/or significant others, and have used available resources and social support systems for their relationships while under supervision.[4]

What Works

It has been well established that providing opportunities to improve educational and work-related skills can reduce the risk of future offending.[5] Further, some have argued that employability is related to criminal involvement[6] considering that a significant number of offenders come to prison with poor work histories.[7] Therefore, it is vital that correctional agencies work with community organizations whose expertise involves employment readiness, workplace culture. and knowledge of job opportunities that commences at the outset of an offender's incarceration, thus preparing him or her for meaningful future endeavors. Although society maintains knowledge that the cost-benefit ratio of meaningful employment for offenders has positive, tangible outcomes over time (for example, reduction in crime, declining prison populations, decreased operating costs), community business leaders continue to review their bottom line in terms of human resources and cannot obviously afford to hire unqualified offenders. As such, the absence of skilled labor on the part of offenders reentering the community can create uncertainty and, in turn, unstable working habits.

Without the development of relevant job skills, offenders will find their ability to obtain sustainable employment challenging. Attaining sustainable employment and acceptance into the workforce can serve as a building block to connecting with the community. As with any member of society and particularly with released offenders, those gainfully employed are capable of taking care of themselves, their families, and are contributing members to the tax base of the community in which they reside. The fiscal burden of caring for the offender is now placed upon themselves and not on the community.

Traditionally, many employers have been reluctant to hire former offenders due to the perceived risks and potential public backlash to the company. However, corrections and the business community must work together to help overcome these barriers. For example, Cleveland's program, Providing Real Opportunities for Ex-Offenders to Succeed, includes workforce skills development, job placement, and federal incentives to employers who hire offenders. The program has shown tangible results with increases in both tax revenues and gross wages. These results are now leading to additional business participation.

Leveraging prosocial support through the community is another venue that aids in the reentry process as offenders attempt to reestablish connections to their support systems. As an increasing number of offenders begin to reenter the community, the importance of providing pro-social support through nonprofit groups or organizations, such as faith-based organizations, can help to alleviate the uncertainty prevalent in many newly released offenders. Developing relationships with community organizations to provide mentoring and peer support to offenders is an area that has shown promise and has recently gained support through the Serious and Violent Offender Reentry Initiative that includes the provision of mentoring services.

However, correctional agencies must be proactive in their approach to soliciting community organizations to participate in a reentry initiative. In Ohio, for example, agency staff attend community functions to provide education and to dispel misinformation about offenders entering their neighborhoods. As such, informed decisions can be made in relation to reentry participation. In the same regard, Ohio has developed "citizen circles" that include members of community organizations, faith-based groups, employment agencies, business and law enforcement, among others. The group meets on a monthly basis with the offender and his or her family or other support person to assist with the reintegration process. Members of the citizen circle address the offender's risk factors and relay their expectations for successful reentry. Concurrently, the offender is able to network with members for opportunities and to demonstrate his or her potential value as a community member.

Mending Families

The development of pro-social support systems within the community is also critical to the reentry process when the concern focuses on family reunification. It has become increasingly apparent that offenders have difficulty reentering the family structure they left behind prior to being incarcerated for any period of time. Family members and the offender change, as does the structure of their relationships. In many instances, children of the incarcerated have not seen their parent since they were incarcerated. Recent estimates by the Bureau of Justice Statistics suggest that 1.5 million children have at least one parent currently incarcerated.

The adjustment back into family life for an offender can create further problems that, if left unattended and without intervention, may produce negative outcomes that make other reentry initiatives ineffective. In essence, the success or failure of any single reentry initiative designed to impact a particular risk factor is not mutually exclusive to another and can determine the outcome of other initiatives geared towards the offender. In other words, if an offender is having a difficult time adjusting back into a relationship with his or her spouse or child, how engaged or encouraged will the offender be to successfully participate in an education or job skills program?

In Ohio, the Department of Rehabilitation and Correction and selected community partners have developed Family Life Centers and the Ohio Family Council to aid in the reunification process. A pilot project of the Family Life Centers, Children of Incarcerated Parents: Breaking the Cycle, provides services to the incarcerated offender and his or her family prior to and after release. The program is based on the premise that family relationships should be reestablished prior to reentry into the community. Similarly, the Ohio Family Council was established to address familial issues that develop and adopt practices that foster family reunification. Along with the offender and his or her immediate family, the Ohio Family Council includes family-counseling practitioners, nonprofit and interfaith organizations, and corrections personnel as well as other state agencies relevant to the offender's case.

Perhaps one of the most successful examples of community engagement into the reentry process has been the development of the reentry court, where Ohio was selected as one of nine states in 2000 to engage in a partnership between the Ohio Department of Rehabilitation and Correction and the Richland County Common Pleas Court. Paralleling the principles underlying drug courts, the Richland County Common Pleas Court is responsible for managing the return of offenders who have been released from prison into their community. The court uses its authority to apply graduated sanctions and positive reinforcement to support the offender's reintegration. An initial needs assessment is completed on each offender with a reentry court case manager periodically meeting with the individual, along with prison staff, to monitor the case plan to ensure the offender's needs and court orders are being fulfilled. While incarcerated, the offender is placed in programs consistent with his or her reentry plan. If programs dictated by the reentry plan are unavailable, the court case manager coordinates with community entities to have these needs addressed upon release. Parole and probation officers work jointly to monitor offenders once they return to the community and assist with helping them meet the program's requirements. Local law enforcement also participate as part of the team to enforce the conditions of release.

Corrections officials' understanding of the reentry process and of what works to assist offenders in becoming participating members of their respective community is still in its infancy, but appears promising. Reentry has certainly taken root in the philosophy of corrections, with communities now beginning to grasp the essential role they play in the process. There are obviously multiple pathways to engage communities in reentry, and this article has discussed only the surface of the many possibilities currently in operation. The community's role in corrections has become a necessary component and essential ingredient to the success of offender reentry. If developing viable community partnerships is aggressively pursued, correctional agencies will embrace the knowledge of the importance of establishing multiple means of working with and through the community to the extent that offenders will be more likely to experience successful transitions home.

ENDNOTES

[1] Glaze, L. E. and S. Palla. 2004. Probation and Parole in the United States, 2003. *Bureau of Justice Statistics Bulletin*. Washington, D.C.: U.S. Department of Justice, Office of Justice Programs.

[2] Petersilia, J. 2003. *When Prisoners Come Home: Parole and Prisoner Reentry*. New York: Oxford University Press.

[3] Wilkinson, R. A. 2001. Offender Reentry: A Storm Overdue. *Correctional Management Quarterly*. 5(3): 46-51.

[4] Laub, J. H. and R. Sampson. 2003. *Shared Beginnings, Divergent Lives: Delinquent Boys to Age 70*. Cambridge, Massachusetts.: Harvard University Press.

[5] Andrews, D. and J. Bonta. 1994. *The Psychology of Criminal Conduct*. Cincinnati: Anderson.

Wilson, D., C. Gallagher, and D. MacKenzie. 2000. A Meta-Analysis of Corrections-Based Education Vocation and Work Programs for Adult Offenders. *Journal of Research in Crime and Delinquency*. 37: 347-368.

[6] Andrews, D. and J. Bonta. 1994. Wilson, D. et al. 2000.

[7] Saylor, W. and G. Gaes. 1996. *PREP: Training Inmates through Industrial Work Participation and Vocational and Apprenticeship Instruction*. Washington, D.C.: U.S. Federal Bureau of Prisons.

Reginald A. Wilkinson, Ed.D, is past president of the American Correctional Association and former director of the Ohio Department of Rehabilitation and Correction.

Citizens' Circles: Community Reentry: Does Working in Prison Result in Greater Employment and Less Recidivism Upon Release?

Edward Rhine, John R. Matthews II,
Lee A. Sampson,
and Rev. Hugh Daley

First printed in *Corrections Today*, a publication of the American Correctional Association, August 2003

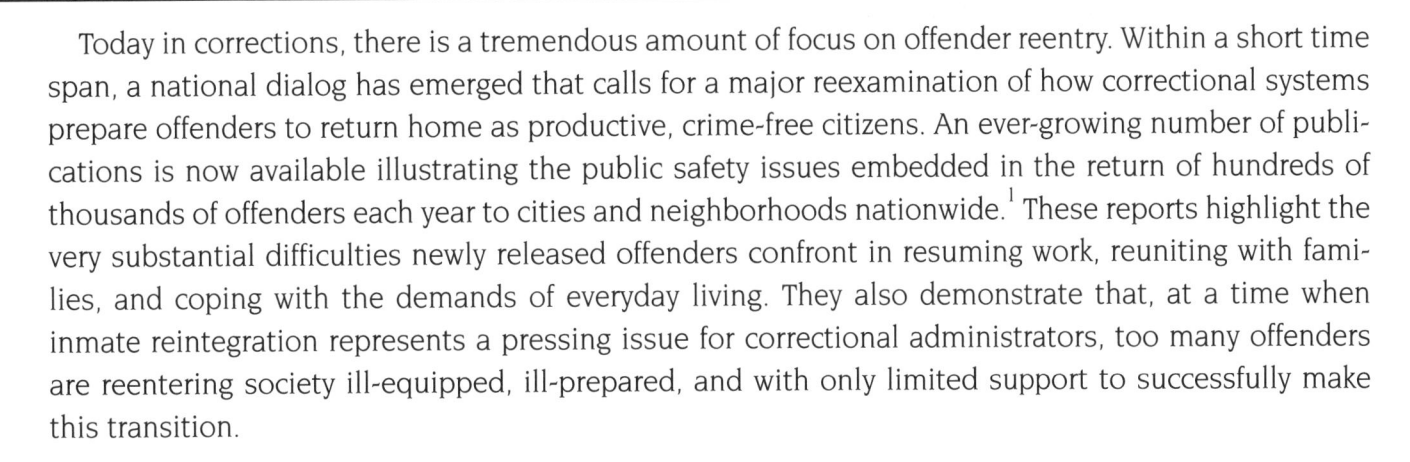

Today in corrections, there is a tremendous amount of focus on offender reentry. Within a short time span, a national dialog has emerged that calls for a major reexamination of how correctional systems prepare offenders to return home as productive, crime-free citizens. An ever-growing number of publications is now available illustrating the public safety issues embedded in the return of hundreds of thousands of offenders each year to cities and neighborhoods nationwide.[1] These reports highlight the very substantial difficulties newly released offenders confront in resuming work, reuniting with families, and coping with the demands of everyday living. They also demonstrate that, at a time when inmate reintegration represents a pressing issue for correctional administrators, too many offenders are reentering society ill-equipped, ill-prepared, and with only limited support to successfully make this transition.

Ohio, like many states, has embraced the myriad challenges associated with reentry. Last year, the Department of Rehabilitation and Correction issued a comprehensive report, *The Ohio Plan for Productive Offender Reentry and Recidivism Reduction*. The Ohio Department of Rehabilitation and Correction has adopted a new vision and mission governing offender reentry and at the core of Ohio Department of Rehabilitation and Correction's approach is the notion that reentry is a philosophy, not a program. Under the plan, reentry calls for a broad systems approach to managing offenders returning to the community. It requires the involvement of every phase of the correctional system beginning at reception, and continuing through to release and community supervision. It expresses a strong commitment to answering the question: What is needed to prepare this offender for successful reentry? This commitment is summarized succinctly in the slogan, "Reentry means going home to stay."

One of the key assumptions behind the Ohio plan is the recognition that community partnerships and collaboration are essential to ensuring successful offender reintegration. It is not possible for any correctional system acting alone to create effective and durable pathways to reentry. The links and connections that are forged with key stakeholders and individuals in the communities to which offenders return carry the potential to reinforce and sustain the reintegration prospects of ex-inmates. The active participation of citizens, as well as local agencies and groups with an interest in public safety, serves to augment the limited operational capacity of the correctional system.

The Ohio Department of Rehabilitation and Correction has long embraced community justice as a framework governing correctional practices in its institutions and parole regions. A community justice cabinet was created in 1997 to improve citizen satisfaction and provide guidance through the participation of victims, the community, and offenders in the process. In addition, the Adult Parole Authority has established community policing partnerships in several areas of the state. One of the department's major new initiatives under the Ohio plan that speaks directly to the importance of citizen involvement and community collaboration is the development of citizens' circles.

Citizens' Circles Development

Community members are often resistant to the idea of offenders living in their neighborhoods. As a result, offenders return to their neighborhoods with little or no support from local citizens. The public often relies on the justice system to supervise and monitor released offenders rather than taking an active role in the reintegration process. Yet, community support is vital for offenders leaving prison. Ex-inmates who make positive life changes while incarcerated but return to environments without guidance and support frequently resume old behavioral patterns that lead to new crimes. Offenders who feel accepted by their community and believe they are valued are less likely to re-offend. The formation of a citizens' circle contributes to this process. Within Ohio's plan, citizens' circles are community justice partnerships forged between the Ohio Department of Rehabilitation and Correction and communities within the state that promote prosocial interaction and offender accountability upon release.

A citizens' circle attempts to address the root causes contributing to offenders' commission of crimes, encourage local ownership of and solutions from the community itself, and achieve agreement on the responsibilities of offenders upon release. The process is based on peacekeeping, negotiation, and consensus-building among the parties involved that, according to the Department of Justice, draws from the principles of the Justice/Sentencing Circles established in Minnesota and Vermont. Community expectations are conveyed to offenders who work with circle members to reach agreement on the final outcomes to be accomplished through their participation. In essence, citizens' circles embrace local citizens and community agencies, alongside the Ohio Department of Rehabilitation and Correction, in decision-making and case management relative to offender rehabilitation and reentry.

Citizens' Circles in Operation

Offenders enter the circle on their own free will to seek restored citizenship. The circle reviews applications for membership from offenders who are incarcerated, those currently under community supervision, and from halfway houses or community-based correctional facilities. Prior to offenders attending their first meeting, circle coordinators conduct an in-depth interview with them. The information disclosed is verified before presenting the application to the entire circle membership. Circle coordinators are individuals drawn from parole or institution staff, most often supervision officers, case managers, or treatment counselors.

Circle members may accept offenders based on the following criteria:

- The circle application process has been completed.

- Responsibility has been accepted for the commission of the crime and the harm resulting from the offense.

- A plan of reconciliation has been developed.

- There is an expressed willingness to accept agreed upon circle recommendations.

- There is a commitment to take part in community service.

- There is a clear willingness to set goals focused on law-abiding and productive community behavior.

The acceptance of an offender into a circle, however, is not solely based on these criteria. The circle members can arrange a face-to-face interview to ask specific questions or to clarify information on the application. Once offenders have met with the circle members, nonapplication-based factors (for example, if offenders are viewed as insincere and/or untruthful) may be a cause for rejection. Once accepted, offenders must communicate their strengths, weaknesses, and needs to the circle to ensure that viable circle accountability plans may be negotiated and developed with the members. Circle accountability plans are formed in concert with parole supervision guidelines and may address:

- Job seeking

- Education

- Family issues

- Mental health

- Substance abuse

- Attitude

- Social interactions

- Community service

- Housing assistance

- Spiritual needs

- Designation of a community sponsor

The circle members meet on a regular basis to discuss offender progress, review and modify their accountability plans, interview new applicants, admit new members, and discharge successful or unsuccessful offenders. Circles involve the offenders, their support systems, victim advocacy groups, and community members.

Citizens' circles offer a powerful forum for community collaboration by providing an opportunity for citizens to communicate their expectations for successful reentry. They also help offenders recognize the harm their criminal behavior has caused others, especially their victims, and develop a viable plan of action to promote responsible citizenship. Circle members inform offenders that society is willing to accept them as restored members and believes that they have paid their debt. Importantly, the circle helps offenders understand that acceptance back into their community requires the fulfillment of certain obligations and commitments. Citizens' circle objectives are centered on opening the lines of communication between citizens and offenders returning home. They foster equality for the parties, promote a problem-solving environment, and encourage mutual respect among the participants.

Looking Ahead

Citizens' circles will play an integral role as the Ohio Department of Rehabilitation and Correction moves forward under the Ohio plan to create stronger links with community partners that support reentry. Since the inception of the first circles in several communities in north central Ohio, they have been, or are in the process of being, implemented in each of the seven parole regions in the state. The Ohio Department of Rehabilitation and Correction envisions that citizens' circles will eventually become a presence in every major city throughout Ohio. In the larger metropolitan areas, citizens' circles will target certain neighborhoods and areas to which significant concentrations of offenders return.

Parole officers in Ohio, as elsewhere, are currently faced with large workloads and fewer programmatic options from which to draw. These conditions present a challenge to field staff and correctional administrators to find new models for effectively supervising offenders in the community. Citizens' circles present an innovative approach to involving the community in effective community-based offender supervision. They enhance offender supervision by securing citizen involvement in offender case management. Through hands-on contact with offenders, community members become more active in reentry, and develop an increased knowledge of the correctional system. They also develop a better understanding of the correctional process and the issues offenders face as they transition from prison to the community. Offenders themselves develop a more positive attitude as they return to their communities and are provided opportunities to give back and to become productive members of the community.

As the expansion of citizens' circles continues, and the lessons that are learned are factored into improvements in the process, community safety will be strengthened. It is expected that offenders participating in citizens' circles compared with nonparticipants will show reduced rates of re-offending, lower rates of unemployment, higher completion rates for provider-based programming, and increased compliance with supervision conditions.

Conclusion

Under the Ohio plan, citizens' circles are designed to address the multitude of challenges that offenders face upon their return to the community. Such circles draw on the social capital provided by linking a network of community-based partnerships with individual citizens and local agencies that have a direct stake in the outcomes that are achieved. Citizens' circles seek to create and sustain collaborative relationships that are able to more effectively supervise offenders, impose greater leverage and accountability over them, and contribute to greater public safety in the process. The operation of citizens' circles incorporates the greater operational and resource capacities of local communities in responding to the crime problem. Ultimately, citizens' circles recognize that it takes a community to successfully transition offenders home.

ENDNOTES

[1] Petersilia, J. 2003. *When Prisoners Come Home: Parole And Prisoner Reentry*. New York: Oxford University Press.

[2] Petersilia, J. and J. Travis. 2001. From Prison to Society: Managing the Challenges of Prisoner Reentry. *Crime and Delinquency*. 47(3): 291-485. Thousand Oaks, Calif.: Sage Publications.

[3] Rhine, E. E. 2001. Rethinking Prisoner Reentry: Implications for Corrections. *Corrections Management Quarterly*. 5(3): V-VIII. Frederick, Maryland: Aspen Publications.

[4] Travis, J., A. L. Solomon and M. Waul. 2001. *From Prison to Home: The Consequences of Prisoner Reentry*. Washington, D.C.: Urban Institute.

Ed Rhine, Ph.D., is chief of the Office of Offender Reentry and Correctional Best Practices for the Ohio Department of Rehabilitation and Correction. John R. Matthews II is regional services coordinator for the Offender Services Network of the Adult Parole Authority-Mansfield Region, Ohio Department of Rehabilitation and Correction. Lee A. Sampson is regional administrator of the Adult Parole Authority-Mansfield Region. The Rev. Hugh Daley is deputy warden of the Toledo Correctional Institution of the Ohio Department of Rehabilitation and Correction.

Adding the Crime Victims to the Reentry Equation

Peter A. Michaud

First printed in *Corrections Today*, a publication of the American Correctional Association, April 2003

Many respected, corrections professionals find it easy to simply acknowledge that crimes have victims. At the same time, these professionals find it difficult to see benefits for corrections becoming more victim-centered in philosophy and practice. This may reflect longstanding views of many experienced correctional staff seeking to protect the public and promote offender accountability. However, with today's renewed focus on offender reentry into the community, there is an important opportunity for additional focus on crime victims' needs and interests. Doing so can improve corrections professionals' public safety role as they encourage released offenders to be responsible citizens.

Many of today's policymakers and justice professionals recognize the importance of continually improving systemic responses to crime. Although a realistic solution for eliminating crime may never be found, there are ways to continue improving the correctional response to crime on behalf of victims, offenders and all citizens.

Responding To the Harm

In its simplest form, crime is behavior that harms someone. It is easy to acknowledge that most crimes have victims. Additionally, most crimes are deemed serious enough to be prosecuted by the state on behalf of its citizens. In corrections, most crimes are addressed in ways that are intended to correct. Correctional efforts to correct are generally viewed as a combination of punishment and opportunities for offender change. Equally critical to success is better integration of individual and systemwide reentry initiatives with a sensible understanding of crime impacts and resulting victim needs.

Although different correctional jurisdictions vary in mission and scope, each strives to respond to factors influenced by the offenders' histories and actions. Prior record, instant offense, and substance abuse are some of the typical factors being addressed. As inmates are poised to reenter communities, much attention is focused on their individual needs. Employability, training, and community-based support are critical for helping offenders successfully reintegrate into the community as responsible citizens.

Although crime can be simply defined as harmful behavior, the responses to crime tend to focus on much more complex factors. Addressing substance abuse, mental health, and employability are examples of factors that have challenged correctional systems for many years. Another challenge is for corrections professionals to continually improve their responses to the harmful behavior itself. To successfully respond, corrections professionals must deal with the harm the offenders have caused. To do that, they must actively inform and involve the people who were harmed—the crime victims and community members.

A victim-centered approach to offender reentry does not merely acknowledge that crimes have victims, nor does it dodge correctional responsibility for public safety and offender accountability. When properly implemented, such an approach enhances safety and accountability. Victims of crime are a central part of the public to be protected.

Being victim-centered promotes safety of the people already hurt and usually most anxious about the offenders' return to the community. It also encourages offenders to accept full responsibility for the harm they caused. Citizens personally experiencing the impact of crime bring an extraordinary perspective to correctional agencies striving for public safety. Crime victims have dealt with the offenders and the crime with truly firsthand knowledge and pain. If the aim is to correct or to help the offender "make it right," then the person harmed by the offending behavior has much to offer.

When addressing offenders' accountability, it is important to consider to whom they should be held accountable. As offending behavior harms real people, offenders should be responsible to those same people: crime victims and other community members. For example, victim-impact programs for all offenders can help them learn, understand, and empathize with the physical, emotional and financial harms experienced by crime victims, families, and communities. Identifying the means for making amends to victims, such as restitution and apologies, helps hold offenders directly accountable to those harmed. Opportunities for meaningful community or public service work can provide a means for offenders to give back to the community and victim-service organizations.

Ideally, effective offender reintegration into the community begins as soon as an individual enters a correctional facility. Connecting classification, facility programming, and release planning, as well as community corrections and community-based supports, help promote successful offender reentry.

Classification staff require not simply knowledge of inmate needs, but also a practical understanding of prison programming. Corrections program staff and support agencies in the community must see the interconnectivity of each other's efforts in encouraging changed behavior by offenders. Similarly, reentry, community corrections, and victim-services professionals must mutually understand inmate progress during incarceration and expectations upon release. Assuring such connectivity is challenging. Moving towards practices that address the victimization factor is no less challenging. All players in the reentry equation must see the advantages of close collaboration and communication—not for their own gain, but for the benefit of changing offender behavior and preventing further victimization in the community.

Addressing Crime: Victims' Rights

Various statutory or constitutional crime victims' rights have been instituted in each state. Typically, these include a victim's right for fairness, respect, participation and input, safety, information, notification of offender status, and restitution. When correctional agencies honor these rights before and during offender reentry, the interests and needs of victims are supported. They can honor these rights by understanding and supporting the following victims' needs:

Fairness and Respect. Crime victims want, and are entitled to, fairness and respect. They are not generally seeking to "have it their way and only their way." They want their concerns known and their voices heard. They need and deserve empathy from skilled corrections professionals who are knowledgeable about the impact of crime and respectful of the crime victims' experiences.

Participation and Input. In the past, crime victims were typically viewed solely as witnesses needed to prove a crime, thus, helping the state achieve an offender's conviction. Today, more and more policymakers and justice professionals view crime victims as critical players in efforts to promote a just response to crime. Victim statements about the impact of crime, including input about sentence and release decisions, should be actively solicited, and reasonably honored. Appropriate victim participation in decisions about inmate release is a critical element of successful offender reentry. For example, the victim should be invited to inform the releasing and supervising authorities about the harm caused by the crime and how the offender might help "make it right."

Safety and Reasonable Protection. Like all citizens, crime victims want to be safe. Yet, unlike all citizens, those who have been victimized have certain concerns about safety and tend to focus on the harm that they were caused and the fear they feel about being revictimized. As offenders approach reentry, victims' anxieties understandably escalate. Victim safety is central to offender reintegration within the community. Reasonable correctional and community efforts to protect the victim are vital components of successful offender reentry planning. Support for victims in developing safety plans and identifying community resources can be helpful in addressing anxiety about an inmate's release.

Notification and Information. Timely and accurate information is fundamental to crime victims' rights. For interested victims, being informed about correctional programs and processes is helpful as they continue to recover from the long-term impact of crime. A general understanding of how offenders are managed in correctional facilities and communities is useful information. A little knowledge goes a long way in helping crime victims on the road to recovery. Formal notification of inmate custody changes, particularly release to the community, is a priority. Availability of victim service and other trained staff is another important resource needed for effective victim support.

Restitution. To be truly accountable for their crimes, offenders must recognize their responsibility for repairing the harm they caused by their behavior. Nationwide, the financial impact of crime on victims, survivors and communities is staggering. For some, the resulting out-of-pocket expenses, such as medical costs, lost wages, and funeral expenses, can be devastating. As reentry plans are developed, specific strategies for offenders' timely and complete payment of victim restitution must be assured. State-based victim compensation funds are also an important resource for victims of violent crime when restitution is not forthcoming from the offenders.

Roles and Relationships

Throughout the nation, correctional efforts to implement and support offender reentry differ in magnitude and design. Each model promotes collaboration within and beyond the correctional agency. While delivery of reentry services may vary with each offender's needs (for example, job training, housing, education, batterers' intervention, and mental health and/or substance abuse treatment), a common denominator for all offenders is that their behavior has harmed someone. In corrections, staff can do more than merely acknowledge that there are victims. With the understanding that each crime forces the victims and community into a painful relationship with offenders, corrections professionals can promote responses, which address the problem of harmful behavior and its impact. Programs teaching the many impacts of crime can improve empathy. Offenders with greater empathy are more likely to feel responsible for the harms they caused and seek ways to make it right. Financial restitution, sincere apologies, and community service are some examples to consider.

With enhanced focus on that one factor shared by all offenders, correctional responses to crime can best meet victim and community needs and better promote offender responsibility. To succeed at holding offenders accountable and preventing recidivism, corrections professionals can lead collaborative efforts in educating offenders about the harm they caused, as well as how to make proper amends to their victims and their communities. Enforcing victims' rights during the correctional phase of the justice system is no less important than doing so prior to conviction and sentencing. Indeed, it is during this stage that many victims can move closer to reasonable recovery from crime's emotional and financial impacts. Effective correctional programming and community support play a significant role in promoting that recovery.

Crime victims and survivors deserve a seat at the decision-making table when the justice system strives to correct offenders. Reparation of victims should be sought when striving for reintegration of offenders. In addition, when seeking to improve the competency of offenders, crime victims' capacity for improving offender understanding of the real impact of crime on real people also should be considered. When endeavoring to hold offenders accountable, corrections professionals should also ask themselves, and remind offenders, accountable to whom?

As corrections professionals focus on offender reentry, they must do more than simply acknowledge that there are victims. While some in corrections do not view public safety as a business, more are recognizing the value of continually improving correctional responses to crime. Bringing the focus towards all of corrections' "customers," including crime victims, can improve the profession's public safety role and strengthen efforts in supporting released offenders in their transition towards more responsible citizenship.

Peter A. Michaud is the victim services coordinator for the New Hampshire Department of Corrections. He can be reached at (603) 271-1937; pmichaud@nhdoc.state.nh.us.

Correctional Industries Preparing Inmates for Reentry: Recidivism and Postrelease Employment

Cindy J. Smith, Ph.D.,
Jennifer Bechtel, M.S.,
and Angie Patrick, M.S.

Introduction

These preliminary findings summarize the first national review of the recidivism and postrelease employment effects of the Prison Industries Enhancement Certification Program (PIECP) engaging state prison inmates in private sector jobs since 1979. The report is based on results from a records' review of outcomes for three matched samples, each of approximately 2,200 inmates, released from five PIECP states between 1996 and 2001. It examines whether sampled inmates participating in PIECP return to prison less frequently (for example, recidivism effects) or enjoy more successful employment (for example, employment effects) than otherwise similar inmates who either participated only in traditional prison industries (traditional industries) or were involved in other-than-work-(other work opportunities) activities while in prison.

Site and Sample Selection

A cluster sampling strategy was used for site selection. The selection process included all major U.S. geographic regions that represented rural versus urban populations. The sample selection included all inmates, both male and female, in five states who worked in PIECP (n=2,408) and were released between January 1996 and June 2001, which permits at least one-year follow-up and a maximum of eight years.

The next step was to answer the question: To whom should we compare? There are two options. First, a random sample of all inmates could be selected and compared to PIECP participants. But, surely PIECP participants would do better because they represent a specific type of inmate. The selection criteria to be eligible for PIECP separate these inmates from others. For example, typical PIECP participant would be disciplinary-report free for six months prior to obtaining a PIECP job and remain report free during employment.

The second option was to use matched samples from those eligible to work in PIECP. The selected control groups (for example, traditional industries, other work opportunities) are comparable or matched to PIECP participants. Therefore, the PIECP sample is representative of PIECP. The traditional industries and other work opportunities control groups are not representative of all traditional industries or all other work opportunities. They are representative of those who match inmates who were hired into the PIECP program.

What does this mean in practice? The study results do not address overall traditional industries or other work opportunities success or failure. It only discusses success or failure for the type of inmate who is matched to PIECP workers. We cannot compare traditional industries or other work opportunities results to the general population of all traditional industries or all other work opportunities results found in the literature. We do not know at this time the percentage of the general prison population that matches PIECP participants.

Findings

The preliminary findings of this research are that state prison inmates who worked in open-market jobs in the PIECP were found to be significantly more successful in postrelease employment and in reducing recidivism than either inmates working in traditional industries or involved in other work opportunities. Results for traditional industries and other work opportunities, while significantly different than PIECP inmates, did not significantly differ from each other. Throughout the analysis traditional industries and other work opportunities releasees had very similar results. On the contrary, the findings for the PIECP releasees stood alone. Based on quarterly survival rates, the slope of the survival curve indicated that the PIECP releasees were employed significantly more quickly after release from prison than either traditional industries or those in other work opportunities and remained employed significantly longer. In addition, the slope of the survival curve for recidivism indicated that the PIECP participants recidivated significantly more slowly and less frequently as measured by any of the three measures (arrest, conviction, or incarceration). The details of these findings follow.

Research Question 1: Does PIECP participation increase post-release employment compared to traditional industries work and other work opportunities? Under what conditions and for which inmates is it more effective?

Table 1: Release to employment duration descriptive measures

Total sample size	6,821 people		
Never employed during follow-up	1,494 (21.9%)		
Range of time from release to employment	5-29 quarters		
	PIE	Traditional industries	Other work opportunities
Never employed after release	404 (16.8%)	485 (24.0%)	608 (25.2%)
Employed first quarter after release	1,324 (55.0%)	802 (40.0%)	963 (40.0%)

Table 2: Postrelease employment duration—descriptive measures (n=6,821)

Characteristic	N=		Percent
Range of time employed	0-30 quarters		(std. dev.)
	PIECP	Traditional industries	Other work opportunities
Never employed	400 (16.6%)	476 (23.7%)	600 (24.9%)
Employed continuously 1yr + (n=2885)	1,171 (48.6%)	798 (39.8%)	916 (38.0%)
Employed continuously 3 yrs + (n=778)	329 (13.7%)	207 (10.3%)	242 (10.0%)

This research question is answered through a variety of measures. Based on a panel of experts' and states' guidance, measures for success include the following criteria: 1) time to first employment after release, 2) duration of first employment, and 3) wage rate during the follow-up period. Details of each analysis are described in the following section.

Length of time to employment

The first measure of success for releasees was the amount of time that lapsed between release and employment. This included a comparison of PIECP, traditional industries, and other work opportunities to each other to determine which group obtained employment faster.

Based on the survival analysis, PIECP participants obtained postrelease employment significantly faster than either traditional industries or other work opportunities (*see* Table 1). The steepest slope indicates that comparably more releasees than other groups have found employment. Approximately 24 and 25 percent of the traditional industries and other work opportunities releasees did not have reported earnings, whereas less than 17 percent of the PIECP's did not have earnings over the course of follow-up (see Table 1).

The second measure of success relative to postrelease employment is the length of the time between first employment and the first full quarter without reported earnings (employment) (see Table 2). A sequence of jobs or multiple jobs in one quarter (in other words, changing employment, working two jobs) is not counted as a loss of employment. Unemployment within a quarter remains counted as employment so long as there are reported earnings within the quarter, and the releasee may be unemployed for large parts of the quarter. Hypothetically, a person only needs to work some part of one day in a quarter to be considered employed for that quarter.

The postrelease duration measures are presented in Table 2. PIECP releasees are more likely to be continuously employed than either those in traditional industries or other work opportunities. Of the 2,408 available PIECP participants, 48.6 percent of them were employed for one year or more continuously and 13.7 percent of them were employed for three years or more continuously, whereas 39.8 percent and 38.0 percent of the traditional industries and other work opportunities releasees, respectively, were continuously employed for one year and approximately 10 percent of both traditional industries and other work opportunities groups were continuously employed for over three years. Because the follow-up period varies across the 5.5 years of postrelease review, some releasees were released less than two years. Therefore, the survival analysis provides a better description of the findings than the periodic time series analysis.

Last, wages earned by the sample were examined. On average, PIECP participants earned higher wages and had reported earnings during more quarters. Approximately 55 percent of the releasees earned at an hourly rate over the quarter that averaged less than the federal minimum wage during the postrelease follow-up period. It is not likely that the releasees were earning less than minimum wage. It is more likely that the sample were under-employed (in other words, working part time or working intermittently).

In addition, there is a significant difference between PIECP and traditional industries, PIECP and other work opportunities, and other work opportunities and traditional industries based on the t test on the amount of wages earned.

Table 3: Wages earned postrelease

	PIECP	traditional industries	other work opportunities
Wages earned (mean)	$43,796	$31,377	$27,138
# quarters employed at least one day (mean)	8.7 quarters	8.2 quarters	7.7 quarters

Table 4: Duration from release to arrest descriptive measures

Total sample size	6,751[1]
No post-release arrests	3,120 (55.1%)
Range from release to arrest	1-2,519 days

	PIECP	traditional industries	other work opportunities
No post-release arrest	1,412 (59.4%)	1,050 (52.8%)	1,258 (52.3%)
Success rate for one year (no post-release arrest during 1st year)	1,940 (81.6%)	1,512 (76.0%)	1,790 (75.0%)

[1] Law enforcement records were not available for 68 people of the 6,819 sample. Therefore, recidivism analyses are based on a maximum of 6,751.

Research Question 2: Does PIECP participation reduce recidivism as compared to traditional industries work or other work opportunities? Under what conditions and for which inmates is it more effective?

The analysis for recidivism is similar to postrelease employment. Recidivism is measured in the three traditional ways: new arrest, conviction, and incarceration. Technical violations were not measured as a new arrest. Survival analysis measures how long a releasee is in the free world community until he or she recidivated. The terminal event for the analysis may be an arrest, conviction, or incarceration. At that time, the individual is removed from further analysis. Therefore, this measure does not take into account future free world time or additional recidivism measures. This analysis technique

Table 5: Duration from release to conviction descriptive measures

Total sample size			6,751 people
Never convicted after release			4,288 (76%)
Range of time from release to conviction			6-2,724 days

	PIECP	traditional industries	other work opportunities
Never convicted	1,841 (77.8%)	1,484 (74.7%)	1,740 (73.2%)

Table 6: Duration of time from release to incarceration descriptive measures

Total sample size			6,751 people
Never incarcerated after release			5,195 (91.8%)
Range of time from release to incarceration			12-1,940 days

	PIECP	traditional industries	other work opportunities
Never incarcerated	2,209 (93.0%)	1,789 (89.9%)	2,119 (88.9%)

Table 7: Success

Measure of success	Finding
1) Time to first employment after release	PIECP participants obtain employment significantly faster
2) Duration of first employment	PIECP participants retain the first employment significantly longer
3) Wage rate during the follow-up period	PIECP participants earn more wages and higher wages
4) Time from release to first arrest	PIECP participants are arrested at a slower rate than other groups.
5) Time from release to first conviction	PIECP participants are convicted at a slower rate than other groups.
6) Time from release to first incarceration	PIECP participants are incarcerated at a slower rate than other groups

allows the survival curve to measure the percentage of those who are still in the free world at the end of each interval for the first recidivism event. Recidivism is measured in units of days.

The three measurements are based on the recidivism definition debates over the years. One school of thought is that the number of arrests overcount crime. Others think that convictions are only incidents that can be proven in court, thereby undercounting crime. And, finally, others think that measuring reincarceration is best because prison should be responsible for reducing prison stays.

Arrest

This matched sample of releasees has relatively low recidivism rates. The average amount of time from release to first arrest is approximately 500 days, suggesting that many (80 percent) of the releasees were arrest free at the end of the first year. Almost 59 percent of those in PIE successfully reentered society, whereas approximately 52 percent of the traditional industries and other work opportunities were not arrested during the follow-up period. The rate of success at the end of the first year is high for all three groups; 81.6 percent of PIECP, and 76 percent of traditional industries, and 75 percent other work opportunities did not get arrested in the first year postrelease.

Convictions

Between 73.2 and 77.8 percent of the releasees remained conviction free at the end of the follow-up period (*see* Table 5). PIECP releasees stay conviction free longer than traditional industries or other work opportunities releasees during the follow-up period. Traditional industries and other work opportunities releasees exhibit little difference. The percentage of those who are conviction free postrelease also continues to decline until about the fourth year.

Incarcerations

Between 88.9 and 93.0 percent of the releasees remained incarceration free at the end of the follow-up period (*see* Table 6). PIECP releasees stay incarceration free longer than traditional industries or other work opportunities releasees during the follow-up period. Traditional industries and other work opportunities releasees exhibit little difference.

Summary

Based on the cluster sampling across five states and forty-six prisons, with a matched sample of 6,827 releasees between January 1, 1996 and June 30, 2001, PIECP participants reenter society more successfully than traditional industries or other work opportunities releasees. Success was defined using seven criteria (*see* Table 7). The survival analysis consistently demonstrates that PIECP participants perform in a significantly different way than traditional industries or other work opportunities releasees.

Cindy J. Smith, Ph.D., is the director of the Criminal Justice Graduate Program at the University of Baltimore. Jennifer Bechtel, M.S. and Angie Patrick, M.S., are research associates with the Schaefer Center for Public Policy at the University of Baltimore.

Releasing Inmates with Mental Illness and Co-Occurring Disorders into the Community

Lance Couturier, Ph.D.,
Frederick Maue, Ph.D.,
and Catherine McVey, M.A.

Editor's Note: A longer version of this article was published in the Jail Suicide/Mental Health Update, a joint project of the National Center on Institutions and Alternatives and the National Institute of Corrections, U.S. Department of Justice. This version was printed in Corrections Today, a publication of the American Correctional Association, April 2005.

In his 2004 State of the Union address, President George Bush proposed a four-year, $300 million initiative for offender reentry into the community. He asserted that "America is the land of the second chance, and when the gates of the prison open, the path ahead should lead to a better life." However, many inmates with mental illness encounter serious obstacles that prevent them from finding that better life.[1]

These obstacles are highlighted in the settlement of the Brad H. v. New York City class-action lawsuit in which New York City agreed to provide mentally ill inmates with treatment and other supportive services when they are released from the city prisons. The plaintiffs charged that the prisons routinely discharged offenders with mental illness into impoverished neighborhoods without adequate release plans, government benefits, housing, or other services. The prisons allegedly released offenders near subway stations between 2 and 6 a.m. with $1.50 and two subway tokens. The plaintiffs argued that failure to provide discharge planning to inmates with mental illness increases the risk that this group will relapse, engage in aggressive acts harmful to others, attempt or commit suicide, be unable to care for themselves, become homeless, and ultimately, be rearrested and returned to jail.[2]

New York City agreed to provide psychiatric treatment, including outpatient treatment, and medication needed to maintain stability after release, assistance obtaining housing and access to and, in cases where the inmate is indigent, the means to pay for those services. This would be a monumental task for correctional agencies across the county considering the following data.

The number of offenders with mental illness is staggering. According to recent Department of Justice estimates, approximately 700,000 adults with mental illness entered U.S. jails, and approximately 75 percent of these individuals suffered from co-occurring disorders, particularly substance abuse.

Also, these offenders may display multiple health and mental health problems due to their lifestyles, which frequently include transient behavior, financial instability, and high-risk behaviors such as intravenous drug use, smoking, and multiple sex partners. Most offenders do not have health insurance and lack supportive, positive, and enduring relationships, which contribute to their emotional and health instability.

Finally, the offenders are reentering communities where the mental health delivery system failed them in the first place. The shortage of community-based mental health services is epidemic. Community agencies that may be available often distance themselves from working with offenders and display reluctance to accept clients with criminal records. Frequently, offenders display excesses in bizarre, unusual, and aggressive behaviors, and deficits in self-care skills.

Discharging from the Pennsylvania Department of Corrections

The Pennsylvania Department of Corrections comprises 26 prisons housing more than 40,000 inmates. Approximately 18 percent of the offenders carry a psychiatric diagnosis, and a subset of approximately 4 percent of the population is rated seriously mentally ill (in other words, they display "a substantial disorder of thought or mood that significantly impairs judgment, behavior capacity to recognize reality or cope with the ordinary demands of life," according to the Department of Corrections' official definition). The department tracks the inmates with mental illness through an automated mental health/mental retardation tracking system. The Department of Corrections compared parole and max-out data for mental health/mental retardation inmates and non-mental health/mental retardation inmates during the twelve-month period from April 2002 to May 2003.

The data show that higher proportions of inmates with mental illness and serious mental illness are more likely to serve their full sentences rather than receive parole, as indicated by the following statistics:

- Inmates with no mental health history were paroled 81.7 percent of the time (n = 4,320) and maxed out 18 percent of the time (n = 969)

- Offenders with a mental health history, but who no longer were considered mentally ill, were paroled 73.7 percent of the time (n = 547) and maxed out 26.3 percent of the time (n = 195)

- Inmates diagnosed with mental illness were paroled 65.3 percent of the time (n = 466) and maxed out 34.7 percent of the time (n = 248)

- Inmates diagnosed with nonserious mental illness were paroled 45.1 percent of the time (n = 78) and maxed out 54.9 percent of the time (n = 95)

Preparation behind Walls

During the past ten years, the department has enhanced the continuity-of-care policies and procedures for inmates with mental illness and co-occurring disorders, and developed programs, described below, to assist inmates with reentry.

Continuity-of-Care Policy for Offenders Retuning to the Community through Parole or Maxing Out. Department of Correction's staff collaborated with other agencies, including the Office of Mental Health and the Pennsylvania Board of Probation and Parole, to develop reentry protocols for inmates with mental illness and co-occurring disorders who either will be paroled in the community, or are unlikely to receive parole, and hence serve their full sentence. The policy requires the facility interdisciplinary mental health treatment team (composed of the facility chief psychologist, psychiatrist, health care administrator, unit management staff, drug and alcohol treatment specialist, and custody staff representative) to meet twelve months prior to the inmate's release, and again six months prior to release, to conduct continuity-of-care planning. The protocol outlines procedures for:

- Obtaining a release of information from the inmate

- Contacting community mental health/mental retardation resources in the inmate's community

- Completing entitlement applications for various benefits to which the inmate might be entitled (for example, medical assistance, veterans benefits, Temporary Assistance to Needy Families, and supplemental security income)

- Arranging civil commitments for clients who meet involuntary commitment criteria

- Notifying law enforcement authorities regarding the release of inmates who were considered dangerous (but not committable)

- Providing inmates with a thirty-day supply of medication

The policy is consistent with both the American Correctional Association and the National Commission on Correctional Health Care standards that mandate correctional settings to show written policy, procedure and practice to provide continuity of care from admission to discharge from the facility, including referral to community care when that is needed.

Community Orientation and Reintegration Program. The Community Orientation and Reintegration program is a two-phase program designed to facilitate inmates' transition from the prison environment to their home community. The program provides for an individualized, targeted approach based on the inmate's risk factors. The first phase of the program is completed in the prison during the several weeks prior to discharge and addresses the critical issues of parole responsibilities, employment preparation, vocational evaluation, personal finances, substance abuse education, Alcoholics Anonymous/Narcotics Anonymous meetings, housing, family and parenting, mental health, life skills, antisocial attitudes, and community (give back) services. The program's second phase includes two weeks of programming in one of the community corrections centers, which are described later in this article. Phase 2 prepares the inmate for a gradual return to family and community during the four- to six-week program. Staff of the community corrections centers, Pennsylvania Board of Probation and Parole and Department of Corrections community corrections determine the date the inmate is released from the community corrections center. Where necessary, program procedures are modified to meet the needs of offenders with special needs.

Model Collaborative Partnership Established with County Mental Health/Mental Retardation Administrators in Philadelphia and Allegheny Counties. The Department of Corrections developed special collaborative relationships with the mental health/mental retardation agencies in Philadelphia and Allegheny (Pittsburgh) counties, which receive approximately half of the offenders (40 percent and 10 percent, respectively) who reenter the community. In 2000, the Philadelphia mental health/mental retardation office approached the Department of Corrections to help the city agency develop a database of Philadelphia inmates with mental illness who were incarcerated in the Department of Corrections and the dates they were returning to the city. The department provides a list of mental health/mental retardation roster inmates who will max out in the next twelve months to assist the counties in identifying aftercare resources. In some cases, Philadelphia mental health/mental retardation staff visit the facilities to review records, discuss the case with Department of Corrections staff members, and interview the inmate.

The mental health/mental retardation agency in Allegheny County also provides "in-reach" services in which caseworkers visit all twenty-six Department of Corrections facilities to review the treatment records and interview the inmates and the Department of Corrections staff. Moreover, Pittsburgh caseworkers also pick up the inmate at the prison on his or her discharge date and escort the inmate back to the city to obtain housing, make final arrangements for entitlement benefits, and/or buy clothes.

The collaborative partnerships with Philadelphia and Pittsburgh mental health/mental retardation agencies address half of the Department of Corrections' reentry problems; however, the department houses inmates from sixty-five other, mostly rural, counties in the state. Mental health treatment resources are scarcer in rural counties, and mental health/mental retardation agencies are more often reluctant to provide services to offenders returning to their communities, probably because in many cases the county resources are strained to meet the needs of mental health/mental retardation consumers in the community who are not involved with the law enforcement or court systems.

FReD Program for Females. In 2000, the Department of Corrections obtained a federal grant to establish the Forensic Community Re-entry and Development project, which is located in Pennsylvania's largest women's facility, the State Correctional Institution at Muncy. Muncy houses the most seriously mentally ill females in the system. Most of the women on the mental health/mental retardation roster also suffer from co-occurring substance abuse disorders and many have mental retardation. The women are placed in the Forensic Community Reentry and Development program twelve months prior to release. The Muncy mental health staff evaluate the female offenders with special needs and assign a community placement specialist who works with the inmates to prepare them for community living, help them develop a reentry plan that addresses their needs, and identify and establish contact with resources for mental health/mental retardation treatment, substance abuse programming, housing, and other services that will be needed in the community. The grant includes monies for subsidized housing as well.

Specialized Community Living Programs

Inmates with mental illness are closely supervised for years, and they are provided mental health services that are typically superior to those that they received prior to their incarceration. The offenders are well-protected from more predatory inmates, and their time is highly structured. When they reenter the community, they will move from two to six hours of free time per day to twenty-four hours of free time per day, with substantially less supervision. To facilitate the transition, the Department of Corrections operates an extensive system of community corrections centers (halfway houses) across the state to transition inmates from institutional life back into the community. Department staff operate fourteen community corrections centers, and vendors run approximately fifty centers. In the past five years, the Department of Corrections has begun to fund community corrections centers for special needs offenders. So far, the Department of Corrections has sponsored the development of specialized transitional community corrections centers for inmates with mental illness and substance abuse problems in Philadelphia, Erie, and Pittsburgh, which help inmates reenter the communities in the counties located in and around those three cities. Examples of these centers are presented below.

FIR-St Program. In 1999, the Department of Corrections funded the Forensic Integration and Recovery-State (FIR-St) Program to transition inmates with mental illness and co-occurring disorders back into the Philadelphia five-county area. The Forensic Integration and Recovery-State is a twenty-five-bed program for men and women, which accepts referrals from the Department of Corrections and the Pennsylvania Board of Probation and Parole. The unit employs a modified therapeutic community treatment model, and where there are parole violations, the model employs graduated parole sanctions, whereby minor infractions of parole rules are dealt with within the community, rather than by bringing the offender back into the prison.

Coleman Center. The Coleman Center is a twenty-bed unit of mentally ill male offenders returning to the Philadelphia County area. The center houses the same clientele as the Forensic Integration and Recovery-State program; however, it can also serve as a "halfway" back program, in which inmates who have encountered problems in the community can return briefly to the halfway house, rather than be reincarcerated. Based on the success of the Forensic Integration and Recovery-State and Coleman Center programs in Philadelphia, similar programs are being planned in Allegheny County.

CROMISA Programs. In 1999, the Pennsylvania Board of Probation and Parole, and the Office of Health initiated the Community Re-Integration of Offenders with Mental Illness and Substance Abuse (CROMISA) programs for parolees returning to the Erie County area. The establishment of a second program in Allegheny County followed this. The focus of the CROMISA programs is to treat primary serious substance abuse disorders in offenders who also have a less serious form of mental illness.

Collaboration among Agencies for a Safer Transition

Mentally ill offenders show high rates of recidivism and cycle through a variety of criminal justice and psychosocial settings, due in part to poor coordination among service providers. Forensic clients have multiple needs for treatment and supervision, and multiple public and private sector agencies must be involved in those services. The Council of State Governments has conducted pioneering work on the problem of offender reentry and recommends "collaboration among correction, community corrections and mental health officials to effect the safe and seamless transition of people with mental illness from prison to community."[3] Unfortunately, public service agencies frequently do not coordinate their mandated activities, and many agencies work unilaterally, rather than employing intra-agency coordination and case management.

In 1999, the Pennsylvania Department of Corrections and the National Alliance of Mentally Ill established the Forensic Interagency Task Force of commonwealth stakeholders interested in continuity of care for mental health/mental retardation inmates. The task force members include representatives from the Department of Corrections as well as numerous other state agencies. The members collaborated in planning the development of new continuity-of-care initiatives described below.

The success of the Forensic Interagency Task Force in developing collaborative relationships among agencies, minimizing turf warfare and addressing forensic problems on a state level, prompted the Office of Mental Heath and Substance Abuse Services to establish a pilot task force to address local forensic problems in the five-county Philadelphia area. The Southeast Regional Task Force included representatives from the Office of Mental Health and Substance Abuse Services, the Department of Corrections, mental health/mental retardation administrators from the counties, mental health and substance abuse services providers, emergency staff, public defenders, district attorneys, prison staff and mental health advocates in the area. The task force has sponsored a local forensic conference, and two of the counties have joined to obtain grant monies to fund a collaborative continuity-of-care program.

The Pennsylvania Department of Corrections, the Department of Public Welfare, and the Board of Probation and Parole are partnering with the Council on State Governments and three other states

(New York, Texas, and Minnesota) to develop strategies to connect inmates with federal entitlements, including Medicaid, supplemental security income, and Social Security disability insurance. Representatives of the four states convened in September 2004 to share strategies and develop action plans to connect/reconnect offenders with benefits when they are discharged. One promising strategy that the Department of Corrections is piloting is the use of the online Commonwealth of Pennsylvania Application for Social Services. This online resource is a single-point access where inmates can apply for a wide variety of programs, including health care coverage, food stamp benefits, and cash assistance, prior to their release. The Department of Corrections is also seeking to establish a seamless relationship with the Social Security offices near each prison to reinitiate benefits prior to release.

Discussion

Prisons and psychiatric hospitals have deleterious effects upon inmates and patients serving long terms of incarceration, which include the development of dependency on the institution to meet their basic needs; acquisition of antisocial attitudes and values that might may be incompatible with the residents' family culture; isolation from family, friends and contacts in the community; and estrangement from the outside world in which the family and/or community may have changed while they were away, making their later readjustment more difficult. These problems are compounded by prison locations that are frequently remote from the offenders' home communities.

Both the American Correctional Association and the National Commission on Correctional Health Care recognize the problem of offender reentry into the community. Both organizations have promulgated standards that mandate correctional settings to show written policy, procedure, and practice to ensure continuity of care from admission to discharge from the facility, including referral to appropriate community resources. Offenders with mental illness also carry the dual stigmas of mental illness and incarceration. They are likely to be extremely anxious about returning to the community where they failed before. Many may suffer from substance abuse and medical problems, which make their treatment needs more complex. Unfortunately, these treatment services are limited or nonexistent in some communities, and some agencies are available, but may be reluctant to provide services to these clients. While offenders have a constitutional right to receive mental health treatment while they are incarcerated, they do not enjoy a similar right to treatment in the community.

There are multiple obstacles to reentry for inmates with mental illness. Pennsylvania's strategies to address this issue include improving aftercare planning while the offender is behind the walls and providing a better "hand-off" from the Department of Corrections to the community agencies, developing community corrections centers located near the offender's community, and collaborating better with community mental health agencies, advocacy groups, and families. Pennsylvania's newest activity is developing mechanisms to enroll the inmates in entitlement programs, including disability payment programs to pay for housing, food, and other needs, and health coverage through Medicaid and Medicare. It is anticipated that success in these endeavors will help the offenders on the path ahead to a better life and promote public safety through reducing recidivism.

ENDNOTES

[1] Honberg, R. 2004. Community Reentry from Prison. *Advocate.* 2(2): 9-11.

[2] Reed, D. B. 2001. Class Action Lawsuit Seeks Discharge Planning for Jail Inmates with Mental Disorders. *Community Mental Health Report.* 1(3): 39-40.

[3] Council of State Governments. 2002. *Criminal Justice/Mental Health Consensus Project.* New York: Council of State Governments.

Lance Couturier, Ph.D., is chief of psychological services, Frederick Maue, Ph.D., is chief of clinical services, and Catherine McVey, M.A., is deputy secretary for administration in the Pennsylvania Department of Corrections.

Iowa Implements Mental Health Reentry Program

Larry Brimeryer

First printed in *Corrections Today*, a publication of the American Correctional Association, August 2004

In July 1999, the Bureau of Justice Statistics reported that more than 250,000 jail and prison inmates—16 percent of the incarcerated population—had or were known to have had a major mental illness. While that trend continues in most jurisdictions, the implications are substantial. Jails and prisons have seemingly become replacements for public mental hospitals.

Iowa's response to this growing population has not been unlike that of many jurisdictions. A 200-bed clinical care unit has been added to the Iowa State Penitentiary in Fort Madison and another 170 beds are under construction at the Iowa Medical and Classification Center at Oakdale. A full complement of psychiatrists, psychologists, and other treatment staff serve this population.

Statistics

According to the Iowa Department of Corrections, virtually all offenders (93 percent), including those who are mentally ill, return to the community and pose particularly difficult challenges when transitioning from prison back into society. Not only is there the stigma of a felony conviction, but there are also needs related to the mental illness. Among those are prescriptions for and supplies of psychotropic medications, treatment appointments at mental health clinics and substance abuse treatment centers, financial support to fill entitlement gaps, and structured time activities. In addition, there are the usual issues of housing, transportation, and work.

For the mentally ill offender going on parole, a prearranged parole plan is required, along with adequate housing, and a supply of medication and finances. Those starting work release must be able to work but typically are ineligible for benefits. These transition issues prompted two of Iowa's community-based corrections programs to apply for a community mental health block grant through the Iowa Department of Human Services to develop mental health reentry programs. The First Judicial District in Waterloo and the Sixth Judicial District in Cedar Rapids are now in the second year of an $80,000 grant for each of these promising programs. The funding supports one parole officer in each district.

Within the project, the parole officer works with the institutional counselor to identify appropriate referrals and to develop release plans while the offender is still incarcerated. Approval for the plan is then obtained from the parole board and release dates are coordinated. Once the offender is released into the community, the project provides wraparound services and links the offender to needed services and agencies.

The mental health reentry program provides a high level of service, intensive supervision and support for offenders who have been diagnosed with chronic mental illness. This program is designed to have maximum impact on the recidivism of clients with co-occurring disorders by providing a higher level of service, support, and supervision than was previously available. Clients are typically diagnosed with an Axis I clinical disorder, a category of psychiatric disturbances, such as schizophrenia and other psychotic disorders, mood disorders—depression, anxiety, panic—and bipolar disorder, as well as substance abuse. Offenders in the program often have more than one diagnosis. There are frequently substance abuse issues, typically of a self-medicating nature through the use of alcohol and illicit drugs.

This population tends to have greater needs because of their diagnoses. The individuals' involvement with the criminal justice system often results from their unmet mental health needs. Often, they are simply unable to access available community resources without support. The reentry program helps make the connection to those services. It is designed to be sensitive and responsive to offenders' needs during the crucial time of transition from institutional supervision to supported living in the community.

Those offenders with co-occurring disorders have some of the highest recidivism rates. Without extra services and support, they fall through the cracks of social service agencies, human service providers and the department of corrections. They not only are caught in the cycle of recidivism, but they also present a potential threat to public safety.

Selection Criteria

Selection criteria for admission into the program aim to differentiate between mentally ill people who end up in the criminal justice system because of inaccessibility or a breakdown in community support systems and offenders who also happen to be mentally ill. This program is for people who have been diagnosed with a chronic mental illness. To be accepted, the offender must have an Axis I diagnosis from a doctor. Axis I diagnoses exclude mental retardation and personality disorders. Applicants must be leaving one of Iowa's correctional institutions and reentering their community under supervision for at least six months. They must agree to the intensive supervision that is essential to the program. Further, they must agree to begin and maintain their mental health and substance abuse treatment programs, take the medications prescribed by their doctor while in the institution and in the program, and attend meetings with the Community Accountability Board about every six weeks.

Applicants are screened for admission by careful assessment in the areas of risk, need, and responsivity. Those who are primarily violent, basically criminogenic, or sex offenders are generally excluded from participation. Finally, there is an expectation that clients present an attitude of desiring a real lifestyle change.

The Community Accountability Board is the cornerstone of the program. It is a model of community collaboration that works with these mentally ill clients. Under the guidance and direction of the respective Judicial District Department of Correctional Services, the Community Accountability Board functions in partnership with community-based corrections to help clients successfully complete their supervision and reintegration into the community. The board is comprised of professional and community volunteers from the following areas:

- Mental health treatment
- Education
- Substance abuse treatment
- Mental health advocacy
- Housing services
- Medical services
- Employment and vocational services;
- Community service
- Law enforcement
- Family/individual therapy
- Neighborhood support

Board members make their experience, expertise, and support available to clients, and come together to meet and support them and provide access to the resources clients need to live in their communities with support. The board's purpose is to:

- Provide information about services and resources in the community

- Help overcome barriers to the resources and services to which clients are entitled

- Recommend plans of action

- Support and mentor clients in achieving their goals

- Hold clients accountable for maintaining progress towards goals

- Help clients successfully complete their supervision with the department of correction

- Restore and repair the harm clients have caused to individual victims and the community

- Complete payment of restitution and fines to victims and the community

At the beginning of each meeting with a client, a board member will read the following introductory statement and mission to the client: "The Community Accountability Board is made up of people from our community who represent mental health treatment and advocacy, substance abuse treatment, housing, employment, community service, family therapy, education and law enforcement. Our mission is to support your return to our community as a productive citizen. We do this by letting you know the services, resources, and entitlements you qualify for as a member of our community. Then, we will support you in overcoming barriers you may encounter in getting these entitlements. We help you form a plan of action to succeed and support you in achieving your goals."

Results

Results thus far are promising. In the First Judicial District, thirty-one clients have been referred since October 1, 2001. The average age was 36.4; fourteen clients were male and seventeen female, of whom twelve were black, seventeen were white and two were Hispanic. All but one had histories of substance abuse. Clients' Axis I diagnoses include depression (fourteen), bipolar disorder (six), schizophrenia (six), schizoaffective disorder (five), depression and borderline personality disorder (one), dementia (one), and anxiety disorder (one). The average score on the LSI-R (Level of Services Inventory-Revised) is 31, which is considered to be in the medium-high range. The average time spent in the program is six to eight months. Of the thirty-one served, four have successfully completed their parole. Only one has been revoked; three have been rearrested: one with an aggravated misdemeanor, one with a serious misdemeanor, and one with a simple misdemeanor.

In March, Dennis DeBerg, the program manager, reported the progress of the program to the Iowa Board of Corrections. He said, "Before becoming involved with this program, I was unaware of the unique challenges this population faces upon their release from the institution. Often, they are overwhelmed in coming from a highly structured environment (prison) to having to secure living arrangements, appointments and locating transportation to make these appointments. By having appointments with mental health, substance abuse, vocational rehabilitation, and so forth, made prior to leaving the prison setting, they have the feeling that there is a safety net of services and assistance in the community already in place. The first couple of months are critical due to the fact that they have the tendency to easily give up and return to the security of the prison setting. Once they see the support in the community, they are more encouraged to try to 'make it' and are more likely to have a successful transition back into the community."

In the Sixth Judicial District, there have been thirty referrals since July 1, 2001: thirteen males and seventeen females; four blacks, twenty-five whites, and one Hispanic; with an average age of 33.3. The average time in the program is six to eight months. The average LSI-R score is 33.5. Twenty-nine have a history of substance abuse. Clients' Axis I diagnoses include depression (thirteen), anxiety disorder (four), bipolar disorder (three), schizophrenia (three), dissociative identity disorder and post-traumatic stress disorder (two), depression and borderline personality disorder (two), panic disorder and depression (one), panic disorder and obsessive-compulsive disorder (one), and depression and post-traumatic stress disorder (one). Of the thirty referrals, four successfully completed their parole. One offender's parole has been revoked and five have been rearrested: one with a felony, one with an aggravated misdemeanor, two with serious misdemeanors, and one with a simple misdemeanor.

Barbara Claire is one of two program staff members associated with the project. In her remarks to the Iowa Board of Corrections in March, Claire reported that clients tend to form a connection with the Community Accountability Board and rarely miss scheduled meetings. She added that some clients have asked to continue contacts with the board after their discharge. Lila Starr, the grant monitor from the Department of Human Services, has been impressed with the results to date and has indicated a desire to extend grant funding beyond the scheduled conclusion.

Conclusion

Program staff believe that these clients require intensive supervision, support, and resources. When they receive these services, they have an opportunity to break the cycle of recidivism and be reintegrated with their families, friends, and their communities. These beliefs serve as the basis for this approach to programming for this unique population. Minimizing the victimization of the mentally ill in the criminal justice system will allow for development of a holistic approach to manageable reintegration in the community and enhance community safety.

Larry Brimeyer is deputy director of Eastern Operations for the Iowa Department of Corrections.

"Step Down" Programs: The Missing Link in Successful Inmate Reentry

Ralph Fretz, Ph.D.

First printed in *Corrections Today*, a publication of the American Correctional Association, April 2005

The sheer volume of inmates being released from federal, state and county prisons is now being recognized as a public safety issue. For example, more than 600,000 state offenders were released in 2002.[1] A significant minority of offenders reentering their communities are parole violators who have been involved in the prison-parole-prison cycle.[2] Released inmates face significant obstacles to successful reentry, including housing problems, lack of education, serious medical conditions, mental illness, and no marketable employment skills, states Joan Petersilia in her *Journal of Community Corrections* article "Meeting the Challenge of Prisoner Reentry."

Research indicates that evidence-based assessment and treatment models reduce recidivism, particularly in high-risk offenders.[3] A critical component of an effective reentry model is a seamless continuum of care with information about the offender's progress being transmitted through each stage of reentry. Within the reentry continuum-of-care process, transitional or "step-down" programming in a secure setting plays a critical role. Community Education Centers, which partner with departments of corrections, parole departments, and universities, has designed a reentry continuum-of-care model that incorporates step-down or transitional programming in a secure setting. The following is a description of a continuum-of-care model that includes a step-down process for offenders before they reenter their respective communities. Outcome research by Fretz and colleagues[4] has indicated that this model is effective in reducing recidivism in a high-risk offender population.

Reentry Issues

The current research on recidivism indicates that more than two-thirds of released offenders will be rearrested within three years of their release, the Bureau of Justice Statistics reports. Almost two-thirds of the recidivists were rearrested within the first year postincarceration. A significant portion (26.4 percent) of the offenders in the Bureau of Justice Statistics study were returned to prison within three years for violations of community supervision. The "supervision failures" have significant treatment needs as they have recently failed while in the community.

Only 7 percent of the offenders are involved with transitional facilities and community release programs prior to their release into the community, Petersilia reported. The offenders involved in transitional services have usually attained a minimum-custody risk level in the prison system. Therefore, inmates who are at the highest risk for re-offending often do not receive treatment prior to their release from custody. A significant portion of the highest risk offenders do not enter a parole supervision program; instead, they are released into their communities after their sentence has been served with no aftercare supervision or treatment.

Characteristics of Released Offenders

A snapshot of offenders expected to be released in 1999 included the following alarming statistics from Bureau of Justice Statistics: 83.9 percent were involved with drugs or alcohol at the time of the offense, 24.9 percent were alcohol dependent, 24.8 percent had used drugs intravenously, and 20.9 percent committed the offense for money for drugs. In terms of criminal history, 56 percent of the released offenders had one or more prior incarcerations with 25 percent having had three or more prior incarcerations, 54 percent were on community supervision (parole or probation) at the time of the arrest, and 33 percent had been convicted of a violent offense. In terms of other needs, 14.3 percent of the released offenders were categorized as mentally ill and 11.6 percent were homeless at the time of their arrest.

Case Example of a Reentry Offender

Thus far, this chapter has described offender reentry from a global or macro-level. Yet, the corrections professional is faced with the task of ameliorating reentry obstacles at a micro- or "ground floor" level. The following excerpt from an initial interview with an offender occurs all too often:

> *Counselor: Mr. Jones, you're getting out soon. What are your plans?*
> *Jones: I don't know. I'm gonna live with my mom. She works at a hospital. She said she can get me a job.*
> *Counselor: What if the job doesn't happen?*
> *Jones: I don't know. I always wanted to own a club.*

Counselor: How would you get the money to own a club?
Jones (in an annoyed tone): I don't know. But I'm gonna be real with you: I'm from the streets—point blank—I'm gonna do what I gotta do to make money.
Counselor: What do you mean?
Jones: I don't know. You know, I'll get work or something.

Since the age of sixteen, Jones has been arrested thirty-three times with sixteen convictions and two state incarcerations. The exchange above highlights the challenges and obstacles faced by reentering offenders and the surrounding system. Similar to many reentering offenders, Jones has a meager plan for postincarceration employment. When asked if he has a secondary employment plan, Jones responds, with a sense of grandiosity, that he was considering opening a nightclub. When pressed by the counselor about this plan, Jones became annoyed and responded to the counselor's inquiry with a criminogenic response, suggesting that he was going to return to drug sales or some other illegal activity if he needed money. Jones then caught himself and responded with a vague answer to the counselor's question.

Jones' vague response may reflect a form of resistance, but also his lack of a realistic plan of action for his aftercare. Similar to many reentering offenders who are at high risk for recidivism, Jones has unrealistic expectations about the outside world. If these expectations continue into the release phase, he will rapidly become angry and depressed when they are not fulfilled. His risk of recidivism will increase significantly as he feels stress with no coping skills to manage the tension.[5] This "slippery slope" into a return to criminal activity often occurs within the first two to three months postincarceration, states Jeremy Travis, formerly of the Urban Institute, in "In Thinking about 'What Works,' What Works Best?"[6]

Jones' situation is a common scenario. He has multiple needs and sees few options other than returning to his old habits to survive "on the street." Given Jones' criminal history, his appraisal of his future, while antisocial, is realistic to him. How to work with Jones to change his criminal attitudes and design a realistic reentry plan is a challenge that confronts corrections professionals on a daily basis.

A Reentry Continuum-of-Care Model

The following is a description of four phases of offender reentry beginning with the offender's time in prison. The contention of this author is that the phases of reentry must be linked together in a continuum-of-care model for recidivism to be effectively reduced. As part of that continuum, a step-down phase plays an important role in terms of assessing the offender's current risk/need level, orienting him or her to treatment and community standards, and developing a master treatment plan. This transitional phase of reentry is considerably enhanced by institutional treatment and the seamless transmission of data from the institution to the assessment center or transitional phase of a program.

The Institutional Phase

Ideally, the rehabilitation process is initiated when the inmate enters the criminal justice system and continues throughout all phases of reentry.[7] A comprehensive assessment of the offender's risk level and treatment needs should be administered soon after the inmate's arrival at the institution. A standardized and validated risk and needs assessment instrument should be used to accomplish this task. The Level of Service Inventory-Revised or the newest version of this instrument is an example of a standardized risk and needs assessment inventory with sound psychometric properties.[8] The newest version of the LSI (Level of Service/ Case Management Inventory) has a case management component that is useful in tracking an offender's progress.[9] After the offender's current risk and needs are determined, an initial continuum-of-care plan should be designed. Inmates should be encouraged through a system of clearly defined sanctions and rewards to participate in the plan.

The Step-Down Phase

The step-down phase of reentry originated from one state department of corrections' request that community education centers develop a secure assessment and treatment program that would provide information about the offender's current risk/needs levels prior to release into a halfway house.[10] This next recommended phase of reentry includes a step-down process in a secure setting. Taxman and colleagues[11] outlined three phases of offender reentry: institutional phase, structured reentry phase, and community reintegration phase. Depending on the offender's sentence, the step-down process occurs between two distinct but interrelated phases (in-prison and in-community) of the structured reentry phase.

The community education center reentry model includes the step-down phase as an integral component of the reentry process. During this phase, the offender is evaluated through a series of relevant assessment instruments whose sequence is determined through a decision-tree approach with higher-risk offenders taking more tests.

Simultaneous with the assessment process, offenders are provided an orientation to treatment with an emphasis on the cognitive-behavioral treatment of criminal thinking. The process of assessment and treatment work in a synergistic fashion with the two components constantly evolving as new data emerge.

During this phase, offenders are immersed in a modified therapeutic community that prepares them for their reentry through a number of mechanisms. For example, the step-down program is designed to reward pro-social behavior and extinguish antisocial behavior. Offenders' antisocial behavior is challenged using a procedural justice model, Travis explained. Following this model, an offender who commits an infraction in any community education center program is dealt with swiftly and fairly. The community education center developed clinical intervention committees to address offender infractions in a respectful and informative manner, allowing the offender time to ask questions during the process. The reason for the rule enforcement is explained to the offender in terms he or she can understand. The consequences for antisocial behavior in a community education center program are designed to be learning experiences, not just punishment. During the step-down phase, staff address inmates as residents to denote their reentry status and move the offenders away from identifying themselves only as inmates.

The step-down assessment and treatment occurs in a secure setting so that offenders are not prematurely exposed to the rigors of the outside world before they are ready. The blend of treatment and control affords the staff an opportunity to observe offenders for a protracted period of time, not just interview behavior. Community education center staff constantly observe the offenders' "walk around" behavior to effectively evaluate their current risk factors and treatment needs. It is postulated that the addition of offenders' observed behavior is more predictive of their postincarceration adjustment than their history alone.

Treatment exercises in the step-down program mimic as much as possible the challenges that offenders will face in the outside world. The program exercises become a "dress rehearsal" for reentering offenders so that they can role-play new skills before being thrust onto the stage of the outside community. The secure setting along with the comprehensive assessment of the offender's current risk/needs factors allow department of corrections' staff to separate offenders who are at high risk for failure during the community-release phase from offenders who will be successful. Higher-risk offenders often have their transitional period extended to monitor and assess their behavior. A subcategory of extremely high-risk inmates is recommended for placement at a higher level of custody for public safety reasons. This subcategory of offenders, often psychopathic, does not benefit from treatment and often becomes a disruptive influence in a program.

The community education center has designed and developed step-down programs in six states, and reentry facilities with a step-down component are being initiated in Colorado and Wyoming. The Colorado facility is designed for prerelease and parole revocation offenders and is scheduled for opening in August; the Wyoming facility opened in January. Since each state has unique needs, the community education center continuum-of-care template is modified to address them. The blend of treatment and assessment in a secure facility sets the stage for the next level of reentry, which takes place in the community for parole violators or offenders leaving prison.

Case Example. Jones was placed at an assessment center when he was sixteen months from his parole-eligibility date. During his initial assessment, he was vague about his reentry goals; his unstated goal was to go back "home" as soon as possible with no planning or forethought involved. During the first month of his stay at the assessment center, Jones received three demerits and was placed on a behavior contract following a clinical intervention committee meeting.

During their individual meetings, Jones' counselor pointed out his self-defeating behavior using his demerits as a point of entry. Initially, Jones denied that he committed the demerit behaviors, then he minimized their importance. The counselor expressed confidence that Jones had the capacity to change his antisocial behavior. After being confronted by his peers during group therapy about his demerits, Jones began to associate his demerit behavior with his criminogenic thinking. The older inmates in his group were particularly effective in "predicting his future" if he did not change his antisocial lifestyle.

The treatment of Jones' criminogenic thinking and behaviors occurred in the secure setting of the assessment center. Had he been placed directly from prison to a halfway house, it is likely that Jones' demerit behaviors would have resulted in his return to prison with an institutional infraction. His situation illustrates another advantage of using a step-down process rather than "jettisoning" inmates from the prison structure into a halfway house or directly into the community.

Research into the step-down process indicated that offenders with this experience are less likely to be returned to custody for disciplinary reasons from a halfway house, and less likely to abscond from a halfway house.[12] Surveys of halfway house personnel indicate that inmates transferred from transitional programs, similar to assessment centers, are better prepared for the structure of a halfway house than inmates sent directly from prison to a halfway house.

Community Release Phase

After the completion of the step-down program, offenders move into the community reintegration phase using as a master treatment plan the continuum-of-care plan developed during Phase 2. Information gathered during the second phase is transmitted in a seamless manner through a comprehensive packet of information that includes cognitive test results, current risk and needs instruments findings, the counselor's rating of the behavior in the program, and a continuum-of-care or master treatment plan.

The seamless transfer of the offender's current risk factors and treatment needs is pivotal in terms of effectively working with an offender as he or she progresses through the phases of reentry. Disconnects between programs as the offender moves through the system often result in a duplication of services or a denial of services. Seamless transfer of data along the continuum of care allows staff at each reentry phase to accurately adjust the intensity of services based on the progress of offenders.[13]

Offenders assigned to community education center community alternative or release centers have their continuum-of-care plan reviewed by their counselor and facility administrator upon admission. Offenders' current reentry needs and risk factors are matched with the release center services. The halfway house treatment team periodically evaluates offenders' progress with revisions to service delivery made as necessary.

Case Example. Given Jones' assessment during the step-down phase, he was placed at a halfway house that included an initial phase of intensive substance abuse treatment followed by a work release phase. Jones' enrollment in the family services program is an example of an effective program that was initiated during the transitional phase of his reentry and continued during his halfway house placement. Initially, Jones met with a family service counselor, the mother of his youngest child, and his child. The reason for including these people was because Jones was still involved with this woman and because he carried a picture of this child on his identification tag.

During the family services program meetings, Jones was guided on how to play with his child and form an attachment or bond with him. Initially, he appeared more interested in having his own needs fulfilled by spending time with his girlfriend rather than bonding with his child. Jones was diplomatically confronted with the counselor's observation about the dissonance between his statements about his devotion to his child and his actual behavior. After many confrontations, Jones began to pay more attention to his child and play with him without his girlfriend's direct involvement.

Jones' participation in family services proved to be an important therapeutic activity in his reentry program. During family service meetings, he reported that he had a distant, almost nonexistent relationship with his father. Jones also acknowledged that he did not know how to be a father to his son. The guidance and support that Jones received during family services increased his confidence in his parenting of his young son. Jones continued his involvement in family services during his placement at the halfway house. It is likely that the bond that he formed with his son played a significant role in his successful reentry back into the community.

Aftercare Services

Aftercare services for the offender are developed during the step-down phase through referrals to community education center alumni services, which are provided at no cost to the offender. Community education center alumni meet with offenders while they are still in the step-down phase to encourage aftercare participation. The alumni also describe their experiences of "life on the outside." Alumni services provide referrals for offenders before they go back to their communities. Also, the monthly alumni meetings anchor the ex-offender to people who have been successful at returning to their communities.

Case Example. After he completed the halfway house program, Jones participated in the community education center alumni program. The alumni services provided employment referrals and supported Jones in his pursuit of his GED. An older alumni member was assigned to mentor him when he returned to his community and accompanied him to his first few Alcoholics Anonymous meetings. Jones has been back in his community for the past two years and has been successful in remaining arrest-free during this timeframe.

Select Subpopulations: Parolees

Parole violators or "churners" are caught in the revolving door of community-prison-parole-prison. These offenders present public safety challenges because they have already been unsuccessful in their reintegration.[14] For this population, the assessment and treatment center is frequently the last stop before their return to the community. The parole officer plays a pivotal role in the reentry process for all offenders conditionally released, but their involvement with churners is critical to the successful implementation of the reentry continuum-of-care plan.

Parole violators need special programming tailored to their unique situation. The most frequent violation of parole is correlated with a substance abuse relapse. This subpopulation has actually taken a "step back" towards returning to prison. They benefit from a comprehensive risk/needs assessment that drives their intense treatment. The parole violators' step-back treatment is focused on relapse triggers and learning more productive ways of coping with the outside community. Parole officers are continuously apprised of the parole violator's progress in the program. A continuum-of-care plan is designed before the parole violator is released into the community. The parole officer receives an assessment package that includes a copy of the reentry continuum-of-care plan, the results of the risk and needs assessment, and the violator's progress in the program.

Another subcategory of reentering offenders comprises individuals who have been granted parole but have significant risk factors, including homelessness and long-term substance abuse. This group of parolees often has served a long prison sentence. Before their release into the community, these offenders often need intensive treatment of their substance abuse and criminogenic thinking. These offenders need referrals to community services, including transitional housing. Also, they often are ill-prepared for living in the community and need basic survival skills, including how to balance their finances and appropriately interact with others. While many offenders need financial counseling and social skills training, these high-risk individuals are usually at the high end of the continuum.

Program Effectiveness

Research by Fretz et al. into the community education center continuum-of-care model has yielded promising results in terms of recidivism reduction. This research, coordinated through Drexel University and the New Jersey Department of Corrections, found that offenders who completed the continuum of care reduced their rate of recidivism by more than 30 percent in terms of rearrest, reconviction, and reincarceration.

In addition, research into the community education center step-down programs has found that this type of programming reduced the rate of absconding from community release facilities. Outcome research has validated the contention that the step-down programming has provided the department of corrections with valuable data that can be used for appropriate community release classification of offenders, Fretz and his colleagues found.

Offenders reentering society are often minimally prepared, particularly high-risk offenders with extensive criminal histories. Providing effective reentry services through a seamless continuum of care that includes transitional programming makes fiscal sense and enhances public safety. To return offenders to their communities without tailoring the level of treatment and supervision to their risk levels increases the risk of recidivism and future victimization.

To accomplish the task of reentry effectively, the continuum-of-care reentry process must be initiated while offenders are still incarcerated, and the reentry plan should evolve as they move through the phases. Providing services in a secure setting through a step-down process allows offenders to experience a "dress rehearsal" before they are thrust onto the community stage. This step-down process serves as a "decompression chamber" for offenders as they transition from a highly secure prison environment to less secure community placement. Also, the process, with its comprehensive risk/needs assessment, separates higher-risk offenders from lower-risk offenders. The risk of recidivism may actually increase for low-risk offenders if they are assigned to an inappropriate level of treatment.

The assessment of offenders' current risk/needs levels should occur before they are transferred to halfway houses or released back into their communities. Offenders need an orientation to the obstacles that they will face before they are exposed to them. Not preparing offenders for the stresses in the community is analogous to throwing someone in the water before he or she is taught to swim.

The successful assessment and treatment of offenders as they reenter society may be the most effective crime control available to the government. If attention is not focused on offenders' reentry needs and risk factors, then the country runs the risk of a whole new generation of offenders due to the intergenerational transmission of antisocial attitudes and antisocial role-modeling to which offenders' children will be exposed.

ENDNOTES

[1] Petersilia, J. 2003. Meeting the Challenge of Prisoner Reentry. *Journal of Community Corrections*. 13(1): 4-6, 23-26.

[2] Taxman, F. S., J. M. Byrne, and D. Young. 2002. *Targeting for Reentry: Matching Needs and Services to Maximize Public Safety*. Unpublished report. Washington, D.C.: National Institute of Justice.

[3] Fretz, R., K. Heilbrun, and D. Brown. 2004. Outcome Research as an Integral Component of Performance-Based Offender Treatment. *Corrections Compendium*. 29(4): 1-4. Bonta, J. and D. A. Andrews. 2003. *The Psychology of Criminal Conduct*, 3rd ed. Cincinnati: Anderson Publishing Co.

[4] Fretz, R. et al. 2004.

[5] Zamble, E. and V. Quinsey. 1997. *The Criminal Recidivism Process*. New York: Cambridge University Press.

[6] Travis, J. 2003. In *Thinking About "What Works," What Works Best?* Address to International Community Corrections Association.

[7] Travis, J. 2000. *But They All Come Back: Rethinking Prisoner Reentry.* Washington, D.C.: U.S. Department of Justice.

[8] Bonta, J. and D. A. Andrews. 2003.

[9] Bonta, J., D. A. Andrews and J. S. Wormith. 2004. *Level of Service/Case Management Inventory: An Offender Assessment System.* User's Manual. North Tonawanda, New York: MHS Publishing.

[10] For a detailed description of the history of the assessment center, see R. Fretz, 2002. Helping Inmates Take the Final Step Before Release. *Corrections Today.* 64(1): 78-81.

[11] Taxman, F. S. et al. 2002.

[12] Mrozowski, B., R. Fretz, E. Silver, K. B. Burchfield, R. Mackey, M. Oliver, and K. Heilbrun. 2002. *Intervention Implications for Reducing Risk of Post-Release Inmates "Walking Away" from Community Correctional Placements.* Paper presented at the Biannual Conference of the American Psychology-Law Society, March, in Austin, Texas.

[13] Taxman, F. S. et al. 2002.

[14] Taxman, F. S. et al. 2002.

Ralph Fretz, Ph.D., *is a licensed psychologist, and assessment and research director for Community Education Centers, Bo Robinson Assessment and Treatment Center, Trenton, New Jersey.*

New Study Proves Jails Are an Important Component of the Reentry Equation

Vanessa St. Gerard

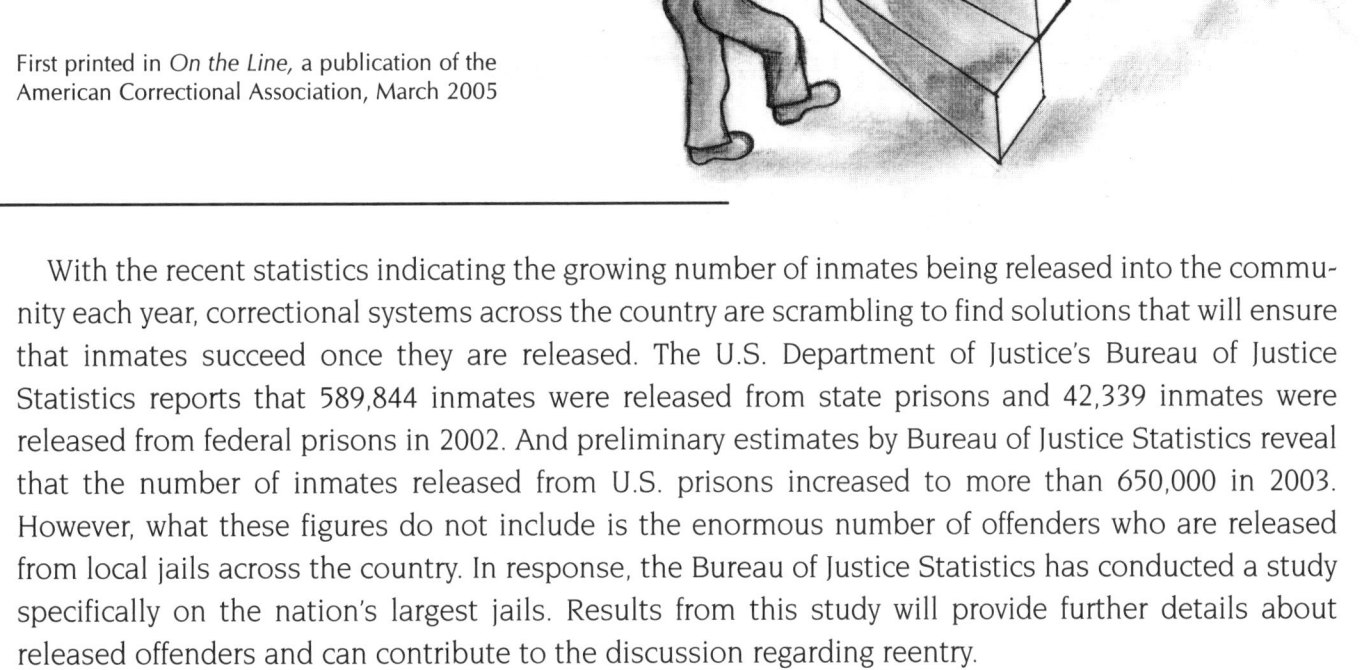

First printed in *On the Line*, a publication of the American Correctional Association, March 2005

With the recent statistics indicating the growing number of inmates being released into the community each year, correctional systems across the country are scrambling to find solutions that will ensure that inmates succeed once they are released. The U.S. Department of Justice's Bureau of Justice Statistics reports that 589,844 inmates were released from state prisons and 42,339 inmates were released from federal prisons in 2002. And preliminary estimates by Bureau of Justice Statistics reveal that the number of inmates released from U.S. prisons increased to more than 650,000 in 2003. However, what these figures do not include is the enormous number of offenders who are released from local jails across the country. In response, the Bureau of Justice Statistics has conducted a study specifically on the nation's largest jails. Results from this study will provide further details about released offenders and can contribute to the discussion regarding reentry.

During the American Correctional Association's 2005 Winter Conference, Allen Beck and Paige Harrison of Bureau of Justice Statistics discussed the agency's newest study, which examined 131 of the largest jail jurisdictions more thoroughly than previous Bureau of Justice Statistics surveys. The study—whose results are expected to be released in a formal report this spring—was conducted in response to a request by the National Institute of Corrections' Large Jail Network to consider new data collections beyond the one-day counts Bureau of Justice Statistics had been examining, Beck explained. "There's real concern that current statistics don't fully measure the jail functions and the importance to public safety and reentry," he added.

Even though jails process more than 12 million admissions annually, local jails are often ignored when it comes to policy discussions. "Successful reentry is pretty much tied to the jail population," Beck said. "I think we need to look to jails, bring jails into the conversation about reentry." In addition, it is evident that jails serve a variety of functions and services related to successful reentry in that they are not only the point of entry into the criminal justice system, but also the point of release and return; jail staff increasingly provide community-based programs as alternatives to incarceration; and jails provide opportunity for assessment and intervention to address offender needs and behavior.

Statistics indicate that on any one day, about half of the nation's jail population is a consequence of failed reentry, Beck said. Thirty-four percent of all jail inmates were on probation at the time of their arrest, 13 percent were on parole, and 7 percent were out on bail/bond. The figures for the year 2003 were about 200,000 parolees and 350,000 probationers who failed and were reincarcerated.

The Bureau of Justice Statistics Survey of Large Jails

In collaboration with the Large Jail Network, composed administrators of the largest U.S. jails and jail systems based on population, Bureau of Justice Statistics used a sample of the largest 146 jurisdictions in which 131 provided data, representing nearly half of the nation's jail population in 2003. The initial focus of the study, Beck said, was admissions and releases, inmates' length of stay, and jail programming.

Jails were asked about their admission rates each month during calendar year 2003, which came out to more than 4 million new admissions into large jails, Beck said, reiterating that this figure does not include readmissions, administrative transfers, and so forth, but only new entries. Bureau of Justice Statistics also found that in January 2004, the last month that data were collected for this study, the large jails admitted about 353,000 inmates and released about 324,000. "What this does is gives us a sense of the volume of flow in and out of the nation's jails," Beck said.

Beck also provided the expected length of stay of the estimated 12.5 million offenders entering local jails on a yearly basis. The Bureau of Justice Statistics estimates that 20 percent (about 2.4 million) of the inmates stay at least one month, while about 12 percent stay at least two months, and only 4 percent stay more than six months, Beck explained. "These are important numbers," he added. "What that means is that population gets released quickly and if you have a treatment program or [an] ... intervention program that takes time," it will not be effective, Beck said, "because you don't have much time in order to intervene." Despite inmates' short lengths of stay, the Bureau of Justice Statistics survey found that most of the large jails provide special programs to inmates, including drug and alcohol treatment, education, and vocational training, Beck said.

In combining results from this most recent survey on jails with those of past Bureau of Justice Statistics surveys that tap into the issue of reentry, such as *Probation and Parole in the United States*, 2002 and *Profile of Jail Inmates*, 2002, a more knowledgeable examination can be made in determining how to ensure that inmates who are released from prison or jail successfully reenter their communities. These past surveys have provided data that offer insight about trends in parole, characteristics of prison releases, and reasons for failure while on community supervision. The most significant findings include:

- Approximately one-third of those admitted to state prison in 2002 were parole violators.

- Among all parole violators in state prisons in 2002, 70 percent had an arrest or conviction for a new offense, 16 percent had a drug-related violation, and 22 percent had absconded.

- Rereleases are an increasing portion of entries to state parole, rising from about 30 percent in 1985 to nearly 50 percent in 1999.

- First releases are three times more likely to succeed on parole than rereleases.

- Of probation and parole violators who were admitted to local jails in 2002, 57 percent for failed community supervision as a result of an arrest/conviction for a new offense, 35 percent a drug violation, and 40 percent absconded.

- One in five returning inmates report a condition that limits their ability to work.

- The annual death rates of parolees are more than double the rates of inmates.

- Slightly more than one-half of all releases were returned to prison within three years.

Based on these statistics, and as has been echoed throughout the corrections field, health care, past failed reentry, drug and alcohol treatment, behavior modification, and employment are among the key factors on which correctional staff must focus in helping inmates to successfully reenter society. According to Beck, the best predictor of failure is past failure. "What you have is a reentry cohort that increasingly is comprised of people who failed before," he said. "The individuals who haven't failed before are more likely to succeed." Beck also identified post-release health care as a significant issue affecting released offenders. "Part of the reentry package is the discussion of health care and health care delivery," he said, indicating that the high rate of deaths among parolees is more a result of illnesses as opposed to suicide or homicide.

As the Bureau of Justice Statistics continues to provide corrections-related data, policymakers, corrections professionals, state legislators, and all other stakeholders must continue to take note of the significant trends related to reentry in their endeavor to abort the rise in recidivism. It is only through collaborated efforts among all involved, including jail officials, that inmates will have a better chance to avoid re-incarceration by becoming law-abiding citizens. When the report on the Bureau of Justice Statistics's survey of large U.S. jails is released this spring, it will certainly add substance to the reentry discussion that has not been considered before. Once the functions and services that jails provide are viewed as an important factor in helping inmates in their reentry effort, more effective solutions can be determined that not will only result in the success of inmate reentry, but also ensure that communities are being made safer throughout the United States.

Vanessa St. Gerard is the former senior editor of Corrections Today *and* On the Line, *American Correctional Association publications.*

Jail Inmates Bake Their Way to Successful Reentry

Susan L. Clayton, MS

First printed in *Corrections Today*, a publication of the American Correctional Association, April 2005

Cakes, cookies, pastries, pies—the keys to success. This may not be the case for everyone, but it is for the inmates enrolled in the "Sweet Release" Bakery Job Training Program at the Montgomery County Correctional Facility in Clarksburg, Maryland. This culinary job training program, which began in 2003, aims to reduce recidivism of ex-offenders in Maryland. It is designed to teach inmates how to obtain and keep a job in the baking/food service industry upon release.

The three-month-long (forty hours per week) program focuses on hands-on commercial baking and sanitation skills, as well as the process of making positive changes to ensure successful reentry to the community. "If someone has a job, a way to earn a living, they may choose that rather than going back to a life of crime and coming back to jail," said Chris Johnson, bakery program manager. She adds that besides reducing recidivism, the goal of the program is to give hope for the future. "We help them realize that they can, in fact, do something besides be criminals. They have skills, and after three months of this program, it really builds a person. They come out different. They have a lot of self-confidence. They have hope for a new life for themselves and their families."

There are five formal goals of the program:

- Reduce the recidivism rate of inmates at the Montgomery County Correctional Facility

- Obtain a job in the baking/food service industry for each program participant

- Teach inmates in the program how to get and keep a job

- Teach basic and advanced elements of baking production so that permanent, full-time employment is possible

- Provide the education necessary so that each graduate can pass a national sanitation exam and obtain a food service manager's license

Program Elements

Eligibility and admission to the program is based on the following:

- Sentencing has taken place and there are at least three months remaining on the sentence

- Pre-screening and selection by counseling and correctional staff

- Expressed interest in full-time employment

- Interest in baking/food service as a career opportunity

- Good record during incarceration (no violent behavior)

- Ability to read at an eighth-grade level

Johnson receives about forty applications every three months for which there are only six available spots. She conducts one-on-one interviews to narrow down applicants. Johnson tries to find the people who are serious about the work and who need the most support when they get out in the community. Ideally, she likes to take people who have about four to six months left to serve, as this allows the perfect amount of time to complete the program and to obtain a job in the community.

Five days a week, program participants report to the kitchen by 6 a.m. for hands-on baking instruction. Recipes and baking techniques begin with simple products and progress to the more difficult as the weeks pass. After a lunch break, formal classroom instruction takes place. This part of the program is divided into six sections: baking skills and techniques, pre-employment skills, job skills, food service sanitation, life skills, and confidence building. All participants are required to complete a resume before graduation.

According to Joanne Zacharias, food service manager, Montgomery County Department of Correction and Rehabilitation, the cost of the program is minimal. All of the food that is prepared is used for inmate desserts or events/programs in the jail. Zacharias notes that both the staff and inmate population have been very supportive of the program. For example, through the inmate canteen fund, inmates have donated money to help defray the costs of licenses and supplies. "I think a lot of people we get in the program are maybe people who haven't had a lot of support most of their life and didn't really have many goals," Zacharias said. "This program gives them goals and a sense of pride and accomplishment."

Upon completion of the program, graduates receive a certified food manger's license from the Montgomery County Department of Health and Human Services. This, Johnson said, is the ticket to a job for them. At this point, they will have obtained bakery training, completed a nationally recognized sanitation course, and attended courses in life skills and job training. Through her contacts in the community, Johnson helps place graduates who are being released in food service jobs.

"Some of us have never known what it is to have a job. This program teaches you how to work with people, teaches you how to be responsible," said William Jaume, a recent graduate of the program. "It changes the way you feel about being released. It helps conquer some of the fears you have about where you're going to work and live and what you're going to do with yourself. . . . It does teach you a way to earn a living and gives you a sense of accomplishment," Jaume added. "It's a program of hope. It gives you a skill when you walk out the door that you can use so that you don't have to end up coming back to jail."

Montgomery County Pre-Release Center

The bakery program works in cooperation with a county residential treatment facility, the Montgomery County Department of Correction and Rehabilitation Pre-Release Center in Rockville, Maryland, which has been cited as a national model by the U.S. Department of Justice. Some of the graduating inmates will be released directly to the community, while others are transferred to the prerelease center. At the center, offenders live in a highly structured residential work release and treatment facility, which closely supervises them and monitors their behavior. Full-time bakery or food service jobs are found in the local community for each resident. Usually within one to three months, the people sent to the prerelease center are discharged. The inmates who are not transferred from the jail serve out the remainder of their sentence and Johnson assists them in finding jobs.

Hillel Raskis, work release coordinator at the center, gets all of the transferred jail program graduates in his unit. "Here at the center, we give residents a chance to change themselves through employment, counseling, education, treatment, housing, money, a job," Raskis said. He works closely with the bakery program and notes that some offenders come to the center for assistance in final job preparation before being placed in a job.

Before bakery program graduates are transferred, Raskis is notified. When they arrive, they must participate in a week of classroom instruction to work on issues that led to their criminal behavior and prepare them for work. Raskis talks to them about their skills and possibilities for employment. Then, the job search begins. Raskis helps identify restaurants and bakeries that might be appropriate for job placement. He sets up interviews and contacts employers to let them know that residents are at the center and what their charges were.

Raskis said that the center stays in contact with employers and tries to do a follow-up at the sixty-day mark to see if people have kept the job. He notes that everyone in the bakery program has been able to get a job in the food service industry. "Many offenders have no job skills but come out of the bakery program with experience and job readiness and a will to work. It's a very well-structured, well-thought-out program."

Johnson maintains contact with graduates for at least the first six months of new employment. At the beginning, she talks to them every week; gradually, it becomes every six weeks. "We get to really know each other," Johnson said. "We have a lot of ups and downs, and at the end of the three months there is a real bonding that takes place."

Results

As far as successes go, Johnson acknowledges that the program is still young. "We need to get three years under our belt of measuring to truly evaluate it," she said. To date, the program has twenty-two graduates. Each of the twenty-two passed the national sanitation exam (ServSafe) and earned a certified food server license. Of the twenty-two, twelve are serving out the remainder of their sentences in jail or at the prerelease center; four are working at local bakeries and restaurants; four have been released and are in residential treatment centers for relapse prevention; one is selling cars; and one has been reincarcerated.

Five women at the jail also have earned their certified food manager license in a scaled-down trial version of the program that taught sanitation and job skills only. They all remain incarcerated. Hands-on baking was not possible for the women due to security issues in the kitchen.

Johnson and Zacharias hope to expand the program in the future to fully include women, who make up about 10 percent of the jail population. In total, twenty-seven inmates at the facility have taken the national sanitation exam and twenty-six have passed.

Helping the program participants succeed is paramount to Johnson. "They've been hopeless for such a long time and then all of a sudden someone is trying to help them," she said. "Structure, attention and the feeling that somebody cares about them and is going to help them find their way and teach them a new skill are key."

Michael Velez, a current program participant is confident that the "Sweet Release" program will help him pursue a career when he is released. "I've never had a career. I've had jobs, but never had anything that would take me anywhere," Velez said. "It's scary to come out of jail and not know what you're going to do. This helps you build self-esteem. I'm twenty-three years old and I've been in jail twice. I've spent every holiday in jail, and I don't want to do it anymore. It's about a lifestyle change for me . . . getting out and staying out, and this program has taught me what I need to do it."

Challenges and the Future

According to Johnson, the challenges of the program are similar to many new reentry projects: funding; reluctance on the part of employers to hire convicted felons; substance abuse relapse; realities of hard work at a regular job; and the lure of a criminal lifestyle. She notes that there are three future goals for the program. The first is a partnership with a local chemical dependency treatment facility. Counselors would come into the jail twice a week to conduct group and individual sessions on drug and alcohol relapse prevention. "Almost all of the graduates of this program have had chemical dependency issues, and the majority of them [issues] contributed to their crimes," Johnson said. "If the addictions are not dealt with, the long-term success of the project will be negatively impacted." The second component is weekly continuation of the relapse prevention therapy after release, which Johnson said would become part of an offender's sentence. Finally, the program would partner with one or more community food service employers to hire the graduates and institute an aftercare component that could be expanded. The work environment could become a support system for these ex-offenders.

Zacharias notes that some of her staff would even like to expand the program beyond baking. "We definitely feel that food service gives them a skill they can use when they go back to the community because there are a lot of food service jobs available," she said. "We can give them the training and the certificate that gives them marketable skills for when they get out. I think the guys really feel a sense of pride in accomplishing something."

Traditionally, Johnson said, people are often released from jail with no money, no job, no home, no hope. However, "when they get released from this program and reenter, whether they go through the prerelease center or not, hopefully we are going to have a job set up, a place to live, a plan," Johnson said, adding, "That's what it's all about—successful reentry."

Susan Clayton, MS, is managing editor of Corrections Today.

Pennsylvania's Approach to Reentry

Jeffrey A. Beard, Ph.D,
and Kathleen Gnall

First printed in *Corrections Today*, a publication of the
American Correctional Association, August 2003

More inmates are leaving prisons and jails now than at any other time in the nation's history. In 2001, nearly 600,000 inmates were released from state and federal prisons. Of these, 10,500 inmates were released from Pennsylvania state prisons and the number of inmates leaving Pennsylvania prisons has grown by nearly 15 percent since 1997.[1] As so many have noted recently,[2] inmates leaving prisons are faced with a multitude of problems, including having few or no employment skills and prospects for meaningful work, low levels of education, and serious drug and alcohol problems. Released offenders must find a place to live, and some will need to reunify with families from which they may have become estranged before or during their incarceration. Often, released offenders have chronic health problems and many suffer from mental illness. These offenders are often returning to communities that are ill-equipped to handle both their sheer numbers and the multiple problems that each individual brings.

Pennsylvania's Approach

Like many departments of correction, the Pennsylvania Department of Correction once viewed its primary responsibility as keeping convicted felons away from the public. There was a heavy focus on staff and inmate safety. Today, many believe the purpose of prison has broadened considerably, and while it is still critical to maintain a safe and secure environment and keep those incarcerated apart from society, it is equally critical to prepare inmates for their eventual reintegration into the community.

National data shows that more than 95 percent of inmates will eventually return to society.[3] A recent Bureau of Justice Statistics report on the recidivism of inmates released from prisons in fifteen states in 1994 indicates that 52 percent of released inmates returned to prison within three years. In Pennsylvania, approximately 40 percent of all released inmates return to state custody at least once within three years. One of the most important ways a department of correction can protect public safety is by preparing offenders for their eventual reintegration into the community. Department of corrections must perform this important function at a time of increasingly tight budgets and, in Pennsylvania's case, a continuing growth in the prison population.

In any case, the preparation of inmates for their eventual release is something departments of corrections are discussing and are taking more steps towards than, arguably, ever before. The Pennsylvania Department of Correction even has gone so far as to change its mission statement to show that corrections is not just a "lock 'em up and throw away the key" business, but a business striving to improve offenders' odds of success in the community. The Pennsylvania Department of Correction's new mission statement is "to protect the public by confining persons committed to our custody in safe, secure facilities and to provide opportunities for inmates to acquire the skills and values necessary to become productive, law-abiding citizens while respecting the rights of crime victims."

In furtherance of its mission, the Pennsylvania Department of Correction has adopted a three-pronged approach to preparing incarcerated men and women for reentry into communities. First, the department conducts a thorough risk and needs assessment of individual inmates. The risk principle measures the likelihood that offenders will commit additional offenses after their release from prison. The classification process also includes a risk measurement of disruption within an institution. The need principle entails the specific issues that contribute to offenders' criminally deviant behavior, such as low education levels and few job skills. Second, the department offers alcohol and other drug treatment and education programs, such as GED preparation and vocational training, aimed at addressing offender needs. Finally, the department provides inmates with the opportunity to participate in the Community Orientation and Reintegration program, which teaches inmates skills to find and keep a job, and how to overcome the obstacles to successful reintegration. The Community Orientation and Reintegration program also acts as a booster, reminding inmates of the important lessons they have learned in prison programming that will help them in their attempt to become law-abiding community members.

Assessment

All new male court commitments entering the Pennsylvania Department of Correction come through the Diagnostic Center at the State Corrections Institution at Camp Hill, while females complete the diagnostic process at State Corrections Institution Muncy. Approximately 13,000 inmates, including 8,000 new commitments and 5,000 parole violators, were admitted to the Pennsylvania Department of Correction in 2002. The department recognizes that preparing inmates for reentry begins the day they enter the front door. The research and evaluation literature point to the importance of conducting thorough risk and needs assessments at intake to best target resources to the particular issues of individual offenders.

During the diagnostic process, the department uses an internally developed and validated classification instrument called the Pennsylvania additive classification tool, which determines each inmate's custody level. The custody level ranges from one to five, with one being the lowest security risk in an institution and five being the highest. Through the process of assigning custody levels, the department of correction staff learn a great deal about each individual inmate's needs. For example, during the diagnostic process, staff determine the reading level of each inmate, how much formal schooling he or she has had, the level of job skills, and whether an inmate has recently been employed, and many other issues, which are then saved in management information systems.

The diagnostic process further involves inmates being screened for their particular level of drug and alcohol dependence or abuse using the Texas Christian University drug screen and assessment tool. Most recent data indicate that nearly 70 percent of the inmate population has a drug and/or alcohol dependency problem. The Test of Adult Basic Education also administered at intake measures each inmate's aptitude in reading and mathematics.

Through the extensive program evaluation the department has undertaken during the past several years, the department of correction has learned that it must do a better job of measuring other important criminogenic needs. In addition to low educational levels and few job skills, criminogenic needs include having antisocial attitudes and associates, and criminal thinking, which are shown to be highly correlated with re-offending. Targeting these needs may result in lower levels of recidivism for offenders.

This past spring, the department pilot-tested four needs assessment instruments and a risks and needs tool to better understand these criminogenic needs. The pilot-tested needs instruments included the Criminal Sentiments Scale-Modified (CSS-M) and the Self-Appraisal Questionnaire, which measure criminal thinking, and the Novaco Anger Scale and the Hostile Interpretations Questionnaire (HIQ), which measure hostility and anger. The instruments were administered to about 1,000 inmates during the pilot phase. After extensive evaluation of the data during this period, the department concluded that all tools provided valuable insight into criminogenic needs. Administration time and cost are two important factors that the department weighed in making a decision on which of the tools to administer to all inmates entering the diagnostic centers.

The department of correction elected to adopt the Criminal Sentiments Scale-Modified and the Hostile Interpretations Questionnaire and began administering these tools last month. The department of correction also administered the Level of Service Inventory-Revised (LSI-R), a risk and needs tool, during the pilot. The Pennsylvania Board of Probation and Parole is already administering the LSI-R to parolees in the community to help determine the level of supervision required and the department of correction began administering the LSI-R to inmates at intake in June. Depending on the results from ongoing program evaluation, the department of correction may consider adopting other instruments to gauge inmates' criminogenic needs. For example, it is considering adopting a specific instrument for sex offenders and an instrument to measure proclivity towards violence.

Treatment Programming

Conducting thorough assessments of individual risk and needs allows the department to identify the most predominant areas that should be addressed through structured treatment programs. The research and evaluation literature dictate that to be most effective, programs must be tailored to the needs of the individual offender and must be of substantial intensity and duration. This is a particular challenge in a system that has less than 5 percent of the $1.1 billion budget dedicated to treatment programs, limited treatment staff, and 40,000 inmates, most of whom have multiple needs. So, how can a large correctional system deal with this tension, providing individual treatment while serving a massive number of incarcerated offenders? One of the most important first steps is to sort inmates by their risk and need level. This process is akin to a medical triage model used to prioritize patients for treatment. Those offenders who are high risk and high need should be the first considered for treatment. Further, they should receive the most intensive services over the longest time period. On the other hand, low-risk/low-need offenders should not be directed into treatment, as they are not likely to re-offend and treatment can actually make them more likely to return to crime.[4] This is because exposing low-risk inmates to high-risk offenders in treatment settings gives the low-risk offenders opportunities to learn the very antisocial thinking patterns and behavior that treatment is trying to counteract. After inmates are classified, the department uses information from the diagnostic process to develop a correctional plan for each of them. The correctional plan is intended to serve as a roadmap for inmates to help them chart behavior and program activities during their incarceration and is updated annually in a meeting between the inmate and his or her counselor.

The department recently standardized treatment programs based on a review of the literature on what factors contribute to criminal offending, as well as a careful analysis of the assessment data being captured in the diagnostic process. Programming under the department's correctional plan is divided into five major areas: work/education; citizenship; family/relationship/self; offense-related; and reentry.

The overall goals of inmate programs are to enable inmates to:

- Understand the effects and consequences their criminal behavior has had on their victims, families, community and self

- Demonstrate an appropriate respect for authority, peers, and self by having a better understanding of what it means to be a member of the community

- Understand their high-risk factors for re-offending

- Describe resources and intervention strategies for support to establish and maintain successful community adjustment

Inmates are assigned to programs based on the results of their assessments, coupled with the clinical judgment of correctional staff observations. Offenders are assigned to these programs as early in their incarceration as possible. The Pennsylvania Department of Correction recognizes that to have the most impact, lessons must be more than didactic exercises. For this reason, instructors use a variety of techniques to deliver programming, including role-playing exercises, homework assignments, and the development of individual relapse-prevention plans. Using these various techniques within larger classroom settings allows for the targeted treatment approach that is so important in helping reduce the chance that an offender will return to prison.

The work/education programs offer a number of academic and vocational programs for inmates of all ability levels. Among the major academic program areas offered are adult basic education, GED and the commonwealth secondary diploma, English as a second language, and special education programs. The department offers numerous vocational training programs, including painting, carpentry, barbering/cosmetology, plumbing, computer repair, computer-aided design, and electronics.

The citizenship program focuses on providing a basis for inmates to function as law-abiding citizens within the institution, as well as productive community members after their release. The curriculum helps provide inmates with the cognitive background they will need to be responsible citizens. Consistent with research findings from national evaluations of programs that work, the citizenship courses provide inmates with ample opportunity to role-play prosocial responses to situations they will encounter in the community.

The family/relationship/self program focuses on developing skills in parenting, as well as addressing the needs of special populations such as long-term offenders, inmates fifty and older, and female offenders. The programs offered under this umbrella are designed to strengthen family ties and prepare inmates to be accountable and accept responsibility as parents.

Programs included under the offense-related category include alcohol and other drug treatment, sex offender treatment, anger management and violence prevention, batterer treatment, and impact of crime. Most inmates participate in some form of alcohol and other drug treatment, which includes alcohol and drug education, outpatient treatment, and therapeutic community treatment. Inmate peer facilitators run 12-step and relapse-prevention meetings.

Community Orientation and Reintegration

The Community Orientation and Reintegration program is the department's transitional program designed to bridge the gap between prison and the community. The Community Orientation and Reintegration program is intended to address the obstacles to reentry, such as securing proper identification and finding employment and housing. The goals of the Community Orientation and Reintegration program are to establish a standard, coordinated release program based on known risk factors and needs; promote effective community linkages; enhance employability and job-readiness; and promote healthy family and interpersonal relationships.

The Community Orientation and Reintegration program has two phases. The first occurs in an institution about one month prior to an inmate's release. The second phase takes place in a community corrections facility and lasts approximately thirty to forty-five days. It is essential that there be continuity of care between the Community Orientation and Reintegration program phases and the inmate's ultimate transition to parole supervision. Staff pay particular care to ensure that the transition between the two phases is smooth and logical.

Phase 1 of the Community Orientation and Reintegration program consists of two weeks of classroom exercises on topics researchers have found to be critical to inmates' success. The entire first week of Phase 1 is devoted to job readiness and retention. During this week, inmates develop their resumes, participate in mock employment interviews and role-play handling conflict situations in the workplace. The second week offers inmates opportunities to actively work on their relapse prevention plans, practice prosocial responses to conflict situations and exercise decision-making and problem-solving skills. Inmates' families are also integral to ensuring a successful transition—program staff encourage inmates to maintain a connection with their families throughout incarceration. Phase 1 of the Community Orientation and Reintegration program includes modules on effective parenting and communication skills.

Most inmates participating in Phase 1 will move on to a community corrections facility to participate in Phase 2, which builds on lessons and exercises learned in the first phase. During the second phase, inmates actively seek employment or work, meet with their family members in counseling situations and connect with substance abuse and other providers in the community.

The department recognizes that collaboration with other state agencies, community providers, churches, and civic organizations is critical to helping inmates make the transition from prison to the community. Thus, the Pennsylvania Department of Correction is sponsoring a series of conferences titled "Bridging the Gap" throughout the state. These conferences are designed to solicit the help of community members in returning inmates to their communities with the support they will need to be successful. The Department of Correction is also actively developing a mentoring program that will link community members with inmates who are about to be released.

Commitment to Improvement

The department is committed to the ongoing enhancement of its programs and approaches to preparing inmates for their eventual reintegration. There are three teams of key staff from the central office and state correctional institutions charged with developing strategic plans in the critical areas of assessment, treatment, and reentry. In addition to department experts in these areas, the department of correction also solicits input from university-based researchers to advise team members on key research findings that will influence the way prisons are operated.

The department maintains an aggressive research and evaluation agenda that allows it to examine what it does and how it can do it more effectively and efficiently by using a three-pronged model with respect to its research initiatives. First, staff identify evaluation needs internally. Next, they seek an outside research partner with expertise in the area being studied to conduct the research on the department's behalf. Finally, third-party funding is sought to pay for the research. The Pennsylvania Department of Correction has used this model to examine its alcohol and other drug programs, and select education and vocational programs, and parenting programs, among others. Most recently, the department partnered with the Urban Institute to conduct a process evaluation of the Community Orientation and Reintegration program. The department of correction has learned a great deal from the studies conducted thus far and has made real changes, such as enhancing assessment and offering more cognitive-behavioral treatment, to programs based on these findings.

In its efforts to respond to the reality that most inmates incarcerated in its system will eventually be released into communities, the Pennsylvania Department of Correction altered its mission to focus on reentry. The department is committed to ongoing improvement of its programs. Therefore, it maintains an ambitious research and evaluation agenda that allows it to become increasingly better at preparing inmates for successful community reintegration.

ENDNOTES

[1] Beck, A. J. 2000. *State and Federal Prisoners Returning to the Community: Findings from the Bureau of Justice Statistics*. Paper presented at the First Reentry Courts Initiative Cluster Meeting in April 2000. Washington, D.C.

[2] Petersilia, J. 1999. Parole and Prisoner Reentry in the United States. In M. Tonry and J. Petersilia, eds. *Prisons*, pp. 479-524. Chicago: University of Chicago Press.

Travis, J., A. L. Solomon and M. Waul. 2001. *From Prison To Home: The Dimensions and Consequences of Prisoner Reentry*. Washington, D.C.: The Urban Institute.

3 Travis, J. et al. 2001.

4 Bonta, J. 1996. Risk-Needs Assessment and Treatment. In A.T. Harland, ed. *Choosing Correctional Options that Work: Defining the Demand and Evaluating the Supply*, pp. 18-32. Thousand Oaks, California: Sage.

Jeffrey A. Beard, Ph.D., is secretary of corrections for the Pennsylvania Department of Corrections. Kathleen Gnall is chief of Planning, Research, Statistics and Grants for the Pennsylvania Department of Correction.

NIC Provides Practitioners Skills to Help Offenders with Reentry

Shelly Morelock, MA, and
Melissa Houston, MSW

First printed in *Corrections Today*, a publication of the American Correctional Association, August 2003

The National Institute of Corrections' Offender Workforce Development Specialist training program is a comprehensive curriculum designed to increase participants' ability to provide adult offenders and ex-offenders with the skills required for employment, retention, and career advancement. The program aims to train professionals who directly or indirectly offer one or more of the following: offender employment training, placement and retention services, or career counseling, such as for personnel in prisons, jails, community correctional facilities, colleges, employment agencies and other community-based organizations. In addition, the program addresses the competencies designed to meet certification as a global career development facilitator.

NIC's Office of Correctional Job Training and Placement developed the training program. One of the primary functions of Office of Correctional Job Training and Placement is to provide staff the training required to develop competencies in working with adult offenders and ex-offenders relative to job training, placement, retention, advancement, and career assistance.

The Office of Correctional Job Training and Placement was established by the Violent Crime Control and Law Enforcement Act of 1994, and became an integral part of the National Institute of Corrections in March 1995. The purpose of this legislation was to support the development and improvement of job training and placement programs for adult offenders in custody or under community supervision and ex-offenders.

Program Design

The training program is 160 hours and consists of three blocks. Each block is four and a half days or thirty-six hours for a total of 108 hours of classroom instruction. Additionally, there are approximately fifty-two hours of practicum and homework assignments.

The three blocks of training are scheduled approximately thirty days apart to allow participants to return to their local jurisdictions and take care of critical job responsibilities. However, the intervals between classroom sessions are used to complete practicum and reading assignments.

This training program is designed for six-person teams. In addition to the required competencies, which include employment assessments, labor market information, and resources, individual facilitation skills, group facilitation skills and employability, the Offender Workforce Development Specialist training program provides instruction in training other offender employment service providers to increase their basic skill level in the areas of workforce development and career facilitation. As part of the Offender Workforce Development Specialist training, state teams create action plans for implementing employment training in their home states. These plans often reflect the teams' excitement about transferring their enhanced skills and knowledge to their colleagues.

Program Evaluation

The impact of NIC's Offender Workforce Development Specialist training program is measured at several levels using Kirkpatrick's four-level training performance evaluation model. Training may be measured for participant satisfaction, new skills and knowledge, learning behavioral changes on the job, and organizational performance results.

Participants' evaluations, tests, and statements indicate that through the training they receive, they have learned new skills and acquired additional knowledge, making it worth all the "blood, sweat, and tears." But what, if anything, is truly changing about the way participants approach offender employment following their intensive training? The Office of Correctional Job Training and Placement followed up with teams requesting brief updates on the progress of their action plans and their efforts to improve offender workforce development in their home states.

The Colorado Team

Following its Offender Workforce Development Specialist training, the team from Colorado trained key stakeholders on offender employment issues and practices at the John Inmann Work and Family Center, a multiagency offender services center focused on work and family services. The center's partners include the Colorado Department of Corrections, Colorado Department of Labor and Employment, Colorado Department of Public Safety/Division of Criminal Justice, Denver Mayor's Office of Workforce Development, Denver Department of Human Services, and a number of community and faith-based organizations. The Offender Workforce Development Specialist team also trained the department of corrections reintegration staff who are responsible for providing prerelease programs and individual transition planning in sixteen facilities across the state; and the community-based reintegration staff associated with workforce centers that provide employment services, such as assessment and job placement, and work with parole and community corrections staff to coordinate employment and service delivery.

The Offender Workforce Development Specialist team training of key partners has resulted in unexpected benefits. For example, a veterans' representative from a workforce center attended the training, liked what was being presented, and became involved in facility employment programs. This later contributed to the development of a possible veterans' grant program.

The Iowa Team

Iowa's Offender Workforce Development Specialist team returned to train the Sixth Judicial District's employment staff, probation officers, residential officer, Workforce Investment Act staff, community college staff, vocational rehabilitation staff, and prison transition counselors. These practitioners now meet the classroom requirements to apply for the nationally recognized Career Development Facilitator certification, which is fortuitous since the Iowa team has developed a career track for correctional staff who work with the following employment programs: offender employment specialist, offender workforce development specialist, and program manager, and has written this eligibility for certification into the job descriptions for each.

One of the staff members who benefited from the Iowa Offender Workforce Development Specialist team's training was Connie Wimer, a job developer for nine years. "I taught myself how to do my job by networking with other agencies. The Offender Workforce Development Specialist training broadened my approach and improved the skills I use to assist the individuals on my caseload," she said. "I believe the offenders and ex-offenders are getting better assistance from me due to my ability to provide multifaceted interventions. Additionally, I feel it has raised the professionalism of my position and allowed my colleagues to see the specialized skills I have learned."

The Sixth Judicial District Department of Correctional Services initiated several programs for the offenders it supervises both in the field and in residential settings. These programs are designed to improve initial job placement, matching, satisfaction and retention, as well as overall career development. Staff use the skills and tools attained through the Offender Workforce Development Specialist training to deliver high-quality services to benefit offenders and the community. Offender workforce development is particularly important in the Sixth District's supervision process given the agency's commitment to the "what works" literature and its use of the Level of Service Inventory. Successful employment and job retention can positively impact many of the risk factors indicated by the inventory.

For the past three years, exit interviews were conducted with successful discharges from the district's residential facilities, which have consistently shown that offenders were happy with the employment programs they received. Programs in the Sixth District also included involvement with Kirkwood Community College, where offenders were referred for assessment and job readiness. Programming in-house included computer assessments, counseling and, based on need, referrals to partner organizations.

The Maryland Team

Members of the Maryland Offender Workforce Development Specialist team report that like many states, Maryland has experienced significant cuts in the state budget resulting in staff reductions, as well as major reductions in employment, training, and transition services for ex-offenders. Rising above these challenges, the Maryland State Department of Education and the department of corrections continued to host periodic real and mock career fairs, employer appreciation celebrations, career exploration, and workforce development programs. Regional staff development activities occur quarterly to address career assessment, documents for employment, retention strategies, accessing community partners, and other Offender Workforce Development Specialist competencies.

Currently, an interagency team is working on a number of initiatives in partnership with state, local, and community service providers. These initiatives include the creation of a job opportunities task force, which hosts policy work sessions to address barriers to employment and serves as an active advocacy group to draw legislative and funding attention to ex-offenders in need of employment, training, and support services upon release from confinement.

Other offender workforce development projects in Maryland include the Transitional Jobs Project Model, a technical assistance grant awarded to the Baltimore National League of Cities, and the YESNetwork Project. The YESNetwork Project provides classroom instruction inside institutions and directed services at two one-stop career centers. The Advisory Council on Offender Employment Coordination addresses policy and practice issues that impact offender employment, and attempts to build the knowledge and skills of ex-offenders (to improve their chances of successful employment when they transition back to the community). In addition, the advisory council expands the network of employers willing to hire ex-offenders in jobs, leading to their self-sufficiency.

The Minnesota Team

After completing its own Offender Workforce Development Specialist training, Minnesota's team facilitated thirty-two hours of distance-learning training on offender job retention and provided a customized sixteen-hour curriculum on offender employment. The team conducted both programs at correctional facilities to introduce community-based practitioners to the environment where offenders are preparing for reintegration.

In Hennepin County, plans are under way to implement an offender employment program in the Department of Community Corrections. The program bridges the gap between incarceration and all other supervision levels. A continuum of services and interventions will be available to deal with employability issues. In Minnesota, reducing recidivism through employability will be the focus for many practitioners who have traditionally been responsible for offender supervision and compliance with court directives. Much of the offender employment program will be based on Office of Correctional Job Training and Placement's 2001 paper and on the Offender Job Retention distance learning training curriculum, which is available from the NIC Information Center.

Minnesota is forming a network of approximately 140 offender employment specialists from fifty different organizations, including community-based programs, jails, and prisons. The network's goal is to increase the knowledge base of professionals relative to what works and best practices in offender employment programs from around the country.

The Missouri Team

Missouri's Offender Workforce Development Specialist team returned to train staff assigned to the Offender Re-Entry Grant Initiative and the Transition from Prison to Community Initiative using the Offender Workforce Development Specialist basic skill modules provided by NIC. Missouri also is providing training for its faith-based organization staff, initiative grant staff, community members, probation and parole officers, and their employability skills and life skills team.

Seven institutions in Missouri offer employability skills and life skills classes, which are taught by certified teachers. The state is looking to expand these classes to additional institutions since they are included in the transition plans for students with special needs and offenders who are targeted for Missouri's reentry grant.

The North Carolina Team

One of the North Carolina Offender Workforce Development Specialist team members is managing the Job Preparation for Offenders project, which focuses on matching job-qualified inmates with prospective employment opportunities at the time of release and on promoting the employment of ex-offenders as a sound business decision. The Offender Workforce Development Specialist team is leading local interagency support groups, comprised of service providers who have a stake in offender job development and employment, including faith-based and other nonprofit organizations. These support groups coordinate transition services available to ex-offenders within the community.

The Offender Workforce Development Specialist team also conducted a series of staff development workshops for community correctional officers and day reporting center staff on career-building skills for offenders. They were sponsored by the North Carolina Workforce Development Institute.

All activities undertaken by the Offender Workforce Development Specialist team have been implemented in partnership with the state's workforce development community as coordinated by the North Carolina Commission on Workforce Preparedness.

Sophia Feaster, a mental health social worker for the department of corrections, who was part of the North Carolina Offender Workforce Development Specialist team, said, "What makes this partnership unique and interesting is that for the first time, community agencies, along with the North Carolina prison system, are working together as a team to address the problem of recidivism." The team attributes the beginning of this partnership, called Project Re-Entry, to its Offender Workforce Development Specialist training experience.

The Oklahoma Team

Some of the more recent Offender Workforce Development Specialist training graduates are from Oklahoma. The Oklahoma Offender Workforce Development Specialist team provided a one-day information session for a group of service providers in its home state.

The U.S. Probation Team

Following their Offender Workforce Development Specialist training, the members of the team from the U.S. Probation Office in the Eastern District of Missouri completed Career Development Facilitator Instructor training, and are now certified instructors of the curriculum. The team is providing Offender Workforce Development Specialist instruction to U.S. probation and pretrial officers from across the country, as well as state and local correctional and employment service providers.

Missouri's federal Offender Workforce Development Specialist team also has provided training and information to offenders at a job seminar; to employers at breakfasts; and to staff of the U.S. Probation Office, Community Corrections Centers, U.S. Bureau of Prisons, and local nonprofit organizations. Training topics have included collaboration, communication, assessment, diversity, barriers, case planning, and offender job retention. The Offender Workforce Development Specialist team, in partnership with twenty-six area agencies, also held the first annual Partnership for Success Career Fair for ex-offenders. More than 1,000 local, state and federal ex-offenders attended the job fair that resulted in nearly 200 offenders becoming employed.

The federal team is embracing a systems approach to ex-offender employment. The foundation of the program is creating collaborative alliances and relationships with the Bureau of Prisons, community corrections centers in the region, community organizations, training providers, and employers. The plan focuses on offender assessment, job-readiness training, job placement in meaningful employment, and job retention with ongoing assessment data while emphasizing research and development on comprehensive programs versus single events.

The Vermont Team

Vermont's Offender Workforce Development Specialist team focused on developing a strategy to bring about local partnerships among the department of corrections, department of employment and training, and department of vocational rehabilitation with the goals of improving offenders' ability to build successful career paths, and find and retain meaningful employment at livable wages.

Following its training, the team organized a statewide conference attended by key managers from across the state, representing each of the three departments, to introduce the plan. The Vermont Department of Corrections is following with training for line staff from all three departments and other appropriate community partners in different regions.

Vermont's Department of Corrections also is creating a workforce development program that combines a high school diploma and GED preparation, vocational training, work experience, and job placement services. This program will function both inside facilities and in community-based settings to provide seamless, integrated transition and service delivery.

The Washington Team

In addition to presenting to law enforcement groups in Washington, members of the Offender Workforce Development Specialist team contributed to the development of a curriculum on offender workforce development issues for offenders. This training has been delivered to staff from state and local agencies, colleges, law enforcement, community-based organizations, and private individuals.

Conclusion

The Offender Workforce Development Specialist training provides an opportunity for state and local jurisdictions nationwide to improve the knowledge and skills of practitioners regarding career development for offenders. But the question remains: Is the training truly having an impact? The progress reports reveal that practitioners are indeed transferring knowledge, coordinating service delivery, and building systems that reflect their increased commitment to providing quality offender workforce development initiatives.

This training program is announced annually in the NIC service plan, which is available upon request from the NIC Information Center and can be downloaded from its Web site at www.nicic.org. To request a service plan, call 1-800-877-1461 or (303) 682-0213; or e-mail asknicic@nicic.org. In addition, announcements will be made through NIC brochures, conference workshops, training programs, and technical assistance.

Shelly Morelock, M.A., is a program specialist based in the Washington, D.C. office of the National Institute of Corrections. Melissa Houston, MSW, is a criminal justice consultant with Houston and Associates in Cleveland. For additional information on Offender Workforce Development Specialist training, contact Morelock at (202) 353-0485.

Reentry Statistics Now Available on the Bureau of Justice Statistics' Web Site

Leon T. Geter

First printed in *Corrections Today,* a publication of the American Correctional Association, August 2003

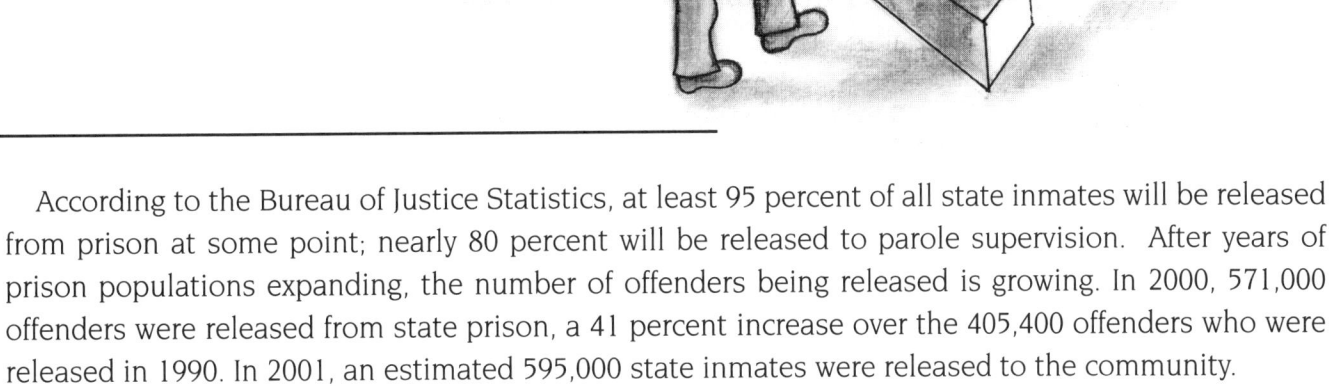

According to the Bureau of Justice Statistics, at least 95 percent of all state inmates will be released from prison at some point; nearly 80 percent will be released to parole supervision. After years of prison populations expanding, the number of offenders being released is growing. In 2000, 571,000 offenders were released from state prison, a 41 percent increase over the 405,400 offenders who were released in 1990. In 2001, an estimated 595,000 state inmates were released to the community.

Faced with a dramatic increase in the number of inmates reentering society, then Attorney General John Ashcroft announced that several federal agencies are collaborating through the new Serious and Violent Offender Reentry Initiative (visit www.ojp.usdoj. gov/reentry), which provides grant funds to correctional institutions and communities for programs that will help ex-offenders make a successful transition to society.

To help keep track of this issue, Bureau of Justice Statistics, the statistical arm of the U.S. Department of Justice, has launched a new web site section "Reentry Trends in the United States" at www.ojp.usdoj. gov/bjs/reentry/reentry.htm. Bureau of Justice Statistics statisticians have compiled all the relevant data from several surveys and numerous Bureau of Justice Statistics reports in one location. The result is a concise, statistical analysis of trends of interest to administrators of correctional facilities, parole officers, policymakers, and academicians. Topics include:

- Growth in state prison and parole populations

- Releases from state prison, including the number of releases, method of release, most serious offense and time served

- Entries to state parole

- Success rates for state parolees, including the number of discharges and parole violators returning to state prison

- Recidivism, including rearrest of released inmates, reconviction and return to prison

- Characteristics of released inmates

- Federal supervised release.

The analyses present key points in bulleted format, accompanied by graphs that illustrate the trends. For example, the page on the growth in the state prison and parole population reports that, on average, the prison population increased 5.3 percent per year between 1990 and 2001, while the state parole population rose 2.4 percent per year during that same period. A downloadable spreadsheet version of each table is also available. Additional easy-to-use features include a page of highlights, definitions of key terms and one-click access to a printer-friendly PDF version of the section's entire contents. Bureau of Justice Statistics plans to update this material as new data become available.

In addition, *Reentry Trends* provides quick links to additional national, state and federal correctional data in downloadable spreadsheets. Other links take users directly to related sections of the BJS Web site that focus on offenders and probation and parole.

About the Bureau of Justice Statistics

The Bureau of Justice Statistics is responsible for collecting, analyzing, and reporting data related to criminal victimization and the administration of justice. It maintains more than two dozen major data collection series from which it publishes and distributes reports nationwide. This year, the Bureau of Justice Statistics will count populations and conduct sample surveys among the more than 6.6 million adults who, during an average day, are subject to the care, custody, or control of criminal justice authorities.

The Bureau of Justice Statistics releases national- and state-level statistical research in a variety of formats each year. Subscribe to JUSTSTATS to receive e-mail notification of new statistical materials from the Bureau of Justice Statistics, the FBI, and the Office of Juvenile Justice and Delinquency Prevention at www.ojp.usdoj.gov/bjs/juststats.htm. Once subscribed, e-mail notifications will be sent from JUSTSTATS when updated or new information becomes available.

Bureau of Justice Statistics' Reentry Data Sources

The analyses presented in *Reentry Trends* are based on data drawn from the following surveys and reports, which can be accessed online at www.ojp.usdoj.gov/bjs/reentry/ addinfo.htm#sources. Printed copies of the reports may be ordered at www.puborder. ncjrs.org.

Surveys

Annual Parole Survey. Collects counts of the total number of people supervised in the community on Jan. 1 and Dec. 31 and a count of the number entering and leaving supervision during the collection year.

Federal Justice Statistics Program. Constructed from source data files provided by the Executive Office for United States Attorneys, the Administrative Office of the United States Courts, the United States Sentencing Commission, and the Federal Bureau of Prisons.

National Corrections Reporting Program. Collects individual-level data on offenders admitted to and released from state prisons, those in custody at year-end, and people discharged from state parole supervision.

National Prisoners Statistics. Obtains year-end and midyear counts of prison inmates from departments of correction in each of the fifty states, the District of Columbia, and the Bureau of Prisons.

Survey of Inmates in Local Jails and Survey of Inmates in Adult State Correctional Facilities. Survey of national representative samples of inmates about every five years, providing self-reported data on information about the current and past offenses of inmates, their sentences, prior use of drugs and alcohol, medical and mental health conditions, family background, use of firearms, and characteristics of the victims of their crimes.

Bureau of Justice Statistics Reports

Prison and Jail Inmates at Midyear 2001, April 2002

Prisoners in 2001, July 2002

Probation and Parole in the United States, 2001, August 2002

Recidivism of Prisoners Released in 1983, April 1998

Recidivism of Prisoners Released in 1994, June 2002

Trends in State Parole, 1990-2000, October 2001

Truth in Sentencing in State Prisons, January 1999

Additional Relevant Bureau of Justice Statistics' Reports

Census of State and Federal Adult Correctional Facilities, 1995, August 1997

Compendium of Federal Justice Statistics, 2000, August 2002

Correctional Populations in the United States, 1997, November 2000

DWI Offenders under Correctional Supervision, June 1999

Federal Criminal Case Processing, 2000, November 2001

Federal Drug Offenders, 1999, With Trends, 1984-99, August 2001

Federal Offenders under Community Supervision, 1987-96, August 1998

HIV in Prisons and Jails, 1999, July 2001

Incarcerated Parents and Their Children, August 2000

Medical Problems of Inmates, 1997, January 2001

Mental Health and Treatment of Inmates and Probationers, July 1999

Mental Health Treatment in State Prisons, 2000, July 2001

Offenders Returning to Federal Prison, 1986-97, September 2000

Prior Abuse Reported by Inmates and Probationers, April 1999

Substance Abuse and Treatment, State and Federal Prisoners, 1997, January 1999

Time Served in Prison by Federal Offenders, 1986-97, June 1999

Veterans in Prison or Jail, January 2000

Women in Prison, March 1994

Women Offenders, December 1999

Leon T. Geter *is project manager for the Bureau of Justice Statistics in Washington, D.C.*

Reentry Resources

National Criminal Justice Reference Service

First printed in *Corrections Today*, a publication of the American Correctional Association, April 2005 and updated January 2006

The National Criminal Justice Reference Service (NCJRS) compiled the following reentry resources. NCJRS, administered by the Office of Justice Programs, U.S. Department of Justice, provides resources offering justice and substance abuse information to support research, policy, and program development worldwide. Additional resources are available on their Web site: http://www.ncjrs.gov. *For criminal justice assistance, please contact NCJRS at: http://www.ncjrs.gov/App/ContactUs.aspx*

Publications

Core

Background Paper: The Effect of Incarceration and Reentry on Children, Families, and Communities
http://www.urban.org/UploadedPDF/410632_HHSConferenceBackground.pdf
Urban Institute, 2002

Development of a Guide to Resources on Faith-Based Organizations in Criminal Justice Final Report
http://www.ncjrs.gov/pdffiles1/nij/grants/209350.pdf
National Institute of Justice Sponsored, 2004

Crime Policy Report: Prisoner Reentry in Perspective
http://www.urban.org/pdfs/410213_reentry.pdf
Urban Institute, 2001

Exploring the Needs and Risks of the Returning Prisoner Population
http://www.urban.org/UploadedPDF/410626_ReturningPrisonerPopulation.pdf
Urban Institute, 2002

The Front Line: Building Programs that Recognize Families' Role in Reentry
http://www.vera.org/publication_pdf/249_476.pdf
Vera Institute of Justice, 2004

Incarceration, Reentry and Social Capital: Social Networks in the Balance
http://www.urban.org/uploadedpdf/410623_SocialCapital.pdf
John Jay College of Criminal Justice, 2002

New Reentry Programs Being Implemented
http://www.saferfoundation.org/graphics/newsletter/Final%20pdf.pdf
Safer Foundation, 2003

Prisoner Reentry and the Institutions of Civil Society: Bridges and Barriers to Successful Reintegration
http://www.urban.org/UploadedPDF/410801_Barriers.pdf
Urban Institute, 2002

Prisoner Reentry–In Perspective
http://www.urban.org/UploadedPDF/410213_reentry.PDF
Urban Institute, 2001

Prisoner Reentry: The State of Public Opinion
http://www.njisj.org/reports/eagleton_report.html
Eagleton Institute of Politics Center for Public Interest Polling at Rutger's University, 2003

Prospects for Prisoner Reentry
http://www.epinet.org/workingpapers/WP125.pdf
Economic Policy Institute, 2003

Reentry and Public Safety: Sample Programs
http://www.reentrymediaoutreach.org/pdfs/publicsafety_ex.pdf
Reentry National Media Outreach Campaign, 2004

Religion, Reform, Community: Examining the Idea of Church-based Prisoner Reentry
http://www.urban.org/UploadedPDF/410802_Religion.pdf
Urban Institute, 2002

Returning Home: Understanding the Challenges of Prisoner Reentry
http://www.urban.org/UploadedPDF/410974_ReturningHome_MD.pdf
Urban Institute, 2004

The Revolving Door: Exploring Public Attitudes toward Prisoner Reentry
http://www.urban.org/UploadedPDF/410804_RevolvingDoor.pdf
Urban Institute, 2002

Services Integration: Strengthening Offenders and Families, While Promoting Community Health and Safety
http://aspe.hhs.gov/hsp/prison2home02/Rossman.htm
Urban Institute, 2001

Serving Incarcerated and Ex-Offender Fathers and Their Families
http://www.vera.org/publication_pdf/fathers.PDF
Vera Institute of Justice, 2001

Transition from Prison to Community Initiative
http://www.nicic.org/pubs/2002/017520.pdf
National Institute of Corrections, 2002

Value-Based Initiative and Value-Based Reentry Initiative
http://www.cops.usdoj.gov/mime/open.pdf?Item=1026
Community Oriented Policing, 2004

Corrections

Beyond the Prison Gates: The State of Parole in America
http://www.urban.org/UploadedPDF/310583_Beyond_prison_gates.pdf
Urban Institute, 2002

Corrections Employment Eligibility for Ex-Offenders
http://nicic.org/pubs/2002/018209.pdf
National Institute of Corrections, 2002

Managing the Transition from Institution to Community: A Canadian Parole Officer Perspective on the Needs of Newly Released Federal Offenders
http://wcr.sonoma.edu/v5n2/manuscripts/brown.pdf
Western Criminology Review, 2004

Navigating a New Horizon: Promising Pathways to Prisoner Reintegration
http://www.calib.com/home/work_samples/files/kairosissuebriefII.pdf
Caliber Associates, 2003

The Practice and Promise of Prison Programming
http://www.urban.org/UploadedPDF/410493_PrisonProgramming.pdf
The Urban Institute, 2002

Prison Overcrowding and the Reintegration of Offenders
http://www.ccja-acjp.ca/en/overc.html
Canadian Criminal Justice Association

Prison Reform through Offender Reentry: A Partnership between Courts and Corrections
http://www.drc.state.oh.us/web/Articles/article93.htm
Ohio Department of Rehabilitation and Correction, 2003

The Practice and Promise of Prison Programming
http://www.urban.org/UploadedPDF/410493_PrisonProgramming.pdf
The Urban Institute, 2002

Prisoner Reentry and the Institutions of Civil Society: Bridges and Barriers to Successful Integration
http://www.urban.org/UploadedPDF/410801_Barriers.pdf
Urban Institute, 2002

Reintegration of Offenders into Communities
http://www.gao.gov/new.items/d01966T.pdf
US General Accounting Office, 2001

Women's Choices, Case Management for Women Leaving Jails and Prisons
http://www.communityalternatives.org/pdfs/The_Source.pdf
Weissman, M., DeLamater, L., & Lovejoy, A. (2003)

Courts

Prison Reform Through Offender Reentry: A Partnership Between Courts and Corrections
http://www.drc.state.oh.us/web/Articles/article93.htm
Ohio Department of Rehabilitation and Correction, 2003

Reentry Courts Process Evaluation (Phase 1), Final Report
http://www.ncjrs.gov/pdffiles1/nij/grants/202472.pdf
National Institute of Justice Sponsored, 2003

Welcome Home? Examining the "Reentry Court" Concept from a Strengths-based Perspective
http://wcr.sonoma.edu/v4n2/manuscripts/marunalebel.pdf
Western Criminology Review, 2003

Employment

Barriers and Promising Approaches to Workforce and Youth Development for Young Offenders
http://www.aecf.org/publications/data/workforce_youth_dev.pdf
Annie E. Casey Foundation, 2003

Building Bridges to Employment for Prisoners
http://www.homeoffice.gov.uk/rds/pdfs/hors226.pdf
Criminal Policy Research Institute, 2001

Can Employers Play a More Positive Role in Prisoner Reentry?
http://www.urban.org/UploadedPDF/410803_PositiveRole.pdf
Urban Institute, 2002

Corrections Employment Eligibility for Ex-Offenders
http://nicic.org/pubs/2002/018209.pdf
National Institute of Corrections, 2002

Employment Discrimination and What to Do About It: A Guide for California Counselors of Individuals with Criminal Records or in Recovery from Alcohol and Drug Dependence
http://www.hirenetwork.org/pdfs/050542_ca_disc.pdf
Hire Network, 2002

Employment Opportunities for Ex-Offenders in New Jersey
http://www.njisj.org/reports/heldrich_report.html
New Jersey Institute for Social Justice, 2003

Every Door Closed: Facts about Parents with Criminal Records
http://www.clasp.org/publications/EDC_fact_sheets.pdf
Center for Law and Social Policy, 2003

From Hard Time to Full Time: Strategies to Help Move Ex-Offenders from Welfare to Work
http://www.hirenetwork.org/pdfs/From_Hard_Time_to_Full_Time.pdf
U.S. Department of Labor, Employment and Training Administration, 2001

Incarceration, Employment and Public Policy
http://www.njisj.org/reports/western_report.html
New Jersey Institute for Social Justice, 2003

Legal Consequences of Incarceration for Reentry
http://www.njisj.org/reports/mukamal.pdf
National Hire Network, 2003

Moving from the Criminal Justice System to Self Sufficiency: Barriers Facing Women Ex-Offenders
http://www.communityalternatives.org/pdfs/Moving_from_CGS.pdf
Center for Community Alternatives, 2001

Prison Industry Enhancement Certification Program
http://www.ncjrs.org/pdffiles1/bja/193772.pdf
Bureau of Justice Assistance, 2002

Systematic Review of the Effects of Non-Custodial Employment Programs on the Recidivism Rates of Ex-Offenders
http://www.campbellcollaboration.org/doc-pdf/reentry.pdf
Urban Institute, 2003

Time to Work: Managing the Employment of Sex Offenders Under Community Supervision
http://www.csom.org/pubs/timetowork.pdf
Center for Sex Offender Management, 2002

Will Employers Hire Ex-Offenders? Employer Preferences, Background Checks, and Their Determinants
http://www.jcpr.org/wpfiles/holzer_raphael_stoll.pdf?CFID=1998894&CFTOKEN=25347158
Institute for Research on Policy, 2002

Female Offenders

A Woman's Journey Home: Challenges for Female Offenders and Their Children
http://www.urban.org/UploadedPDF/410630_FemaleOffenders.pdf
Urban Institute, 2002

Female Mentally Ill Offenders and Community Reintegration Needs: An Initial Examination
http://www.ihhcpar.rutgers.edu/cmhs-cjr/pdf/female_mentally_ill.pdf
International Journal of Law and Psychiatry, 2001

Leaving Jail: Service Linkage and Community Reentry for Mothers with Co-Occurring Disorders
http://www.gainsctr.com/pdfs/women/LeavingJail.pdf
National GAINES Center, 2002

Moving from the Criminal Justice System to Self Sufficiency: Barriers Facing Women Ex-Offenders
http://www.communityalternatives.org/pdfs/Moving_from_CGS.pdf
Center for Community Alternatives, 2001

Reentry Programs for Female Offenders
http://www.ncjrs.org/pdffiles1/jr000252.pdf
National Institute of Justice, 2005

Health

A Best Practice Approach to Community Re-entry from Jails for Inmates with Co-occurring Disorders: The APIC Model
http://www.gainsctr.com/pdfs/reentry/apic.pdf
National GAINS Center, 2002

Assertive Community Treatment: A Reentry Model for Seriously Mentally Ill Offenders
http://www.sconet.state.oh.us/ACMIC/resources/assertive.pdf
Supreme Court of Ohio, 2002

Corrections Agency Collaborations with Public Health
http://www.nicic.org/Downloads/pdf/2003/019101.pdf
National Institute of Corrections, 2003

Criminal Justice / Mental Health Consensus Project
http://consensusproject.org/downloads/Entire_report.pdf
Consensus Project, 2002

Female Mentally Ill Offenders and Community Reintegration Needs: An Initial Examination
http://www.ihhcpar.rutgers.edu/cmhs-cjr/pdf/female_mentally_ill.pdf
International Journal of Law and Psychiatry, 2001

Health Status of Soon to be Released Inmates: A Report to Congress
http://www.ncchc.org/pubs/pubs_stbr.html

National Commission on Correctional Health Care, 2002
Health Status Report: Infectious Diseases in Corrections
http://www.hivcorrections.org/archives/oct02/oct2002.pdf
HIV and Hepatitis Education Prison Project, 2002

Helping Inmates Return to the Community
http://www.cdc.gov/idu/facts/cj-transition.pdf
Center for Disease Control, 2001

Investing in Health and Justice Outcomes: An Investment Strategy for Offenders with Mental Health Problems in New Jersey
http://www.njisj.org/reports/wolff_report.html
New Jersey Institute for Social Justice, 2003

Leaving Jail: Service Linkage and Community Reentry for Mothers with Co-Occurring Disorders
http://209.132.230.103/pdfs/Women/series/LeavingJail.pdf
National GAINES Center, 2002

"New" Public Management of Mentally Disordered Offender, Part I: A Cautionary Tale
http://www.ihhcpar.rutgers.edu/cmhs-cjr/pdf/new_public_management_partI.pdf
International Journal of Law and Medicine, 2002

"New" Public Management of Mentally Disordered Offender Part II: A Vision with Promise
http://www.ihhcpar.rutgers.edu/cmhs-cjr/pdf/new_public_management_partII.pdf
International Journal of Law and Medicine, 2002

Predicting Incarceration of Clients of a Psychiatric Probation and Parole Service
http://www.ihhcpar.rutgers.edu/cmhs-cjr/pdf/predicting_incarceration.pdf
Psychiatric Services, 2002

Prisoner Reentry Initiative: Substance Abuse and Mental Health Disorders: The Challenges and Solutions
http://www.workforceinnovations.org/speaker_docs/robertson.pdf
Department of Labor, 2005

Prisoner Reentry: What are the Health Challenges?
http://www.rand.org/publications/RB/RB6013/RB6013.pdf
RAND, 2003

The Public Health Challenges of Prisoner Reentry: Addressing the Health Needs and Risks of Returning Prisoners and Their Families
http://www.calendow.org/reference/publications/pdf/special/TCE1214-2002_The_Public_Hea.pdf
Urban Institute, 2002

The Psychological Impact of Incarceration: Implications for Post-Prison Adjustment
http://www.urban.org/UploadedPDF/410624_PyschologicalImpact.pdf
Urban Institute, 2002

The Skill Sets and Health Needs of Released Offenders
http://aspe.hhs.gov/hsp/prison2home02/Gaes.htm
Federal Bureau of Prisons, 2002

Re-entry Issues for Offenders Living with HIV
http://www.njisj.org/reports/jacobs_report.html
New Jersey Institute for Social Justice, 2003

Release Planning for Inmates with Mental Illness Compared with Those Who Have Other Chronic Illnesses
http://www.ihhcpar.rutgers.edu/cmhs-cjr/pdf/release_planning_for_inmates.pdf
Psychiatric Services, 2002

Residential Substance Abuse Treatment for State Prisoners (RSAT)
http://www.ncjrs.gov/pdffiles1/bja/206269.pdf
Bureau of Justice Assistance, 2005

The Skill Sets and Health Care Needs of Released Offenders
http://www.urban.org/UploadedPDF/410629_ReleasedOffenders.pdf
Urban Institute, 2002

Housing/Homelessness

A Guide to Reentry Supportive Housing: A Three Part Primer for Non –Profit Supportive Housing Developers, Social Service Providers, and Their Government Partners
http://consensusproject.org/downloads/housing-guide.pdf
The Consensus Project, 2002

Guide for Developing Housing for Ex-Offenders
http://www.ojp.usdoj.gov/ccdo/pub/pdf/NCJ203374.pdf
Community Capacity Development Office, 2004

Homeless Shelter Use and Reincarceration Following Prison Release: Assessing the Risk
http://melvilletrust.org/uploads/dennis_culhane_prison_paper.doc
Center for Studies on Addictions, 2002

Integrated Services Reduce Recidivism among Homeless Adults with Serious Mental Illness in California
http://gainscenter.samhsa.gov/pdfs/integrating/Iintegrated_Services_Calif.pdf
National GAINES Center, 2001

Preventing Homelessness Among Reentering Prisoners
http://www.naeh.org/reentry/
National Alliance to End Homelessness, 2003

Preventing Homelessness: Discharge Planning From Correctional Facilities
http://www.csb.org/What_s_New/FinalReportAug2002/Final%20Report%20August%202002.doc
Community Shelter Board, 2002

Inmate Rehabilitation

Partnership with Purpose: Breaking the Ice of Recidivism
http://www.corr.state.mn.us/publications/pdf/recidivismproceedings.pdf
Minnesota Department of Corrections, 2002

Juvenile Justice/Delinquency Prevention

Aftercare as an Afterthought: Reentry and the California Youth Authority
http://www.cjcj.org/pdf/aftercare.pdf
Center for Criminal Juvenile Justice, 2002

Aftercare Services
http://www.ncjrs.org/pdffiles1/ojjdp/201800.pdf
Office of Juvenile Justice and Delinquency Prevention, 2003

Community Re-Entry of Adolescents from New Jersey's Juvenile Justice System
http://www.njisj.org/reports/stout_report.html
The New Jersey Institute for Social Justice, 2003

The Dimensions, Pathways, and Consequences of Youth Reentry
http://www.urban.org/UploadedPDF/410927_youth_reentry.pdf
Urban Institute, 2004

The Effective Management of Juvenile Sex Offenders in the Community: Case Management Protocols
http://www.csom.org/pubs/JuvProtocols.pdf
Center for Sex Offender Management, 2002

Intensive Parole Model for High-Risk Juvenile Offenders
http://www.wsipp.wa.gov/rptfiles/Ipmodel.pdf
Washington State Department of Social and Health Services, 2002

"Re-Entry" of Students
http://www.dese.state.mo.us/divimprove/fedprog/instrucimprov/reentry.pdf
Missouri Department of Education, 2002

School Related Problems Confronting New Jersey Youth Returning to Local Communities and Schools from Juvenile Detention Facilities and Juvenile Justice Commission Programs
http://www.njisj.org/reports/giles_report.html
The New Jersey Institute for Social Justice, 2003

Street Law for Juvenile Justice Programs
http://www.streetlaw.org/juvenilejustice.html
Street Law, 2003

State and Local Programs Descriptions/Evaluations

A Portrait of Prisoner Reentry in Illinois
http://www.urban.org/UploadedPDF/410662_ILPortraitReentry.pdf
Urban Institute, 2003

Aftercare as an Afterthought: Reentry and the California Youth Authority
http://www.cjcj.org/pdf/aftercare.pdf
Center on Criminal and Juvenile Justice, 2002

A Portrait of Prisoner Reentry in Maryland
http://www.urban.org/UploadedPDF/410655_MDPortraitReentry.pdf
Urban Institute, 2003

A Portrait of Prisoner Reentry in New Jersey
http://www.njisj.org/reports/portrait_present.html
New Jersey Institute for Social Justice, 2003

Applying Problem Solving Approaches to Issues of Inmate Re-Entry: The Indianapolis Pilot Project, Final Report
http://www.ncjrs.gov/pdffiles1/nij/grants/203923.pdf
National Institute of Justice, 2004

Assertive Community Treatment: A Reentry Model for Seriously Mentally Ill Offenders
http://www.sconet.state.oh.us/ACMIC/resources/assertive.pdf
Supreme Court of Ohio, 2002

Briefing Paper: An Overview of Prisoner Reentry in New Jersey
http://www.njisj.org/reports/prisoner_reentry.pdf
New Jersey Institute for Social Justice, 2002

Briefing Paper: Legal Barriers to Prisoner Reentry in New Jersey
http://www.njisj.org/reports/barriers_report.html
New Jersey Institute for Social Justice, 2003

Chicago Communities and Prisoner Reentry
http://www.icjia.state.il.us/public/pdf/Bulletins/chicago_communities.pdf
Urban Institute, 2005

Comprehensive Reentry Strategy for Adults in the District of Columbia
http://www.csosa.gov/reentry/Comp_Reentry_Action_Plan.pdf
Court Services and Offender Supervision Agency, 2003

Criminal Justice and Health and Human Services: An Exploration of Overlapping Needs, Resources, and Interests in Brooklyn Neighborhoods
http://www.urban.org/UploadedPDF/410633_CriminalJustice.pdf
Urban Institute, 2002

Families: A Critical Resources for New Jersey's Prisoner Reentry Strategy
http://www.familyjustice.org/assets/publications/New_Jersey_Paper.pdf
New Jersey Institute of Social Justice, 2003

Greenlight, in Transition, Sharing Lessons about Reentry
http://www.vera.org/publication_pdf/200_384.pdf#greenlight_in_transition_sharing_lessons_about_reentry
Vera Institute of Justice, 2003

Memorandum of Agreement between the North Carolina Department of Correction And the North Carolina Department of Health and Human Services and the North Carolina Department of Commerce and the North Carolina Community College System
http://www.dhhs.state.nc.us/mhddsas/sas/tasc/ReEntrymemorandum.PDF
North Carolina Department of Health and Human Services, 2003

The Michigan Prisoner Reentry Initiative
http://www.nga.org/cda/files/reentryupdateMI.pdf
A Collaborative Effort of the Governor's Office and the Departments of Corrections, Community Health, Labor & Economic Growth and the Family Independence Agency, 2004

The Network Program of Episcopal Social Services: A Process Evaluation
http://www.vera.org/publication_pdf/181_328.pdf
Vera Institute of Justice, 2002

New Reentry Programs Being Implemented
http://www.saferfoundation.org/graphics/newsletter/Final%20pdf.pdf
Safer Foundation, 2003

North Carolina Department of Corrections Transition/Reentry Plan
http://www.doc.state.nc.us/rap/DOC_Transition_Workplan.pdf
North Carolina Division of Corrections, 2003

Offender Reentry Initiative Launched
http://www.michigan.gov/documents/103003_77257_7.pdf
Michigan Department of Corrections, 2003

Pilot Program Offers Reentry Transition Services to Offenders
http://www.vadoc.state.va.us/offenders/institutions/programs/reentry.htm
Virginia Department of Corrections

Preventing Homelessness Among Reentering Prisoners: Ohio
http://www.endhomelessness.org/reentry/Reentry-OH.pdf
Ohio Department of Rehabilitation and Corrections

Prisoner Reentry in Idaho
http://www.corrections.state.id.us/facts/annual/Reentry.pdf
Urban Institute, 2004

Prison Reform Through Offender Reentry: A Partnership Between Courts and Corrections
http://www.drc.state.oh.us/web/Articles/article93.htm
Ohio Department of Rehabilitation and Correction, 2003

Serving Incarcerated and Ex-Offender Fathers and Their Families: A Review of the Field
http://www.vera.org/publication_pdf/fathers.pdf
Vera Institute of Justice, 2001

Voting Rights for Prisoners and Ex Prisoners in New York
http://www.cssny.org/pdfs/factsheet.pdf
Community Service Society, 2003

Works for Everyone
http://www.fcnetwork.org/reading/philadelphiareentry.pdf
Philadelphia Consensus Group on Reentry & Reintegration of Adjudicated Offenders, 2003

Sex Offender Monitoring

Analysis of Risk Factors Contributing to the Recidivism of Sex Offenders on Probation
http://www.ncjrs.gov/pdffiles1/nij/grants/203905.pdf
National Institute of Justice Sponsored, 2004

An Overview of Sex Offender Management
http://www.csom.org/pubs/csom_bro.pdf
Center for Sex Offender Management, 2002

Case Studies on CSOM's National Resource Sites, 2nd Edition, Revised
http://www.csom.org/pubs/casestudies2.pdf
Center for Sex Offender Management, 2001

Community Notification and Education
http://www.csom.org/pubs/notedu.pdf
Center for Sex Offender Management, 2001

Community Supervision of the Sex Offender: An Overview of Current and Promising Practices
http://www.csom.org/pubs/supervision2.pdf
Center for Sex Offender Management, 2001

The Effective Management of Juvenile Sex Offenders in the Community: Case Management Protocols
http://www.csom.org/pubs/JuvProtocols.pdf
Center For Sex Offender Management, 2002

Engaging Advocates and Other Victim Service Providers in the Community Management of Sex Offenders
http://www.csom.org/pubs/advocacy.pdf
Center for Sex Offender Management, 2001

Managing Sex Offenders in the Community: A Handbook to Guide Policymakers and Practitioners through a Planning and Implementation Process
http://www.csom.org/pubs/managehandbook.pdf
Center for Sex Offender Management, 2002

Recidivism of Sex Offenders
http://www.csom.org/pubs/recidsexof.pdf
Center for Sex Offender Management, 2001

Summary of State Sex Offender Registries, 2001
http://www.ojp.usdoj.gov/bjs/pub/pdf/sssor01.pdf
Bureau of Justice Statistics, 2002

Time to Work: Managing the Employment of Sex Offenders Under Community Supervision
http://www.csom.org/pubs/timetowork.pdf
Center for Sex Offender Management, 2002

Nongovernmental Organizations

American Correctional Assocaition
http://www.aca.org

American Probation and Parole Association
http://www.appa-net.org/

Annie E. Casey Foundation
http://www.aecf.org/

Center for Alternative Sentencing and Employment Services
http://www.cases.org/

HIV Prison Education Project
http://www.hivcorrections.org/

International Community Corrections Association
http://www.iccaweb.org/

The Sentencing Project
http://www.sentencingproject.org/

The Council of State Governments
http://www.csg.org/csg/default

National Commission on Correctional Health Care
http://www.ncchc.org/

National Governors Association
http://www.nga.org/

National HIRE Network
http://www.hirenetwork.org/index.html

National Institute of Corrections Community Corrections
http://nicic.org/CommunityCorrections

Reentry Policy Council
http://www.csgeast.org/programs/criminal_justice/rpc/index.htm

Reentry National Media Outreach Campaign
http://www.reentrymediaoutreach.org/index.html

Research Triangle Institute
http://www.rti.org/

Street Law Juvenile Justice Reentry Program
http://www.streetlaw.org/reentry.html

Federal and National Resources

Bureau of Justice Statistics Reentry Trends in the United States
http://www.ojp.usdoj.gov/bjs/reentry/reentry.htm

Bureau of Labor Statistics
http://www.bls.gov/

Office of Correctional Education
http://www.ed.gov/offices/OVAE/AdultEd/OCE/index.html

Social Security Agency Serious and Violent Felon Reentry Initiative
http://www.ssa.gov/homelessness/doj.htm

United States Department of Housing and Urban Development National Alliance to End Homelessness
http://www.hud.gov/news/speeches/endhomelessness.cfm

U.S. Department of Labor
http://www.dol.gov/

Putting The Ex-Offender To Work, Not Back Behind Bars

Managing a Job-Retention Program for Ex-Offenders: A Step-By-Step Guide

T. A. Ryan, Ph.D.

One of the primary reasons for recidivism is the offenders inability to find and maintain work upon their release. This resource provides practitioners with a blueprint for creating programs which will help offenders retain employment. The programs within this resource are time- and cost-effective. The book is broken down into four sections. The first documents the need for programs to decrease recidivism, which can occur through increased job retention. Section Two presents a generalized model that sets forth directions and guidelines for developing delivery system models to achieve ex-offender job retention. Part Three presents guidelines for implementing the delivery systems. The last section of the book provides conclusions and a discussion (2004, 104 pages, 1-56991-217-3).

ABOUT THE AUTHOR

T. A. Ryan, Ph.D. is an esteemed researcher and former associate dean of the College of Criminal Justice at the University of South Carolina. She has been an American Correctional Association member for many years and has served on the ACA Delegate Assembly, the Board of Governors, and the Offender Program and Ethics Committees. She was awarded the E. R. Cass Correctional Achievement Award in 1997 for her distinguished service to ACA and the field of corrections.

1-800-222-5646, ext. 0129
American Correctional Association
P.O. Box 201
Annapolis Junction, MD 20701
Order online at www.aca.org

ACA
FOUNDED 1870

A Blueprint for Life on the Outside

Heading Home: Offender Reintegration Into the Family

Vivian L. Gadsden, Editor

Most people assume when offenders return from prison, their life picks up where it left off before their incarceration. This is far from the truth. The incarceration process affects the offender and the family. How can you best prepare the offender and family for this reunion? **Heading Home** has some answers. Chapters include: Parent Education for Incarcerated Parents: Understanding What Works; Families, Prisoners and Community Reentry; Children of Prisoners; What Works in the Treatment of Family Violence in Correctional Populations; What Works in Faith-Based Programming; and The Viability of Mentoring. (2003, 307 pages, index, 1-56991-165-7)

Contributors Include:

Creasie Finney Hairston
Chris Carr
Dwight Cuff
Natalie Gabora-Roth
Denise Johnston
Betsy A. Mathews
David Molzahn
Glen F. Palm
Lynn Stewart
R. Karl Rethemeyer
Vivian Gadsden

1-800-222-5646, ext. 0129
American Correctional Association
P.O. Box 201
Annapolis Junction, MD 20701
Order on the Web at www.aca.org

ACA
FOUNDED 1870